There are vast riches  1
Obadiah. This comn
stand the grammatic.   .e
connecting them with the Bible's salvation story. As you preach through
this part of God's inspired word, this commentary series, written by pas-
tor-scholars, will help you prepare sermons that are exegetically sound,
theologically rich, and full of practical application. This is one resource
you will want in your library.

Daniel Darling, director of The Land Center for Cultural
Engagement at Southwestern Seminary, author of several books including *The Characters of Christmas, The Characters of Easter,* and *The Characters
of Creation*

A constant frustration for biblical expositors is that most commentaries
are helpful on either the scholarly matters or on the pastoral application, but rarely combine the best of both. As two trusted Old Testament
scholars who also happen to be excellent preachers, Moseley and Akin
resolve those frustrations in this helpful commentary on Hosea, Joel,
Amos, and Obadiah. Their work offers clarity on the text, useful background and explanation, and homiletical frameworks that help any
expositor convey the Scriptures to their people. I will definitely be adding this to my library, and so should you!

Jamie Dew, president and professor of Christian philosophy, New
Orleans Baptist Theological Seminary

This well-written, carefully outlined, and thoughtfully organized commentary on Hosea, Joel, Amos, and Obadiah is textually faithful, warm
hearted, applicable, and, as the series title suggests, Christ centered.
Allan Moseley and Jonathan Akin have provided an invaluable service
for readers of these four often-neglected Old Testament books. The
introductory materials for each book and the questions for reflection at
the end of each section strengthen this helpful resource. It is a delight
to joyfully recommend this readable work to pastors, church leaders,
Bible teachers, and students alike.

David S. Dockery, president and distinguished professor of theology, Southwestern Baptist Theological Seminary

As a pastor, I want to be faithful in preaching the whole counsel of God. If I am being honest, the Minor Prophets can be intimidating as I seek to be faithful to the text and preach Christ-centered sermons that edify the church for today. Thanks to this commentary by Jonathan Akin and Allan Moseley, I now have a helpful, clear, and convictional resource to engage with as I study Hosea, Joel, Amos, and Obadiah for my own soul and also for the church. The Christ-Centered Exposition series has been a helpful tool for Bible study leaders in our church and for our pastors who seek to preach in a manner that honors and points to Christ. This is a great new addition to a fantastic series and will be a helpful resource for many.

Dean Inserra, founding and lead pastor of City Church, Tallahassee, and author of *The Unsaved Christian*

For the expository preacher, approaching prophetic books like Hosea, Joel, Amos, and Obadiah comes with multiple challenges. Preaching from these books effectively requires answering questions such as these: What were the historical and political factors that shaped the prophets' messages? How should the preacher treat the recurring themes that continually resurface in their prophecies without seeming redundant to our listeners? How can the preacher authentically bridge the applicational gaps between the original recipients of the prophecies and today's audience? And, most significantly, how do the messages of these prophets connect with God's redemptive purposes in Jesus Christ? In this volume, Old Testament scholars and gifted preachers Allan Moseley and Jonathan Akin not only consider these kinds of questions, but they answer them with perception and aplomb. This commentary provides a wonderful starting place for expositors with clear outlines, skillful explanations of the biblical text, and thought-provoking illustrative and applicational materials. Bible teachers and preachers for years to come will benefit from this helpful and insightful resource.

Stephen N. Rummage, executive director-treasurer, Florida Baptist Convention

CHRIST-CENTERED
Exposition

AUTHORS **Allan Moseley and Jonathan Akin**

SERIES EDITORS **David Platt, Daniel L. Akin, and Tony Merida**

CHRIST-CENTERED
Exposition

EXALTING JESUS IN

HOSEA, JOEL, AMOS, OBADIAH

REFERENCE

BRENTWOOD, TENNESSEE

Christ-Centered Exposition Commentary: Exalting
Jesus in Hosea, Joel, Amos, Obadiah
© Copyright 2024 by Allan Moseley and Jonathan Akin

B&H Publishing Group
Brentwood, Tennessee
All rights reserved.

ISBN: 978-0-8054-9808-0

Dewey Decimal Classification: 220.7
Subject Heading: BIBLE. O.T. HOSEA, JOEL, AMOS, OBADIAH—
COMMENTARIES\JESUS CHRIST

Printed in the United States of America
1 2 3 4 5 6 7 8 9 10 • 29 28 27 26 25 24

SERIES DEDICATION

Dedicated to Adrian Rogers and John Piper. They have taught us to love the gospel of Jesus Christ, to preach the Bible as the inerrant Word of God, to pastor the church for which our Savior died, and to have a passion to see all nations gladly worship the Lamb.

—David Platt, Tony Merida, and Danny Akin
March 2013

AUTHORS' DEDICATIONS

For
Josiah, Caleb, Micah, Jacob, Luke, Beth, Abigail, Eli, Joy,
and any little ones yet to arrive in our family,
with my love.
— Allan Moseley

For
Maddy, Emma Grace, and Judson
"Tell your children of it, and let your children tell their children,
and their children to another generation." Joel 1:3 (ESV)
— Jonathan Akin

TABLE OF CONTENTS

Hosea

Commentary by Allan Moseley

Joel

Commentary by Jonathan Akin

Amos

Commentary by Allan Moseley

Obadiah

Commentary by Allan Moseley

ACKNOWLEDGMENTS

Profound gratitude is due my wife, Sharon, who supports me wonderfully in all I do and shows extraordinary patience when I attempt to do too much. My work in the text of Hosea and Amos began when I was a doctoral student. Dr. Billy K. Smith taught a seminar in those two books. I wrote my dissertation on Hosea's polemic against Baalism, and with the completion of this exposition of Hosea, Amos, and Obadiah, the circle seems complete. I'm grateful to Dr. Smith, who went on to write the New American Commentary volume on Amos and Obadiah. To me, he was a valued professor and a formidable tennis competitor. I am also grateful to my own students in Hebrew exegesis courses in Hosea and Amos. Our shared close reading of the text together was a joy. Readers will notice a varied assortment of resources in the citations and works cited. I attempted to read widely in an effort to be careful with interpretation and helpful in illustration. Finally, I'm grateful to Danny Akin, my friend and boss who invited me to write this, and to David Stabnow, the editor who helped me and waited for me to finish.

— Allan Moseley

Many people deserve my deepest thanks for their help in making this contribution a reality. I am grateful to the wonderful people of First Baptist Church, Charlotte, North Carolina, who listened to every sermon I preached from Joel with kindness and interest. One talented member even wrote a song based on Joel as a result. I am thankful for the legwork my graduate assistant Jasmine Russell, a Carson-Newman University student, did to make this work better. I owe much gratitude to Duane Garrett, who was my professor for prophetic literature and whose commentary on Joel was a vital resource in my study.

I am grateful to my family. Nothing God has allowed me to do in ministry would be humanly possible without the love and support of my wife, Ashley. She gives herself every day to our family and helps us make our dreams come true. She is a "grace gift" far beyond what we deserve. Our children, Maddy, Emma Grace, and Judson, are the biggest joys in our life outside of the Lord Jesus. I am grateful to my mom and to my dad, who asked me to write this work. They have obeyed Joel 1:3 and passed the deep truths about God to their children and grandchildren.

Most importantly, I am eternally grateful to the Lord Jesus Christ. He took on the judgment of the day of the Lord for me at Golgotha so that when the final day of the Lord comes in the valley of decision, I know what my sentence will be: righteous with the righteousness of Christ!

— Jonathan Akin

SERIES INTRODUCTION

Augustine said, "Where Scripture speaks, God speaks." The editors of the Christ-Centered Exposition Commentary series believe that where God speaks, the pastor must speak. God speaks through his written Word. We must speak from that Word. We believe the Bible is God breathed, authoritative, inerrant, sufficient, understandable, necessary, and timeless. We also affirm that the Bible is a Christ-centered book; that is, it contains a unified story of redemptive history of which Jesus is the hero. Because of this Christ-centered trajectory that runs from Genesis 1 through Revelation 22, we believe the Bible has a corresponding global-missions thrust. From beginning to end, we see God's mission as one of making worshipers of Christ from every tribe and tongue worked out through this redemptive drama in Scripture. To that end we must preach the Word.

In addition to these distinct convictions, the Christ-Centered Exposition Commentary series has some distinguishing characteristics. First, this series seeks to display exegetical accuracy. What the Bible says is what we want to say. While not every volume in the series will be a verse-by-verse commentary, we nevertheless desire to handle the text carefully and explain it rightly. Those who teach and preach bear the heavy responsibility of saying what God has said in his Word and declaring what God has done in Christ. We desire to handle God's Word faithfully, knowing that we must give an account for how we have fulfilled this holy calling (Jas 3:1).

Second, the Christ-Centered Exposition Commentary series has pastors in view. While we hope others will read this series, such as parents, teachers, small-group leaders, and student ministers, we desire to provide a commentary busy pastors will use for weekly preparation of biblically faithful and gospel-saturated sermons. This series is not academic in nature. Our aim is to present a readable and pastoral style of commentaries. We believe this aim will serve the church of the Lord Jesus Christ.

Third, we want the Christ-Centered Exposition Commentary series to be known for the inclusion of helpful illustrations and theologically driven applications. Many commentaries offer no help in illustrations, and few offer any kind of help in application. Often those that do offer illustrative material and application unfortunately give little serious attention to the text. While giving ourselves primarily to explanation, we also hope to serve readers by providing inspiring and illuminating illustrations coupled with timely and timeless application.

Finally, as the name suggests, the editors seek to exalt Jesus from every book of the Bible. In saying this, we are not commending wild allegory or fanciful typology. We certainly believe we must be constrained to the meaning intended by the divine Author himself, the Holy Spirit of God. However, we also believe the Bible has a messianic focus, and our hope is that the individual authors will exalt Christ from particular texts. Luke 24:25-27,44-47 and John 5:39,46 inform both our hermeneutics and our homiletics. Not every author will do this the same way or have the same degree of Christ-centered emphasis. That is fine with us. We believe faithful exposition that is Christ centered is not monolithic. We do believe, however, that we must read the whole Bible as Christian Scripture. Therefore, our aim is both to honor the historical particularity of each biblical passage and to highlight its intrinsic connection to the Redeemer.

The editors are indebted to the contributors of each volume. The reader will detect a unique style from each writer, and we celebrate these unique gifts and traits. While distinctive in their approaches, the authors share a common characteristic in that they are pastoral theologians. They love the church, and they regularly preach and teach God's Word to God's people. Further, many of these contributors are younger voices. We think these new, fresh voices can serve the church well, especially among a rising generation that has the task of proclaiming the Word of Christ and the Christ of the Word to the lost world.

We hope and pray this series will serve the body of Christ well in these ways until our Savior returns in glory. If it does, we will have succeeded in our assignment.

David Platt
Daniel L. Akin
Tony Merida
Series Editors
February 2013

Hosea

Introduction

Date

The first verse of the book of Hosea dates Hosea's prophetic ministry to "the reigns of Uzziah, Jotham, Ahaz, and Hezekiah, kings of Judah, and of Jeroboam son of Jehoash, king of Israel" (1:1). The outer limits of the reigns of those kings, from the beginning of the reign of Jeroboam II to the end of the reign of Hezekiah, are 793 BC to 686 BC (Kaiser, *History of Israel*, 491). Of course, Hosea 1:1 does not state that Hosea prophesied during the entire reigns of all those kings, so we can conclude that his ministry extended from sometime near the end of Jeroboam's reign to a time near the beginning of Hezekiah's reign. Also, Hosea does not mention the fall of Samaria. Samaria, the capital city of the northern kingdom of Israel, fell to the Assyrians in 722 BC as God's punishment for Israel's long history of sin and covenant unfaithfulness (2 Kgs 17). It is reasonable to conclude that the book of Hosea was finished before 722 BC, since surely Hosea would have referred to such a decisive event if the book were not completed until after that date. However, Hezekiah did not begin to reign until 715 BC, based on a twenty-nine-year reign (2 Kgs 18:2; cf. v. 13) ending in 687 BC. Most likely, Hezekiah served as coregent with his father, Ahaz. He began reigning as king about 727 BC, which agrees with 2 Kings 18:1-10, in which Hezekiah's sixth year is 722 BC. Thus, Hosea's ministry can be dated to approximately 755 BC to 725 BC. It seems likely that such a long ministry began when he was a young man. The fact that Hosea's ministry began before he was married also supports the conclusion that he became a prophet early in his adult life.

God called Hosea to prophesy during the final years before Israel's fall to Assyria. God was calling the people of Israel back to faithfulness to God and to his covenant with them, and Hosea was his man to issue that call. Because God loved the people of Israel, he was offering them salvation and restoration once more before the final curtain fell. God chose Hosea to issue love's final call. Sadly, Israel did not heed that call, and Assyria became God's instrument of punishment.

Biographical Information

The name *Hosea* is borne by five persons in the Old Testament. In addition to the prophet, it was Joshua's original name, changed by Moses (Num 13:16). "Hosea" was also the name of three other individuals: an officer of King David (1 Chr 27:20), the last king of Israel (2 Kgs 17:1), and a signatory of a covenant made in postexilic Jerusalem (Neh 10:24). Though the history and meaning of the name are not certain, it seems clear that it derives from the root meaning "to save, or deliver" (Andersen and Freedman, *Hosea*, 152–53). This is a fitting name for someone whose message included liberation, and in fact, *Jesus* is its Greek form (Matt 1:21).

The biographical information about Hosea that is most central to the message of his prophecy relates to his marriage and the birth of his children. Those subjects are addressed in the first section of the commentary below. In addition to his immediate family, the book tells us that Hosea was the son of Beeri (1:1). We know nothing about the identity of Beeri, and that name occurs elsewhere only in Genesis 26:34. Hosea's familiarity with God's law could lead to the conclusion that he was from a priestly family, but that may be difficult to reconcile with his negative descriptions of the corrupt cult. Hosea's agricultural references have led some to believe he was a farmer before his call to prophecy (Riggs, *Hosea's Heartbreak*, 14). If Hosea's choices of vocabulary and imagery are the basis for our speculation regarding Hosea's background or vocation, based on Hosea 7:4-10 we could conclude that he had been a baker. We must concede that such conclusions are speculation. All we know about Hosea is what his book records, and it does not specify any vocation except that of prophet.

In the practice of his prophetic vocation, Hosea was clearly skilled in poetic expression. The book of Hosea includes a wide range of Hebrew rhetorical techniques, making the book of Hosea "among the most poetic of the prophetic collections in the OT" (Dearman, *Book of Hosea*, 3). Perhaps most central to the contemporary application of this part of Scripture, the book reveals Hosea as a faithful man of God who lived with the double trauma of his wife's unfaithfulness to him and Israel's unfaithfulness to God.

Historical and Cultural Circumstances

Hosea was one of four biblical prophets who preached and wrote during the eighth century BC. Isaiah and Micah prophesied in the southern kingdom of Judah, and Amos and Hosea prophesied in the northern kingdom of Israel (see the introduction to the book of Amos for further historical information). Jonah also lived and preached during the eighth century in Israel, but little is known about his life or the content of his preaching, except for what we read in one verse (2 Kgs 14:25) and in the book of Jonah. Some scholars also date Joel to the early part of the eighth century, though Joel's date is debated.

The books of the eighth-century prophets reveal that the people of Israel had strayed far from God and were consistently unfaithful to his covenant and its stipulations. Drunkenness, sexual licentiousness, cheating in business, empty ritualism in religion, and pagan idolatry were among the sins condemned by the prophets of the one true God. Archaeological evidence suggests that during the eighth century the monarchy exercised increasing control of the economy. Royal herds increased and larger tracts of land were enclosed for more centralized production of agricultural goods (Matthews, *Social World*, 70–71). The preaching of the prophets indicates that such a situation led to the exploitation of the poorer classes by the wealthy and powerful.

The elite class also supported a corrupt religion. Religion had become syncretistic, mixing elements of God's revelation to Israel with elements of the Baalistic cult of the Canaanites. Hosea made his signal contribution here, strongly denouncing Baalism and stating that the practice of such pagan religion amounted to committing adultery against the one true God. To portray the relationship God intended with Israel, Hosea referred to Israel as both wife and child of the true God.

Hosea lived during dark days, days when God's judgment through the fall of Israel was imminent. Hosea was a light in that darkness, preaching God's truth in the midst of a culture turning away from God and believing lies. We, too, live in times that are spiritually dark. The book of Hosea is a word from God that shines the light of God's truth in the darkness of our times.

A Broken Family, a Broken Nation, a Holy God

HOSEA 1:1–2:1

Main Idea: God's plan for Hosea's life included painful challenges in his family relationships, but God communicated his truth through those challenges and through the words he gave Hosea.

I. Sometimes God Calls His People to a Painful Task (1:2).
II. God Calls His People to Share His Word (1:1).
III. God Calls All People to a Covenant Relationship (1:3).
IV. God Sends His Judgment against Sin (1:4-9).
V. God's Plan Is Restoration (1:10–2:1).

When I was a teenager, one summer I attended a youth camp sponsored by my home church. One of the evening worship services during that week had an especially powerful impact on the people present. Several young people came to faith in Christ, and others recommitted themselves to live for him. I had a powerful and memorable encounter with God, too, but in the room with all those people, I felt a compelling impulse to speak to God alone. I wanted the worship service to be over so I could find a quiet place to pray. When we were dismissed, I went out into the woods in the dark. I fell to my knees and poured out my heart to God. I remember one thing I said to God that night. I told God that for the rest of my life I would do whatever he wanted me to do and I would go wherever he wanted me to go. It's likely I remember that moment because it was a significant commitment to God. I also remember wondering how that commitment might change my life and where God might lead me.

We have no record of Hosea's call experience, but Hosea must have made a commitment something like that. Why else would he have obeyed God when God told him to marry a prostitute? Verse 2 says that God told Hosea, "Go and marry a woman of promiscuity, / and have children of promiscuity." For "promiscuity," other translations use "harlotry" (NASB, NKJV) or "whoredom" (ESV, NRSV). *Whore* is a vulgar word, an offensive word, but it's an appropriate word. What Hosea's wife was doing away from Hosea was offensive, and what the people of

6

Israel were doing away from God was offensive. The word is not *adultery*; that's another Hebrew word (Hosea uses "adultery" too, 4:14; 7:4). The word used to refer to Hosea's wife and Israel appears often in Hosea in its verbal and nominal forms, singular and plural (1:2; 2:4,6; 3:3; 4:10,11,12,13,14,15; 5:3,4; 9:1). In the singular form, this word regularly refers to a prostitute. Tamar, Rahab, and Jephthah's mother are examples (Gen 38:24; Josh 2:1; Judg 11:1). In the plural form, as it appears in Hosea 1:2 with reference to Hosea's wife, the meaning is broader and includes prostitution as well as promiscuity that did not include payment (Koehler and Baumgartner, *HALOT*, 1:275–76; Andersen and Freedman, *Hosea*, 157–63). The King James Version's "whoredoms" is not a word people use today, but that word helps express the meaning here. We could conclude further that Hosea's wife surely received payment for her promiscuity. Such payment is mentioned in Hosea 2:5, and she became a financial asset to someone, since at one point Hosea had to purchase her away from that arrangement (3:1-2). Also, Hosea 4:14 refers to three types of sexual sin: adultery, cult prostitution, and whoredom/promiscuity. Such a grouping suggests distinctions among three different forms of sexual sin, thus differentiating "promiscuity" from "mere" adultery and from the more specific cult prostitution. It seems clear, then, that the sin of Hosea's wife was not only adultery; it was repeated and remunerated sexual sin. If she participated at any point in the prostitution of the Baal cult, she would have been guilty of all three categories of Hosea 4:14—adultery, cult prostitution, and whoredom/promiscuity. Hosea 1:2 emphasizes her sin by means of repetition: "promiscuity" occurs three times in verse 2; in the Hebrew it appears four times.

Sometimes God Calls His People to a Painful Task
HOSEA 1:2

God called Hosea to marry a prostitute (v. 2). Marrying a prostitute was costly obedience for Hosea. God's command to Hosea to marry a harlot sounds strange coming from God. God is holy and moral, and he had given a strict code of conduct to Israel that forbade sexual activity outside marriage. The idea of God's giving such a command creates a moral or theological problem for many people, and it has given rise to numerous interpretations of Hosea's marriage. Some people have said the marriage was not actual but allegorical. Hosea told the story of marrying a prostitute to portray to the people a spiritual point, namely the spiritual harlotry of Israelites in their relationship with God. Other people have said the marriage took place only in a vision Hosea had. Still others have suggested Hosea took a prostitute not as a wife but as a concubine, but that hardly solves the moral problem. Probably the most common interpretation is that God told Hosea to marry an actual prostitute, since the Bible quotes God as saying that, with no elaboration or explanation. Maybe Gomer was chaste when Hosea married her. We don't know, but we do know she was unfaithful to Hosea and she committed sexual sin. It's even possible, as some have suggested, that Gomer was a cult prostitute, serving in the fertility worship of the pagan god Baal (Wolff, *Commentary*, 13–16).

Let's not miss the big point. God told Hosea to marry a woman who committed sexual sin for payment. Maybe she did that for a short period of time or maybe a long period of time, but think about what that meant for Hosea. Hosea was God's prophet, the one who spoke God's word to God's people, but he was married to a hooker. Being a preacher married to a prostitute would be humiliating. If he were living today, he would have to say to the deacons and other leaders of the church, "I need to tell you that I went downtown last night and I talked with several prostitutes on the street. I wasn't there for their business, but I had to do it; I was looking for my wife. She's been working as a prostitute; please pray for her and for me." Probably a lot of Hosea's speaking engagements would be cancelled. His story would be great fodder for exposés in the tabloids, with headlines like, "The Preacher and the Prostitute" and "A Man of God and a Woman of the Night." Ministerially it was humiliating, but it also had to be personally devastating. "Where were you last night, honey? I love you. When you do that, and I know you do, it hurts so much that I feel like I'm being stabbed in the heart."

God called Hosea to that. "Go and marry a woman of promiscuity." Do you know what it's like for God to call you to something hard? Noah did. "Noah, I want you to build an enormous boat in a place where a major body of water is nowhere in sight. I want you to live a blameless life surrounded by people whose actions and thoughts are 'nothing but evil all the time'" (Gen 6:5). God called Abraham to a hard task. Abraham lived among people who worshiped the gods of Mesopotamia and whose families were patriarchal, and God said, "Abraham, follow the true God and leave your family." Sometimes God calls us to a painful task.

God's plan for my life has been easy in comparison with Hosea, Noah, or Abraham. There was a time in my life when God led me to a hard place. I'm not proud of the fact that more than once I said to God, "I must have misunderstood your call. You could not have called me here. You would never do this to somebody who just wanted to serve you and please you." But sometimes God calls his people to a painful task. In today's world there are a lot of hard things to do for God and a lot of hard places to go for God. So this is an important question: If God calls you to do something hard in a hard place, are you up for that? Will you do what God calls you to do?

God Calls His People to Share His Word
HOSEA 1:1

The first verse of the book of Hosea refers to the entire book as, "The word of the LORD that came to Hosea." That may be the most important statement in the book. What is in this book is "the word of the LORD"— not the words of a man but the word of God. Even in the dark days in which Hosea lived, God did not leave himself without a witness. We live in times that are morally and spiritually dark too. God has not left himself without a witness. We, his church, are his witnesses who speak his Word to this world.

"The word of the LORD"—that's what God's people today are to share with the world. Certainly, we're not prophets in the sense that Hosea was a prophet, but numerous times in the New Testament followers of Christ are told to share, to preach, God's Word. We share God's Word, not just our opinions. One reason social media exist is so people can share their opinions immediately about the issues of the day. At the end of the day, when everyone has shared opinions and agreed or disagreed with one another, what has been accomplished of any eternal value? Has anyone been born again? Has anyone been made more holy? Wouldn't it be helpful if a lot of Christians stopped reading social media and started reading God's Word? Wouldn't it help all followers of Jesus to immerse themselves in book after book of the Bible until they cannot encounter any idea in the world without thinking about what God says about that idea in his Word? Then maybe we'll be ready to enter the world of social media to speak not our words but God's. That's what our world needs, and that's what God calls us to give—his Word, his truth. We share not our commentary on the crisis of the day—not human ideas, philosophies, or remedies—but God's words. "The word of the LORD . . . came to Hosea." And it comes to us in God's Word, the Bible.

God Calls All People to a Covenant Relationship
HOSEA 1:3

God called Hosea to speak his word in difficult circumstances. If God calls us to do something, he has a good purpose for that task. He had a good purpose for Hosea's life. In Hosea's marriage God was illustrating the fact that he calls all people to a covenant relationship. A covenant relationship is built on faithful, steadfast love. Genesis 12 says God made a covenant with Abraham and his descendants. God also made a covenant with Moses and Israel at Mount Sinai. God made a covenant with David in which he promised that a descendant of David would reign forever. When the church shares the Lord's Supper together, we celebrate the new covenant that Jeremiah prophesied and that Jesus announced as the new covenant in his blood. God desires to relate to people in a covenant relationship—a relationship built on faithful love. He desires to relate to *every* person in that way. In his covenant with Abraham and his descendants, God said his intention was to bless "all the families of the earth" (Gen 12:3). In his covenant with Moses and Israel, God said they would be "a kingdom of priests" (Exod 19:6). Priests teach people about God, and Israel was to be an entire "*kingdom* of priests"—every Israelite in a covenant relationship with God and showing the nations what that relationship looks like. In the new covenant in Jesus, Jesus commands his followers to make disciples of all nations. God has always had a plan to call all people into a covenant relationship with him.

God used Hosea's marriage as an illustration of his covenant relationship with his people. Hosea was the first to receive the revelation of that comparison from God. Later, God would inspire Jeremiah and Ezekiel to make the same comparison. Marriage is a clear and profound illustration of our relationship with God. Marriage is personal; it's between a man and a woman. A covenant with God is also personal; it's a relationship between a person and God. Marriage is a commitment—through thick and thin, for richer for poorer, 'til death do us part, we're together, *bound* together by our covenant. A relationship with God is also a commitment to a person, God himself. Marriage is not *exactly* the same as a covenant relationship with God; he is *God* so a relationship with him is possible only because of the salvation he gives us and his gracious offer of a covenant relationship with him. But a relationship with God is similar to marriage—he loves us, we love him, we walk together through life, and we're committed to each other.

Hosea's wife, Gomer, did not get that. She had a distorted view of the marriage relationship, the same distorted view Israel had of a covenant relationship with God. It's important for us to understand that distortion because it's key to understanding the book of Hosea, and it's still with us today. In 2:5 God refers to Gomer's children and says,

> *"Their mother is promiscuous;*
> *she conceived them and acted shamefully.*
> *For she thought, 'I will follow my lovers,*
> *the men who give me my food and water,*
> *my wool and flax, my oil and drink.'"*

Far from living in a committed, loving covenant relationship with her husband, she was playing the whore. She was living in sin.

God Sends His Judgment against Sin
HOSEA 1:4-9

Israel and Gomer were unfaithful in covenant relationships; they were prostituting themselves. How did God respond? Through Hosea, God repeatedly stated that he was going to send his punishment. In chapter 1 God announced his punishment by means of the names he told Hosea to give to his children. During that time, names often had symbolic meaning, and the names of Hosea's children carried dark premonitions.

God told Hosea to name the first child "Jezreel." Jezreel was a place of bloodshed—in fact, massacre.

> *"Name him Jezreel, for in a little while*
> *I will bring the bloodshed of Jezreel*
> *on the house of Jehu*
> *and put an end to the kingdom of the house of Israel."* (v. 4)

Jezreel was a city in Israel. As God stated in verse 4, it was a place of blood. In Jezreel a man named Jehu executed the wicked Queen Jezebel. Jezebel's husband, King Ahab, had already died, but he had seventy sons. Jehu sent a letter instructing some men to bring the heads of the seventy sons of Ahab to him. So they murdered all seventy of the sons of Ahab, beheaded them, and brought the heads to Jehu at

Jezreel (2 Kgs 9–10). Second Kings 10:11 summarizes: "So Jehu killed all who remained of the house of Ahab in Jezreel—all his great men, close friends, and priests—leaving him no survivors." The death in the house of Ahab and Jezebel was God's punishment for their sin, but that did not exonerate Jehu of guilt because it's clear that Jehu did it to fulfill his own will, not God's. He continued the idolatry practiced in Israel, and he did not walk with God. In other words, God used Jehu to bring judgment on the house of Ahab for sins Ahab and his court were committing, but Jehu committed the same sins.

God told Hosea he was going to "bring the bloodshed of Jezreel / on the house of Jehu" (Hos 1:4), and he told Hosea to name his firstborn child "Jezreel." God wanted to remind his people that his judgment was coming because of the horrific sins that were virtually uninterrupted throughout the history of Israel, represented famously by the murders committed in Jezreel. It was like God telling his prophet to name his child after the busiest abortion clinic in the country, or after the concentration camp Auschwitz—a place of wanton, grisly murder—so every time someone called the name of the child, people would remember that God was not going to allow that horrific sin to remain unpunished.

God's judgment did come. Second Kings 15:29 says King Tiglath-Pileser III of Assyria marched his army into Israel and conquered much of northern Israel, including Jezreel, and he carried the inhabitants into exile. Hosea lived to see the prophetic word of God fulfilled.

Hosea named his second child Lo-ruhamah, which means "no mercy" or "no compassion." God told Hosea to give her that name because "I will no longer have compassion / on the house of Israel" (1:6). The people of Israel had turned their backs on God for centuries, and finally through Hosea God announced that the time of his judgment was coming—no more mercy; the time of compassion had passed, and the time of punishment had come.

The second announcement of God's judgment against sin is worse than the first. To hear of the loss of the city of Jezreel was shattering news, but it was even more shattering to hear of the loss of God's mercy. God was announcing that he would no longer be a party to Israel's sin; he would not give his forgiveness because they were not seeking it. They were set in their sinful ways, and God would not continue to bless them. Whether Israel remembered it or not, God had established a covenant relationship with Israel. The nations knew he was the God of Israel. So

Israel's sin reflected on him; their sin brought shame on him. "Hosea, name your child No Compassion; I will no longer have compassion on the house of Israel."

Hosea 1:9 says when the third child was born, God said, "Name him Lo-ammi." "Lo-ammi" means "not my people." That's a weird name. Can you imagine seeing a little child with his dad and asking the dad, "What's the little fella's name?" And the father answers, "This is Not-My-Child." You say, "Okay. Whose child is he?" And the dad says, "You don't understand; that's his name—'Not-My-Child.'" So you politely say, "Nice to meet you, Not-My-Child," while you're thinking, *These people need professional help.*

God had a reason for telling his prophet to give his third child such a strange name. God said to Hosea, "Name him Lo-ammi, / for you are not my people, / and I will not be your God" (v. 9). Like the other two children, this child's name carried a message for Israel: "You are not my people, and I am not your God." When God called Moses to be his deliverer in Egypt, God told Moses that his name is, "I AM WHO I AM" (Exod 3:14). God's statement to Hosea here was effectively, "I am not 'I am' to you." "Hosea, give your third child the name 'Not My People' because Israel has forgotten *my* name. My name is 'I am,' but I'm not 'I am' to them anymore." The people of Israel did not know God anymore. The great majority of them were not worshiping and serving him, so the name of Hosea's third child was an acknowledgment of the truth: they were not God's people. So every time someone called the name of one of Hosea's children, he was reminded of those messages from God—egregious sin in Israel's past, Israel was leaving the time of God's mercy and approaching God's judgment, and Israel had so broken the covenant with God that they were no longer his people. God's covenant promises were still in effect, but Hosea's generation was forfeiting God's covenant blessings.

God's Plan Is Restoration
HOSEA 1:10–2:1

The final statement in verse 9 is, "You are not my people, / and I will not be your God." Then, suddenly and without any indication of transition, verse 10 opens with God's promising numerous blessings to his people. And if you think that abrupt shift in theme looks strange, then welcome to Hosea. That kind of sudden shift in subject is characteristic of this book of the Bible.

What did God promise Israel here in verse 10? He promised them multiplication: "The number of the Israelites / will be like the sand of the sea, / which cannot be measured or counted." Do you recognize that promise? It's the promise God gave Abraham. In Genesis 15:5 God told Abraham, "Look at the sky and count the stars, if you are able to count them." Can you see Abraham starting to number the stars and losing count, like we all do? Then God told him that was the number his descendants were going to be—so many he couldn't count them. God said, "Your offspring will be that numerous" (Gen 15:5). Then in Genesis 22 God added another illustration. He told Abraham that his offspring would be "as numerous as the stars of the sky and the sand on the seashore" (Gen 22:17). Abraham surely knew God's point; his descendants would be numberless.

That is the promise God repeated to Israel through Hosea during a time when the people of Israel were so far gone in sin that God could say to them, "You are not my people." Here is a powerful statement of God's grace. The people who had abandoned God, had broken the covenant, were living in rebellion against God's moral law, and were worshiping other gods were indeed not God's people. Israel was in the process of forfeiting God's covenant blessings, and God was going to send his final judgment so they would cease to exist as a nation. But God's covenant with Abraham was and is eternal. Even in the dark days in which Hosea lived, still God had a plan to restore his people. And God *did* restore his people. After Judah was conquered and exiled from the land as God's punishment for their sin, God saved a remnant that returned to the land after the exile—a remnant of God's people who continued to worship him and seek him.

God goes on to say, "And in the place where they were told: / You are not my people, / they will be called: Sons of the living God" (Hos 1:10). The people who were not God's people will become God's people. And in verse 11 God even promises the reunification of Judah and Israel and the return of fertility to the valley of Jezreel. Days of blessing were to come.

In this Messianic Age in which we live, God has indeed created a people through faith in the gospel of Jesus. All people who put their faith in Jesus become the people of God. Hosea 1:10 is the verse the apostle Paul quoted in Romans 9 when he wrote,

As it also says in Hosea,
"I will call Not My People, My People,
and she who is Unloved, Beloved,
and it will be in the place where they were told,
you are not my people,
there they will be called sons of the living God." (Rom 9:25-26)

In Romans 9 Paul was describing the church as the fulfillment of this prophecy in the book of Hosea. The apostle Peter also looked to these verses to define the church of Jesus. He wrote in 1 Peter 2:10, "Once you were not a people, but now you are God's people; you had not received mercy, but now you have received mercy."

So, in this age, the church is the people God has called to himself, into a relationship of covenant love with him. This is the story of the Bible, the story of history—God calling people to life with him. For Israel in the time of Hosea, God had called and called, but most of the people turned away from God again and again, going their own sinful way. The time of repentance was about to end for them, and the time of punishment was about to arrive.

In the remainder of the book of Hosea, God continued to call his people to repentance and to offer his mercy and forgiveness all the way to the end. But God's mercy is only for those who are willing to repent and receive it. The choice is clear; it was clear then and it is clear now. Either turn to God, believe his Word and his way, enter a covenant relationship with him and receive mercy, and become one of his people. Or else, turn away from him and rebel against the truth of his Word, and receive his divine judgment. It's amazing, is it not? Even though we are sinners, God still pursues us and offers us the opportunity to live in a love relationship with him. No matter what we do, no matter how we feel, God pursues us. Even when we're full of pain and regret, he can find us and heal us. He follows us in radical grace based on nothing but his infinite love for undeserving sinners.

God called Hosea to a painful task. He called Jesus to a more painful task. Jesus, God the Son, took our sin and God's righteous wrath against sin on himself when he died on the cross. He became the sacrifice for our sin that he might reconcile us to God. He poured out his love on the cross, taking our sin and its penalty upon himself as our sacrifice. Then he rose to show he has the power to give life, and he gives us life abundant and eternal when we put our faith in him. This is the gospel. Praise his name! May we be warned by the reality of God's coming judgment, may we feel welcomed by his love and grace, and may we run to the one who pursues us while there is still time before his final judgment comes.

Reflect and Discuss

1. Can you identify moments in your life when God spoke to you in an especially memorable way? What was the message, and how did it affect your life?
2. Make a list of the roles to which God has called you. Which of those include painful tasks? Why are they painful?
3. How are you sharing God's Word with people? What motivates you to do so?
4. After reading the descriptions of a covenant in this chapter, how is your relationship with God a covenant relationship?
5. How is God's judgment of sin today like or unlike the judgment God announced in the births of Jezreel, Lo-ruhamah, and Lo-ammi?
6. How do the story of the Bible and the story of history represent God's calling people to life with him? How can that be demonstrated from the Bible? How is that story continuing today?
7. In what ways are nations and families broken today? What is your role in offering God's healing?

East of Eden

HOSEA 2:2-23

Main Idea: People are perennially tempted to turn religion into a way to secure material profit, but God calls all people into a covenant relationship in which he is the only object of worship and faithfulness to him is the priority.

I.   **God Pursues Sinful People (2:2).**

II. **God Promises Punishment for Unrepentant Sin (2:3-13).**

III. **God Provides Reasons for His Punishment (2:5-17).**

    A. Materialism (2:5-7)

    B. Idolatry (2:8-17)

IV. **God Has a Plan for Complete Restoration (2:14-23).**

    A. A renewed relationship with God (2:14-16)

    B. A repudiation of false gods (2:17)

    C. A reversal of the effects of sin (2:18-23)

In John Steinbeck's novel *East of Eden*, Adam Trask finds a woman named Cathy Ames after she's been beaten and left to die along the road. Adam nurses her back to health, falls in love with her, marries her, and they go to California together to begin a new life. After giving birth to twins, Cathy shoots and wounds Adam, then packs her bags and runs away. Years later, Adam discovers that she's running a house of prostitution in a nearby city and has changed her name to Kate Albey. It's obvious he still loves his wife and would take her back if only she would love him in return. Finally, he confronts her as she is sitting at her desk in her place of business. He says to her,

> Just now it came to me what you don't understand. . . . You know about the ugliness in people . . . , but you . . . don't believe I loved you. And the men who come to you here with their ugliness . . . you don't believe those men could have goodness and beauty in them. You see only one side, and . . . you're sure that's all there is. . . . There's a part of you missing. (*East of Eden*, 70)

Like Adam Trask, Hosea married a woman who was unfaithful to him, and unfaithful in the same way—through prostitution. And yes, a part of Hosea's wife was missing, too, the part that can see and understand faithful love—the faithful love of her husband for her and the faithful love she was to have for him. If we're going to understand the book of Hosea, especially the first three chapters, we need to see the parallel between Hosea's wife and Israel and the parallel between Hosea's love for his wife and God's love for Israel. Hosea's wife, Gomer, was unfaithful to her marriage covenant with Hosea, and Israel was unfaithful in their covenant relationship with God.

God Pursues Sinful People
HOSEA 2:2

The covenant relationship between Israel and God began with the wonderful truth that God seeks a relationship with sinful people, and he calls them to enter a covenant with him. That seeking began as soon as the first sin was committed. After Adam and Eve sinned, God pursued them in the garden of Eden. He announced his holy judgment on their sin, but he also continued to pursue a relationship with them. They moved east of Eden, a phrase John Steinbeck borrowed as the title of his book, and God pursued them. We all live east of Eden now, outside paradise and in a world that is saturated with sin and alienated from God. But God has not changed; he pursues sinful people. That pursuing, holy God told Hosea's children in verse 2,

> *Rebuke your mother; rebuke her.*
> *For she is not my wife and I am not her husband.*
> *Let her remove the promiscuous look from her face*
> *and her adultery from between her breasts.*

At points in Hosea 2, it's difficult to determine whether a statement refers to Hosea's wife, to Israel, or to both. Verse 2 is one of those statements that can refer to both. Hosea's wife was not behaving as his wife, and Israel was not behaving like they were in a covenant relationship with God. But God's desire was reconciliation, so he said, "Rebuke your mother; rebuke her." "Rebuke" translates a word that refers to contending with someone or bringing a legal case against someone. Contend with your mother, contend with Israel, show them the error of their ways, prove to them their guilt in this relationship. God's point in stating that "she is not my wife and I am not her husband" was not to announce a permanent divorce from the entire nation of Israel; it was to acknowledge reality and to call Israel back to him, as Hosea's children were to call their mother back to her husband.

The speaker here is the one true God of the universe. He pursues sinful people. He is perfectly holy. He does not know sin. Sin is an offense against his perfect character, his perfect law, and his perfect love, and he expresses his righteous wrath against sin. Still, he pursues sinners. Nothing in us compels God to seek us. Nothing in the universe is capable of compelling God to do anything; he is God. He is compelled to pursue us solely by his own gracious decision to do so. Could there be any greater demonstration of grace and love than a perfectly holy God pursuing people who have never done anything perfectly except sin? This is infinite, divine grace and love.

This is the God of the Old Testament, and he is the God of the New Testament. Jesus, who is God, said he came "to seek and to save the lost" (Luke 19:10). To seek us and save us, he left the glories of heaven to take on flesh as a man who was a servant and to die in agony on the cross for our sins to reconcile us to God (Phil 2:6-8). So we who know Jesus as Savior can say with Paul in Ephesians 2 that though we were "dead in [our] trespasses and sins . . . God, who is rich in mercy, because of his great love that he had for us, made us alive with Christ. . . . You are saved by grace!" (vv. 1-5). God pursues sinful people. This is grace.

God Promises Punishment for Unrepentant Sin
HOSEA 2:3-13

In Hosea 2 God alternates between stating Israel's sin and announcing his punishment for that sin. If people would turn from their sin to God, he was ready to forgive and restore. But as long as the people were unrepentant, his punishment for sin was on the way. God announces his judgment with vivid pictorial images: he was going to strip Israel naked and make her like a wilderness (v. 3), block her way with a hedge and thorns (v. 6), and withhold the harvest of grain, wine, wool, and flax (v. 9). In fact, the vines and fig trees would be abandoned so that they would become a forest (v. 12). If the people did not repent, God's judgment was coming.

God still punishes sin. God is holy and hates sin. God's judgment is found from Genesis to Revelation: it began with God's throwing Adam and Eve out of the garden of Eden, and it will end with God's throwing the godless into the lake of fire. Preaching judgment has largely gone out of fashion, but throughout the history of the church, God's judgment of sin has been prominent in preaching because it's prominent in the Bible. Furthermore, in order for us to fathom the height of God's love expressed on the cross, it is necessary to fathom the depth of our sin and the perfection of God's holiness. Octavius Winslow, a Puritan pastor in the nineteenth century, preached this:

> The cross of Calvary exhibits God's hatred and punishment
> of sin . . . to an extent which the annihilation of millions of
> worlds . . . could never have done! . . . *The wrath of God was
> poured out upon Him* [Jesus]. . . . Go, my soul, to Calvary, and
> learn how holy God is, and what a monstrous thing sin is, and
> how . . . solemnly . . . bound Jehovah is to punish it, either
> in the person of the sinner, or in the person of a Surety [the
> Savior]. . . . Oh, to learn . . . these two great facts: sin's infinite
> hatefulness and love's infinite holiness! (*Christ's Sympathy*, 3;
> emphasis in original)

God has condemned and will condemn sin. But thank God he has poured out his judgment for our sin on Jesus on the cross as our great and final sacrifice. Jesus has taken the just penalty for our sin on himself. That is how God loves us. At infinite cost to himself, he has taken our punishment for sin upon himself so he maintains his holiness and offers the gracious gift of salvation to unworthy sinners who put their faith in Jesus. Praise his name!

God Provides Reasons for His Punishment
HOSEA 2:5-17

At the moment Hosea preached, Israel was unrepentant. Therefore, God's judgment was coming to them. God did not leave Israel to wonder why his judgment was coming. He provided reasons for his coming judgment. Such reasons appear repeatedly in the book of Hosea and throughout the prophetic books. God states explicitly why his wrath is on its way—what sins the people are committing that are inviting his imminent punishment. It's important that we understand God's indictments against Israel's sin because the same sins are with us today, and we are tempted to commit them.

We could summarize the sins God mentions in these verses with just a few words. The first is **materialism**. Verse 5 says, "Their mother is promiscuous; / she conceived them and acted shamefully." How was she promiscuous, and how did she act shamefully? Still in verse 5, God says, "For she thought, 'I will follow my lovers, / the men who give me my food and water, / my wool and flax, my oil and drink.'" She left her husband to go after illicit lovers. Why? For greater income. Her husband and her covenant relationship with her husband were not as important to her as getting the bread and water, wool and flax—those were important, not her husband and faithful love to him.

In verse 6 and the first part of verse 7, God announced that he was going to discipline Gomer. As a consequence of her sin, he was going to block her from receiving prosperity. He would "block her way with thorns; / . . . enclose her with a wall." So, in verse 7, Gomer announces that she will return to her husband. Why? "Then she will think, / 'I will go back to my former husband, / for then it was better for me than now.'" She still doesn't get it. She went into prostitution for prosperity—more wool and flax, oil and drink—but she learned it wasn't as prosperous as she had hoped. Perhaps she thought, *After I paid the overhead, found a different place to stay and paid for that, I really didn't clear as much as I thought I would. I had more wool and flax when I was with Hosea. Might as well go back to him.* As verse 7 says, "I will go back to my former husband, / for then it was better for me than now." She didn't comprehend that prosperity is not the point. The point is faithful, steadfast love to her husband with whom she shared a covenant relationship. That's what God values and what he expects us to value—love and faithfulness in a covenant relationship.

Here we arrive at the central theme of the book of Hosea. The sin Gomer was committing in her relationship with Hosea was the sin Israelites were committing in their relationship with God. The people of Israel were unfaithful in their relationship with God and worshiped the false god Baal. Why? Israel was unfaithful to God for the same reason Gomer was unfaithful to Hosea: for the wool and flax, the oil and drink. Baal was a patron deity of fertility. Somehow the Canaanites convinced the Israelites that Yahweh was sufficient for the wilderness, but in agricultural matters he was out of his depth. For fertility, one had to worship Baal. The Israelites wanted prosperity more than they wanted faithfulness to God. God told them that kind of idolatry was prostitution—being unfaithful to God because unfaithfulness pays better. They were whores.

The kind of idolatry Israel was committing is still with us today. People serve God so they can get the blessings because it's the blessings they want. That way of thinking diminishes God so that he becomes only a dispenser of things. We could call it vending machine theology. God no longer has value in himself; he has value only for what he can give us. It's the fundamental error of the health and wealth movement: they use prayer, they use faith, they use God as tools to get what they really want, which is prosperity. That's not the gospel; it's paganism, yet it's the philosophy many people live by, and some of those people are in church. They attend and serve, wondering what they will get. We get God! *He* is the great treasure. A love relationship with the one true and holy God of the universe is the prize who meets every need we have, needs we cannot even name. To desire something other than him, something in addition to him, is the essence of idolatry.

This discussion leads us to a second word that summarizes Israel's sin that would lead to God's punishment—**idolatry**. In chapter 2 God referred to the worship of Baal four times (vv. 8,13,16,17). That was idolatry, worshiping a god other than the one true God. Verse 13 mentions some of the idolatrous rituals the Israelites were observing: setting aside special days devoted to the worship of Baal, burning incense, and donning special jewelry as a Baalistic ritual. Verse 8 shows us that idolatry is not just ideological; it's personal for God. God says, "It is I who gave her the grain, / the new wine, and the fresh oil. / I lavished silver and gold on her, / which they used for Baal." God gave them blessings, they received them from God without acknowledging that they came from God, and then they used those blessings in the service of a false god. It was like a husband giving a beautiful diamond ring to his wife, but she's thrilled to receive it because she can pawn it and use the money for a trip to visit her adulterous lover.

An obvious but important application here is to acknowledge everything we have as a gift from God. James 1:17 says, "Every good and perfect gift is from above, coming down from the Father of lights." Everything we have—every material possession, every opportunity, every ability, every relationship, every breath—is a gift from God. That's why we pray before every meal and thank God for the gift of the food. That prayer is not just a meaningless religious ritual; it's a healthy, essential spiritual discipline. We recognize that everything we have comes from God—not from ourselves, not from the boss or the company, and not from fate or destiny. God gives all good things. If we *don't* thank God as the Giver of what we have, we are likely failing to recognize that all we have comes from him, and that's idolatry.

Today, people don't worship Baal or Asherah. They worship a higher salary, beachfront property, sex, a bigger car or house; we worship ourselves. Someone has said that Americans are tuned in to WII FM—What's In It For Me? We worship the god of more for me. But the covenant relationship of love to which God calls us is an exclusive relationship. God allows no rival lovers. The first of the Ten Commandments is, "Do not have other gods besides me" (Exod 20:3). *Prostitution* and *whoring* seem like unpleasant, even offensive words to use to refer to people like us, but they are biblical words. Unfaithfulness to our covenant relationship with God is spiritual adultery. Seeking or wanting anything more than we desire him is selling ourselves to another lover; it's spiritual prostitution.

God stated to Israel that their spiritual prostitution would lead to dissatisfaction, not satisfaction. "She will pursue her lovers but not catch them; / she will look for them but not find them" (v. 7). The book of James refers to the same frustration. "You desire and do not have. You . . . covet and cannot obtain. . . . You ask and don't receive because you ask with wrong motives, so that you may spend it on your pleasures. You adulterous people!" (Jas 4:2-4). Thus, James also referred to desiring something other than God as adultery, and he also said it leads to frustration, not satisfaction.

The worldly person is not fulfilled. When worldliness is in our hearts, we pursue what we want, thinking it will result in more for us. What actually happens is that, as we turn away from God, we forfeit our claim to the abundant blessings God wants to give us. Living for God leads to fulfillment; living for self leads to disappointment. Being Christ centered leads to satisfaction; being self-centered leads to frustration.

The frustration we feel when we pursue pleasure has been called the hedonistic paradox. Hedonism is the philosophy that makes pleasure the center of our life. When we're hedonistic, we make decisions based on what will be most pleasurable for us. There are two possible outcomes to the pursuit of pleasure. One possible outcome is that we will not obtain the object of our pleasure. That's frustrating, not pleasurable. The other possible outcome is that we will obtain the object of our pleasure. That's pleasurable, but the trap of pleasure is that the next time we seek that object of pleasure, we need more of it to reach the same level of pleasure. Then, when the object of pleasure does not satisfy as it once did, that also is frustrating, not pleasurable. So, either way, the pursuit of pleasure leads to pain. It's the hedonistic paradox; the selfish pursuit of pleasure leads to the opposite of pleasure, and that's the point of James 4 and Hosea 2. The pursuit of false gods and personal pleasure is a treasure hunt with no treasure. But Christ is the greatest treasure in the universe (see Matt 13:44). Pursuing him leads us to fulfillment and joy, not frustration.

God Has a Plan for Complete Restoration
HOSEA 2:14-23

In the first verses of chapter 2, God reviews the sins of Israel and Hosea's wife. Then verse 6 begins with "therefore," and what follows is an announcement of the punishment Israel's sin has earned from God. They had sinned; *therefore* judgment for sin was coming. Verses 7-8 mention Israel's sin again. Verse 9 begins with another "therefore," and God states again his punishment for their sin. Verses 12-13 present even more sin Israel has committed, and verse 14 has a third "therefore." At this point we expect another announcement of judgment, and we're prepared for the punishment to be even more severe—perhaps the final, ultimate expression of God's judgment against this rebellious, idolatrous, unrepentant people. God has said that Israel has sinned and he is going to pass judgment. Israel continued to sin, and he is going to pass more severe judgment. Then God gives a third statement of their sin, so we're ready for the final curtain to fall, for God to announce the end of these people who will not turn to him. But that's not what he says. Instead, he says, "Therefore, I am going to persuade her, / lead her to the wilderness [an allusion to the wilderness wandering at the beginning of Israel's relationship with God], / and speak tenderly to her" (v. 14).

What an amazing statement of God's grace! Just when readers of Hosea expect God to give these people what they deserve, he offers them what they clearly do not deserve. He speaks tenderly to them and offers them love, **a renewed relationship with God**. The chapter began as a court case—a rebuke, a contention against Israel—and the mountain of evidence of Israel's sin is presented and proves that they were guilty beyond any doubt. When we expect the final gavel to fall and the sentence to be announced, instead God says, "Let's start over. I love you." He persuades Israel and speaks tenderly to them. "Speak tenderly to her" is literally "speak to her heart."

In this future day of renewal, God says, "You will call me 'my husband' / and no longer call me 'my Baal'" (v. 16). They were confusing the one true God with a false god, the not-god named Baal, actually calling God "Baal." But if they would come to God to be restored, they would know God in a loving covenant relationship and would call him "my husband."

So this restoration would also result in **a repudiation of false gods**. In the day of restoration, God says, "I will remove the names of the Baals / from her mouth; / they will no longer be remembered by their names" (v. 17). "Remembered" is often used in the Old Testament to refer to invoking someone or something, calling it to mind, not merely recalling information instead of forgetting (e.g., Gen 8:1). The point here is that idolatry would not be a part of this renewed relationship with God. The people of Israel would no longer invoke the names of false gods in worship.

Further, as part of God's future restoration, he was offering **a reversal of the effects of sin**. Verses 18-23 provide a beautiful description of universal renewal. The word *covenant* occurs five times in the book of Hosea. Twice it refers to God's covenant with Israel (6:7; 8:1), though the idea of the covenant relationship between God and Israel is in view at almost every point. Twice Hosea uses "covenant" to refer to treaties between Israel and neighboring countries—international alliances Israel made in an attempt to secure protection (10:4; 12:1). But the first use of "covenant" is here in chapter 2 as God extends his covenant to the entire natural order. War is no more; everything is at peace. Righteousness, justice, steadfast love, and mercy are practiced as Israel walks with God in a faithful covenant relationship. And they will know God. This is the renewal God plans for his people if they will turn from sin and turn to him. He'll restore them.

A pastor named Jud Wilhite published a book titled *Pursued*, and in that book he tells the story of Randy and Joanne. Randy was a pastor and Joanne was his wife. Joanne was caring for three children at home while serving constantly at the church and leading the women's ministry. She hit an emotional wall, was diagnosed with clinical depression, and spent some time in a hospital. Some leaders in the church found out. They were concerned that Joanne's struggles might leak out, and then the church would know that a pastor's family was having trouble.

They encouraged Randy not to tell anybody at church and act like everything was OK.

It got worse. Joanne met a fellow patient and had a short-term affair with long-term consequences. When the church leaders found out, they panicked and fired Randy. From Randy's perspective, he had done nothing wrong, and his friends had turned their backs on him when he needed them most. Randy did what a lot of people do. He told God what he thought of his people, and he checked out of church altogether. For years, Joanne stayed depressed and Randy stayed angry. He lost his secular job and became even more bitter, but Joanne found a job and learned that she felt good when she served people. After eight years away from any church, Joanne suggested they consider trying to find a church. Randy told her, "No way"; he was never going back to a church. But eventually Randy relented. When they went to church, they heard the gospel, and they were reminded of the God who loves people who are not OK. With all of their anger, bitterness, and emotional exhaustion, they knew they were *so* not OK.

They attended that church for two years, just trying to soak it all in, trying to believe God, trying to believe his love and his Word again. And they did. God restored them. Eventually the church asked them to be part of a video in which people shared their stories in bite-sized headlines. Randy's headline was "Burned by the church. Restored in Jesus Christ." Joanne's was, "Abuse, adultery, and suicide. Healed, forgiven, and alive" (Wilhite, *Pursued*, 24–27).

They were restored, healed by God, after running for a long time. Through everything, God did not quit on them, even when they quit on God. They were unfaithful. God never was; he kept pursuing them. No matter what we do, no matter how we feel, God pursues us. Even when we're full of pain and regret, he can find us and heal us. He follows us in radical grace based on nothing but his infinite love for undeserving sinners. He poured out that love on the cross, taking our sin and its penalty upon himself as our sacrifice. Then he rose to show he has the power to give life. This is the gospel. Praise his name!

Reflect and Discuss

1. Why does God pursue a relationship with sinful people? When we see why God pursues us, what should be our response?
2. What can we learn about God, ourselves, and the world when we consider God's punishment of sin displayed in Israel and on the cross?
3. How do material things distract people away from God? Name some ways this temptation is manifested today and some ways it affects you.
4. What does this chapter identify as the central theme of Hosea? How do you see that central theme being expressed in the world today?
5. Define "vending machine theology." In what ways is such a theology inadequate and faulty?
6. How is idolatry personal to God? How are you tempted to commit idolatry? What can you do to eliminate idolatry?
7. How do you see the "hedonistic paradox" manifested in the lives of people in the world today?
8. Describe God's plan for complete restoration. How will such restoration occur in your life and in the lives of people you know?

Redeeming Love

HOSEA 3

Main Idea: Without a personal relationship with God, all people are slaves to sin, but because God loves us, he has paid the price for our freedom and offers us a new life in Christ.

I.   **God Offers a Relationship to All People (3:1).**
    A. A relationship of love
    B. A covenant relationship
II. **God Sets Us Free from Sin (3:2).**
III. **God Requires Exclusive Worship (3:3-4).**
IV. **God Promises Full Restoration (3:5).**

Hosea lived during dark days. We, too, live in times that are spiritually dark. The book of Hosea is the proclamation of God that shines God's truth in the darkness of our times. In this section we'll consider the message of the third chapter of Hosea. Here Hosea the prophet continues to address the crisis in his family that illustrated the crisis in Israel.

To recap, in the second verse of the book, God gave Hosea a command that must have been difficult to obey: "Go and marry a woman of promiscuity, / and have children of promiscuity." Hosea obeyed that command, so God's prophet was married to a woman who was promiscuous and at least sometimes received payment for sex. Hosea had a wife who was unfaithful to him. Her name was "Gomer." That sounds strange to us; we think of Gomer Pyle and "Shazam!," but in Hosea's Israel "Gomer" was a woman's name. In this case, the woman was unfaithful to her husband. Gomer was an adulteress, and chapter 2 makes clear that Gomer received payment for her unfaithfulness. God draws a parallel between Hosea's wife and Israel—her conduct and Israel's conduct, her unfaithfulness to her covenant with her husband and Israel's unfaithfulness to their covenant with God. That parallel is repeated in chapter 3. And God told Hosea to continue to love his sinful wife as God still loved sinful Israel.

God Offers a Relationship to All People
HOSEA 3:1

Hosea's third chapter begins, "The LORD loves the Israelites though they turn to other gods and love raisin cakes" (v. 1). Those "raisin cakes" were sometimes part of legitimate worship in the Old Testament period (2 Sam 6:19; 1 Chr 16:3), but they were also part of the Canaanite pagan worship in which Israelites were participating (Jer 7:18; 44:19). God said that's what Israel was loving and worshiping—other gods. Yet God was seeking those people who were turning away from him to other gods. God was offering sinners a relationship with him. He loved them even though they were turning to other gods.

Though Israel was unworthy of a relationship with God at this point, we should not think that when God originally chose them they *were* worthy of him. Israel's worth was not the reason God loved Israel. In the book of Deuteronomy, God says explicitly that he did not love and choose Israel because they were the biggest or the best. He loved them and chose them because he loved them. In Deuteronomy 7 God says, "The LORD had his heart set on you and chose you, not because you were more numerous than all peoples, for you were the fewest of all peoples. But because the LORD loved you" (Deut 7:7-8). He loved them because he loved them. Nothing in them elicited God's love. He loved them because of his divine, self-directed choice to love them. The merit was not in the people; it was solely in God.

God's love that led him to choose Israel reminds us that the relationship to which God calls us is **a relationship of love**. In the book of Hosea, God illustrates his relationship with his people by means of the marriage relationship, which is to be a relationship of love. God initially called Israel into a relationship of love—he loved them, and he told them, "Love the LORD your God with all your heart, with all your soul, and with all your strength" (Deut 6:5). In Hosea 3 God reiterates his love for Israel. He says, "The LORD loves the Israelites" (v. 1).

The relationship God wants with us is a relationship of love. Just as God used Hosea's marriage to his wife as an illustration of his love for Israel, God's relationship of love with Israel is an illustration of the love relationship he wants with all people. All people. The object of God's affection is not one person or one group of people but all people. Jesus said, "For God loved the world in this way: He gave his one and only

Son, so that everyone who believes in him will not perish but have eternal life" (John 3:16). That's the reason God gave his only Son—he loves "the world," "everyone." That's also the reason Jesus died on the cross. He was demonstrating God's love for us. Romans 5:8 says, "God proves his own love for us in that while we were still sinners, Christ died for us." God offers a relationship of love to all people.

One of the most common reasons people turn away from God is that they don't like God's punishment of sin and his requirement of holiness. The Bible repeatedly states that God *does* punish sin and call us to holiness, but he also loves us and offers us a relationship of love with him. He wants us to walk with him in a love relationship, and he wants to provide all good things to us. In God's Word he tells us that he wants to relate to us as a father loves his children, as a shepherd cares for his sheep, as a farmer cares for his crops, and as a husband loves his wife. God offers a relationship of love to all people.

The relationship God offers all people is **a covenant relationship**. The relationship between Hosea and his wife was a covenant relationship; they shared the covenant of marriage (Mal 2:14). God had established a covenant relationship with Israel—through Abraham, later through Moses, and still later with King David. This is another parallel between Hosea's relationship with Gomer and God's relationship with Israel—both were covenant relationships. Gomer had been unfaithful in her covenant relationship with Hosea, but the covenant with Hosea was still in place. Israel had been unfaithful to God, but the covenant God had made with them was still in place.

In the world in which Israel lived, covenants could be between two equal parties (parity treaties/covenants) or between a party who was greater and one who was lesser (suzerainty treaties/covenants). In the covenants between equal parties, the obligations and the benefits of the covenant were also equal. But in covenants between a greater party and a lesser, the greater party determined the stipulations of the covenant, and the lesser party was obligated to obey those stipulations. And typically the benefits of the covenant relationship would apply only if the stipulations were obeyed.

Marriage was a covenant between equal parties. But morally, Hosea and his wife were not equals. The fact that Gomer was living in prostitution created moral inequity. That, too, reflected God's covenant with Israel because obviously the covenant God offered to Israel and offers to us is a covenant between a greater party and a lesser party. God is forever the greater party. In that sense God's covenant relationship with us has no parallel with any human covenant because he is God. In Romans 11 the apostle Paul wrote about God's covenant with Israel and his extension of that covenant to Gentiles. Then suddenly, Paul broke into praise because of how sublime, how inconceivable it is that the God of the universe offers a covenant relationship to us. Paul wrote,

> *Oh, the depth of the riches*
> *and the wisdom and the knowledge of God!*
> *How unsearchable his judgments*
> *and untraceable his ways!*
> *For who has known the mind of the Lord?*
> *Or who has been his counselor?*
> *And who has ever given to God,*
> *that he should be repaid?*
> *For from him and through him*
> *and to him are all things.*
> *To him be the glory forever. Amen.* (Rom 11:33-36)

We should consider the truth of those verses when thinking about God's covenant with Israel, with us, or with any sinful human. We should not contemplate God's offer of a covenant relationship with him without stopping to *marvel* that he would do so. Because he is God, he has no need of us. If he had a need, he wouldn't tell us. He says, "If I were hungry, I would not tell you, / for the world and everything in it is mine" (Ps 50:12). May we all marvel that the God of the universe offers a love relationship to all people.

God Sets Us Free from Sin
HOSEA 3:2

Hosea's wife needed to be set free. She was with some lover, and evidently she sank so low that she was being sold as a slave (v. 2). God told Hosea to go and buy her. Did someone in town go to Hosea and say, "Hosea, I just saw your wife in the market. She's being sold as a prostitute. I thought you'd want to know." Imagine Hosea's humiliation. The man of God going to buy his wife, bidding against other men. Surely, Gomer was humiliated too. A man bid five shekels of silver. Another said ten . . . twelve . . . thirteen. Hosea said, "Fifteen shekels of silver." Another said, "Fifteen shekels of silver and a homer of barley." Hosea said, "Fifteen shekels of silver and a homer and a lethech of barley." The auctioneer declared, "Sold, to Hosea."

Hosea and his wife are in the foreground of this story because they are central to the book. We should note in passing the figures in the background—the men who owned, used, and sold a woman as if she were a commodity to be exploited for their profit, not a valuable human being made in God's image. As we acknowledge the sin committed by Hosea's wife, and promiscuous women like her, let us not forget to denounce likewise the sins of the men who use women for their pleasure and sell them for their profit. Such men were present at the auction described in Hosea 3. They are not at the center of Hosea's story of domestic tragedy; the prophet's interest lies in his wife's relationship with him and Israel's relationship with God. But the men participating in promiscuity and promoting it were guilty nonetheless, and the book of Hosea never exonerates them.

As for Hosea, he took his wife and led her home. Hosea did something God does. He loved someone who was unworthy of his love; he was faithful to someone who was unfaithful to him. It's not that Hosea loved his unfaithful wife that way and concluded that God's love must be like that. On the contrary, Hosea first saw the way God loved sinful Israel, and God told him to love his sinful wife in that way. First John 4:11 says, "Dear friends, if God loved us in this way, we also must love one another." We see the way God loves sinners like us, and we know how to love sinners too.

Years ago, a man in vocational ministry came to me to share his struggle. His wife was having an emotional affair with another man. She said she loved the other man and no longer loved her husband. She moved out of the house, and my friend wondered what to do. I turned to Hosea 3 and told him that if he wanted to love like God loves, he would pursue his unfaithful bride, and he would not give up. I suspect he was already inclined to do that, and that's what he did. He had no assurance she would respond to him or even listen to him. But she did. And as her husband loved her, gradually God performed a miracle in her heart. She returned to him, and afterward their marriage was stronger than ever and a wonderful joy to both of them.

Like Hosea's wife, and like Israel, we have sinned, and we have been enslaved by sin. Jesus said, "Everyone who commits sin is a slave of sin" (John 8:34). But just as Hosea purchased his wife and set her free from slavery, God purchases us and sets us free from slavery to sin. That's the meaning of the New Testament word *redeem,* or *ransom*—"to set free from slavery by payment." First Peter 1 says to followers of Jesus, "You were redeemed from your empty way of life inherited from your ancestors, not with perishable things like silver or gold, but with the precious blood of Christ" (vv. 18-19). Christ, God the Son, shed his precious blood, giving his life as the payment for us so that we may be set free from sin, rescued, and reconciled to God. "He erased the certificate of debt, with its obligations, that was against us and opposed to us, and has taken it away by nailing it to the cross" (Col 2:14). Christ "erased" and "has taken away" the debt our sin had incurred. He eradicated our debt by "nailing it to the cross," thus setting us free. Christ's payment for our sin led Paul to write to Christians, "You are not your own, for you were bought at a price" (1 Cor 6:19-20). Hosea purchased his wife and set her free from slavery. God purchased us and set us free from slavery. Hosea had to endure humiliation. Jesus had to endure humiliation and death on a cross.

One of the devil's biggest lies is that living for ourselves is freedom and living for Jesus is slavery. It's tragic that so many people believe that lie when the truth is actually the opposite: a life ruled by the world, the flesh, and the devil is slavery, but Jesus sets us free from such slavery and gives us abundant life. The sad truth is that many people are enslaved to sin, and they don't even know it. Surely Hosea's wife never intended to be enslaved. Her goal was freedom—freedom from the constraints of her marriage covenant with Hosea, freedom to pursue pleasure and prosperity as she pleased. But when she pursued sin, the result was not freedom; it was slavery. She needed to return to the one who really loved her. Israel needed to return to the God who really loved them. So many people today are missing life with the one who loves them infinitely and settling for things that promise love but give only slavery.

Perhaps Hosea's wife can be compared to Estella, a character in Charles Dickens's book *Great Expectations.* Pip, the central character of the story, fell desperately in love with Estella when he was a young man. But Estella was cold toward him. It seemed that not only did Estella not love Pip, but she did not even have the capacity to understand his love. Pip's love only intensified, and he intended to marry her, but she turned away from him and married someone else, and Pip never married. Estella's husband, a man named Drummle, treated Estella cruelly and abused her for years until he was killed in an accident. Then, two years later, Estella and Pip happened to see each other again. Dickens described Estella as a woman whose suffering had transformed her. Her eyes had once been proud; now they were soft. Her heart had once been cold; now she was friendly. The one constant in her life, through all the years, had been Pip's love for her. And now, finally, suffering without love in her life had prepared her to understand and receive his love (Dickens, *Great Expectations*).

I suggest that this is the story of every person in the world. The one constant in their lives is that God loves them, no matter what. So many people respond to God's love like Estella responded to Pip, like Hosea's wife and Israel responded to love. In the face of limitless love, their hearts are cold, and they turn away from it. But to turn away from God's love is always to choose a way of suffering. So we pray for such people, that one day, after they have suffered and come to realize their idols are dead, they will wake up and realize that God loves them so much that he's willing to pay the highest price to redeem them. God sets us free from sin.

God Requires Exclusive Worship
HOSEA 3:3-4

In Hosea 3 God provides another parallel between Hosea's relationship with his wife and God's relationship with Israel. Hosea told his wife, "You are to live with me many days. You must not be promiscuous or belong to any man, and I will act the same way toward you" (v. 3). The next verse presents the parallel with Israel: "For the Israelites must live many days without king or prince, without sacrifice or sacred pillar, and without ephod or household idols" (v. 4).

Hosea's wife was breaking her marriage covenant by going to another man instead of staying with Hosea. Israel was breaking their covenant with God by trusting in kings and princes instead of trusting in God. They also broke their covenant with God by worshiping false gods. They kept "household idols"—little representations of pagan gods—in their homes. The "ephod" was most likely an implement of divination used to consult the will of pagan gods. A "sacred pillar" was typically erected to represent false gods, and in God's law he had said that he hates such pillars (Deut 16:22), and he told his people to destroy them (Deut 7:5; 12:3).

The point of verses 3 and 4 is that somehow God was going to deprive Israel of all those idols, just as Hosea was going to deprive his

wife of the opportunity to go to another lover. The marriage relationship is an exclusive relationship, and a relationship with God is also
exclusive: we worship the one true God and only him.

In the Ten Commandments, the first commandment is, "Do not
have other gods besides me" (Exod 20:3). The second commandment is,

> Do not make an idol for yourself, whether in the shape of anything
> in the heavens above or on the earth below or in the waters under the
> earth. Do not bow in worship to them, and do not serve them; for I, the
> LORD your God, am a jealous God. (Exod 20:4-5)

The word translated "jealous" refers to fervent emotion. It's used in the
Old Testament to refer to a husband's jealousy for the love of his wife
(Prov 6:34) and the love that burns in the hearts of a bride and groom
(Song 8:6). God has that intense emotion for our loyalty and faithful-
ness to him (see Zeph 1:18; 3:8). He has zeal for our devotion to him.
Adultery and idolatry are personal. Yes, adultery and idolatry violate
God's moral code, but they also violate a relationship with a person, a
person who is supposed to be beloved above all. That's true for a per-
son's relationship with a spouse, and it's true in our relationship with
God. Worshiping anything or anyone other than him is personal—it
grieves him, it betrays him, and it arouses his holy jealousy.

The sin of idolatry is still committed today, even by people who
are followers of Jesus. Whenever something or someone becomes as
important as God to us, that's idolatry—putting something in the place
that is to be occupied only by God. Whenever doing something we
want to do becomes as important as doing what God tells us to do,
that's idolatry.

We work hard and get a promotion and a raise. That's not idolatry.
But the company says, "To take this promotion you're going to be trav-
eling a lot on Sundays, and you'll be away from your family much of the
time." At that point, we face the question of what's really important to
us and how that may compare or contrast with what God has told us to
do. Participating in a hobby like sports is fun—playing sports or watching games—and it's not idolatry. But when we calculate the amount
of time we spend watching sports and compare that with the amount
of time we spend in God's Word, or the time we spend worshiping or
serving God, we're back to the question of what's really important to
us and the possibility that an idol exists in our hearts. God requires
exclusive worship.

God Promises Full Restoration
HOSEA 3:5

In verse 3, when God spoke to Israel about living without the objects of their idolatry, he used the words "many days." Again in verse 4, he said "many days." Then, in verse 5 God refers to "the last days." Hosea doesn't record for us *when* these events will take place. But the prophecy in verse 5 does reveal *what* will happen when God's people are restored. God says his people "will return and seek the LORD their God." God's people will turn from sin to him. They'll enjoy fellowship with God unhindered by sin. They'll also seek "David their king." King David had been deceased for almost 250 years at this point, so this refers to a descendant of King David. Also, since this is a prophecy about the future, it's reasonable to take it as a reference to *the* descendant of David—the messianic King who will reign forever—and the New Testament tells us that Jesus is the Davidic ruler who reigns forever (Acts 13:22-23).

Through Hosea, God reveals what he has in store for his people in the end: freedom from sin, fellowship with him, worshiping him, and enjoying the blessings of his presence—full restoration. I know a man who pastors a church named Restoration Church. One day all followers of Jesus will be members of Restoration Church. That's what God has in store for us because of his love and grace for unworthy sinners.

Years ago, when I was serving as a pastor, on a Sunday morning a young lady named Jessica was driving around Raleigh with a shotgun in her truck planning to pull over somewhere and kill herself. She was involved in a sinful lifestyle, she felt stuck in it, her boyfriend had been abusing her, and she was at the end of her rope. She pulled into the parking lot of our church. That's where she was going to kill herself, but for some reason she got out of the truck and walked into the building. It was Sunday morning, and we were in worship. But we always had some people praying during our worship time; we called that prayer meeting our Boiler Room. Somehow Jessica was directed to Charles, who was one of the people praying.

Jessica told Charles what she had planned to do, and she showed him the shotgun shell she had planned to use to kill herself. Charles told her, "First of all, give me that shell; you won't be needing that today." Charles then shared the gospel with her and urged her to come to Christ. Jessica said she wasn't ready to do that, but she ambled into the worship center and stayed for worship. She talked with a few folks after church and eventually with me. Jessica was like Hosea's wife. I asked her where she worked, and she said she worked in the adult entertainment industry. She seemed angry at the church in general and angry at God. She challenged some of the things the Bible says about Jesus; she said they didn't make sense to her. I answered her questions as well as I could, but she was far from satisfied. I told her she needed Jesus, and when I asked her if she wanted to put her faith in him, she laughed and said, "If that ever happens, I'll make sure you're there to see it!"

Jessica came back to worship again, and she had more questions. We began to love her in every way we could. My wife and I spent time with her over meals, and we talked with her through some crises in her life. A few other people in the church did the same. Jessica seemed to be stabbing at God while at the same time reaching out to him. Then one day she told us she was moving to another city in our state, but she said she wanted to stay in touch. Sure enough, not long after she moved, I received an email from her. She said she wanted my wife and me to meet with her. We arranged a day to drive to her city, we sat down at a table together, and she asked me, "Do you remember when I told you I didn't want to receive Christ, but if that ever happened, I would be sure you're there to see it?" I told her, "No, Jessica, I don't remember that." I had forgotten, but she had not. Then she told us that's why she wanted to meet. She was ready to put her faith in Jesus and become a Christian, and she wanted us to be there to help her to do it. So we prayed with Jessica, and she asked Jesus into her life as her Savior and Lord.

A few weeks after Jessica was saved, she called me. After catching up with her, I asked, "Jessica, why did you get out of the truck and come into the building that morning instead of pulling the trigger?" She said, "I really don't know why." I told her, "I think I know why. God loves you, and *he* got you out of that truck to save your life. Even when you were running from God, he kept loving you, and he didn't give up on you—not only to save your life but to save your soul forever." After over ten years, Jessica still calls occasionally. She seems eager for us to know how happy she is in the new life she has in Christ and how God is blessing her.

God gave Jessica a new life, a life of joy and blessing. God wants to do that for every person. Regardless of what we have done, God is ready to receive us and forgive us when we're ready to turn to him, confess sin, believe in him, and enter a covenant relationship with him. The holy, almighty God who holds the universe in his hands wants a love relationship with sinners like us. Like Hosea's wife, we're not only sinners, but we were also slaves to sin. But just as Hosea bought his wife, God has paid our sin debt and purchased us for himself with the blood of God the Son. Jesus, God the Son, died as the sacrifice for our sins and rose again. When we put our faith in him, he forgives our sin, reconciles us to God, and gives us new and eternal life. This is the gospel. Don't turn away from God's redeeming love.

Reflect and Discuss

1. Why did God choose Israel? What does his choice of Israel teach you about God and your relationship with him?
2. Can you think of a modern parallel to Hosea's purchase of his wayward wife from slavery?
3. How is Hosea's purchase of Gomer like and unlike God's purchase of us?
4. What are some ways you can express love to someone who is turning away from God, as Hosea loved Gomer and God loved Israel?
5. In what ways does God's jealousy for our faithfulness help us avoid sin and walk closely with him?
6. Make a list of activities or items people make into more of a priority than God and faithfulness to him. Which of those are temptations for you?
7. What are some ways a redeemed life is better than an unredeemed life?

Love God; Hate Sin

HOSEA 4–5

Main Idea: Sin arises from the heart, breaks fellowship with God, and hurts us; so when we love God, we hate sin and run from it.

I.   **Sin Starts in the Heart (4:12; 5:4).**
II. **Sin and Broken Fellowship with God Go Together (4:1,10; 5:4, 7,13).**
III. **Sin Hurts the Sinner (4:7,11; 5:4).**
IV. **Wrong Worship Is Sin (4:12-14).**
V.   **Sinful Leaders Harm Everyone (4:4-6; 5:1,10).**
VI. **God Punishes Sin (4:9-10; 5:6,10,12,14-15).**

Years ago, I lived in Gulfport, Mississippi, where I pastored a church. The year we arrived in Gulfport, it had been sixteen years since Hurricane Camille made landfall in that city. Still, we heard the horror stories as if Camille had made landfall the week before we arrived. It was Sunday, August 17, 1969, when Hurricane Camille reached the Mississippi Gulf Coast. Sustained winds exceeded 200 miles per hour, with gusts over 230. It's still the only Atlantic hurricane in United States history to reach the shore with winds of that intensity. Death tolls vary in various reports, but according to one source Camille killed 143 people along the coast and another 113 as a result of catastrophic flooding in Virginia (National Weather Service, "Camille").

One of the worst tragedies of Hurricane Camille was that so many people did not have to die. The people were told to evacuate. About ten hours before landfall, the residents of the Gulfport area knew Camille was going to be a major threat. About four o'clock in the afternoon, the weather was stormy. By six o'clock the winds were about forty miles per hour, and the rain was coming down in torrents. Sometime after eight that night the area lost power. Most of the residents in harm's way had evacuated. But the residents of the Richelieu Apartments in Pass Christian decided to ride out the storm. Twenty-three people stayed in that three-story building. The building was destroyed, and fifteen of the twenty-three people were killed.

When people in Gulfport told stories like that to me, and when people heard those stories, the reaction was always the same. People would say, "How foolish!" or "I would never do something so foolish!" Every person who is sane and sensible reacts in that way. But people face something far more dangerous than a devastating hurricane. Sin is a destructive force that has done more damage to people and nations than all the hurricanes in history combined. It wasn't a hurricane that was about to destroy Israel; it was turning away from God. And like those officials in Gulfport who warned people of the danger of the hurricane, Hosea the prophet was warning people about the danger of continuing in sin. In 5:8 Hosea wrote, "Blow the ram's horn in Gibeah, / the trumpet in Ramah; / raise the war cry in Beth-aven!" In 8:1 again he wrote, "Put the ram's horn to your mouth!" Like an emergency alarm from the Federal Emergency Management Agency, Hosea was sounding the warning trumpet. And he opened chapters 4 and 5 with the imperative, "Hear"—listen to this! Then he proceeded to warn them about the danger of continuing in sin. If they remained unrepentant, the arrival of God's judgment and the destruction of the nation were certain. Just as surely as Hurricane Camille was approaching the Gulf Coast, God's punishment for sin is on its way. Of course, God's punishment is different from a hurricane. Hurricanes cause temporal, physical damage; God's punishment is eternal for people who do not put their faith in Jesus. Hurricanes can be unpredictable, but in his Word God tells us exactly why and on whom his punishment is coming.

The Bible teaches that sin leads to death (Gen 2:17; Rom 6:23). Hosea preached that Israel's sin was leading to their death. For individuals in every generation, sin leads to death and eternal separation from God. We ought to hate sin and love God. In fact, we could summarize Christian growth by saying it's a process of loving God more and more and hating sin more and more. Chapters 4 and 5 of Hosea constitute a manual on sin—what sin is and why it's so dangerous. Sin is doing something God says in his Word we ought not to do, or not doing something God says in his Word that we ought to do.

Sin Starts in the Heart
HOSEA 4:12; 5:4

In Hosea 4:12 God says of Israel, "A spirit of promiscuity leads them astray." In 5:4 again God says, "A spirit of promiscuity is among them."

They were committing spiritual adultery because they had an adulterous spirit. They were prostituting themselves with pagan gods and pagan sins because their hearts were not right with God. In 7:14 God says, "They do not cry to me from their hearts." Sin is the result of a sinful heart. The sinful deed is motivated by the sinful spirit.

Jesus said, "What comes out of the mouth comes from the heart, and this defiles a person. For from the heart come evil thoughts, murders, adulteries, sexual immoralities, thefts, false testimonies, slander" (Matt 15:18-19). Sinful words and sinful deeds arise from the condition of our hearts. What's in your heart?

As I was writing these expositions of Hosea, I underwent two heart procedures. In preparation for that work on my heart, physicians and technicians looked at my heart in various ways. One test they performed was a heart ultrasound, which is essentially watching a black-and-white video of the heart. While they were performing the ultrasound, the technician let me watch my heart on the screen. I could see inside my heart, and I could watch the way it was functioning. For me, those moments were some of the most difficult of the entire experience. It was so obvious on the screen that something was wrong with my heart. Afterward, I had that image in my mind. I knew my heart was not right.

Of course, Hosea was referring to the heart not as a physical organ but as our spiritual condition. God sees inside our hearts; he watches how they are functioning. What does your heart look like? Sin starts in the heart. Every sin ever committed and every kind of sin began as a sinful thought. When sinful thoughts or sinful inclinations are in our hearts, we should confess them to God and turn from them immediately, before the consequences cause pain for us and for a lot of other people. Proverbs 4:23 says, "Guard your heart above all else, / for it is the source of life." Guard your heart because sin starts in the heart.

Sin and Broken Fellowship with God Go Together
HOSEA 4:1,10; 5:4,7,13

Sin leads to broken fellowship with God, and broken fellowship with God leads to sin. We have already seen that fact in the book of Hosea. The sin of Hosea's wife was unfaithfulness to her marriage covenant with Hosea, and that led to other sins. Israel's sin was unfaithfulness to their covenant relationship with God, and that, too, led to other sins. In chapters 4 and 5 Hosea refers again to that broken relationship.

In chapter 4 he writes, "There is no . . . / knowledge of God in the land" (v. 1). In verse 10 he says, "They have abandoned their devotion to the LORD." In chapter 5 Hosea wrote, "They do not know the LORD" (v. 4), and "They betrayed the LORD" (v. 7). Clearly, Israel's fellowship with God was broken.

When we're not walking in fellowship with God, we're susceptible to temptation and sin. We're sitting ducks for the world, the flesh, and the devil. And when we sin, we break fellowship with God even further. Isaiah 59:2 says, "Your iniquities are separating you / from your God." Think about that: our sin separates us from God. Sin and broken fellowship with God go together.

Hosea 5:13 says,

"*When Ephraim saw his sickness*
and Judah his wound,
Ephraim went to Assyria
and sent a delegation to the great king.
But he cannot cure you or heal your wound."

The people of Hosea's day were not looking to God for help; they were looking "to the great king" of Assyria. That decision to look to a man instead of God for help was yet more evidence that their fellowship with God was broken. When they were in trouble, they turned to people, not to God. When you're facing a problem, where do you go for help?

The problem with my heart was not a big problem, but it did need to be mended. I'm glad I could go to a doctor who could repair it. How foolish would I have been to know that something was wrong with my heart but refuse to seek help, or decide to go to somebody for help who is not able to help? If there is something wrong in our hearts, God is the one who can heal it. Turning away from him is foolish. But Israel was turning to other people, not to God.

Sin and broken fellowship with God go together. The wonderful flip side of that fact is that purity and fellowship with God also go together. Jesus said,

"*Blessed are the pure in heart,*
for they will see God." (Matt 5:8)

We can have intimacy with God when we're pure in heart. When sin is in our hearts, we confess it to God, ask for his forgiveness and cleansing, and he restores us to close fellowship with him.

Sin Hurts the Sinner
HOSEA 4:7,11; 5:4

In 4:11 Hosea wrote, "Promiscuity, wine, and new wine / take away one's understanding." In the original Hebrew, that's literally, "They take the heart." When we sin, our hearts are not the same. We think we can sin, and afterward everything returns to normal. But it doesn't. When we sin, it affects us. Our hearts are no longer pure. We're more likely to be comfortable with sin than we were before. Sin dulls our conscience and distorts our thinking. Even people who profess Jesus as Savior can commit a sin so often they no longer even see it as sin. Instead, they justify sin. Sin has changed them. A young man and woman once came to me for counseling. They were living together outside of marriage. I told them God says such behavior is sin. In response, they tried to justify fornication to me, and they said they thought God would accept what they were doing. Their thinking had been so distorted, so corrupted by sin that they actually thought they could make that case to a Baptist preacher—and to God! So many people think the same way: they're so accustomed to sin that they think their sin is somehow justifiable. Sin will never be justifiable to a holy God. Sin never helps us; it only hurts us.

In 4:7 God says, "The more they multiplied, / the more they sinned against me." Some books on the history of Israel focus on Israel's economic history and note their development from being nomadic pastoralists, to agriculturalists, to city builders with a more complex economic system. Some books focus on Israel's political history, noting that Israel progressed from being a disorganized group of slaves to being led by judges and tribal elders, then organized around a united monarchy, and then the divided monarchy. Hosea gives us God's concise history of Israel: "The more they multiplied, / the more they sinned against me." God's central concern was not their living conditions, their occupations, or the structure of their government, but their communion with him and their submission to his word. The growth of sin in Israel reminds us that sin is never stagnant. Sin affects us, and the more we sin, the worse sin gets and the more it affects us. "The more they multiplied, / the more they sinned against me."

Hosea 5:4 says, "Their actions do not allow them / to return to their God." Sinful Israel had gone so far down the road of sin that they could no longer even see what it meant to be pure. As long as Israel continued to participate in their sin, a return to God would not happen. Sin and returning to God are incompatible; we cannot return to God while engaged in sin. Something has to go—either sin or fellowship with God. Israel's sin changed them. Dare we think we are immune to that condition? Dare we think we can commit sin and our character will not be affected? Jesus said, "Everyone who commits sin is a slave of sin" (John 8:34). We weren't slaves before we sinned; committing sin made us slaves. That's what sin does: it enslaves, and the more we sin the more we're enslaved. Maybe someone reading these lines is in the grip of sinful deeds, a prisoner of some sin, not in fellowship with God. Turn from sin now before you go further down the road of hurting yourself and other precious people in your life.

Wrong Worship Is Sin
HOSEA 4:12-14

It's possible to commit sin while being religious. Even though the Israelites were involved in all kinds of sin and rebellion against God's word, they were also involved in religion. In John 4 Jesus said, "God is spirit, and those who worship him must worship in Spirit and in truth" (v. 24). The problem was the Israelites were not worshiping in truth. They had religion, but they had the wrong religion. In Hosea 4 God refers to the fact that they were practicing pagan religion. "My people consult their wooden idols, / and their divining rods inform them" (v. 12). A literal translation would be, "My people ask their wood, and their staff declares to them." Israelites were following the common practice of using wooden objects in divination. That practice is called rhabdomancy—using sticks or wood in an effort to discern the will of the gods. The "staff" could have been a divining rod or a walking staff they also used for divination. To paraphrase, Hosea was sarcastically saying, "You guys have got this figured out! You use one stick for multiple purposes. It's a walking staff, and when you want to communicate with some deity, you can throw it on the ground, and the way it lands tells you what the gods think. It's a multiuse stick!" How tragic that Israelites were resorting to such absurd practices to try to divine the will of the gods when the one true God had already communicated his will in his word he had given to them.

In his law, God had told his people how to worship him, what sacrifices were to be offered, and where they were to be offered—at the temple in Jerusalem. But through Hosea God says they were offering sacrifices "on the mountaintops, / and they burn offerings on the hills, / and under oaks, poplars, and terebinths" (4:13). Such locations were common sites for pagan fertility religions—near sacred trees or on elevated locations. It was common for people to imagine that higher places were holy because they were thought to be closer to the gods or they symbolized an imagined cosmic mountain where the gods dwelled. But Hosea was again sarcastic; he wrote that people liked worshiping pagan gods under the trees "because their shade is pleasant" (v. 13). "Let's go worship Baal." "No way, it's too hot!" "Let's do it in that shade." "Oh, then OK." How far they were from worshiping God in spirit and in truth.

Some Israelites were even participating in cult prostitution (v. 14). In his law, God had forbidden Israelites from involvement in such practices (Deut 23:17-18). How widespread this phenomenon was is uncertain. It is certain, though, that the Israelites learned such practices from Baal-worshiping Canaanites. Verse 12 refers to the "spirit of promiscuity" that was leading them astray. The people were straying spiritually, and their straying resulted in following other gods and unfaithfulness to the one true God who had made a covenant with Israel. One part of such illicit religion was physical, and somehow liturgical, prostitution. Thus, Israel's apostasy was spiritual adultery, and physical adultery was the result (Moseley, *Critical Evaluation*, 109–13).

Why did people in antiquity make prostitution part of their "worship"? Such acts were thought to induce gods like Baal to behave similarly and thus provide fertility (Oswalt, *Bible among the Myths*, 47–56). The capitulation of Israelites to the Canaanite practice of committing fornication and adultery as a part of "worship" demonstrates, perhaps better than anything else, just how far Israelites had strayed from the one true God and his word. Some people surely thought they were worshiping, but God rejected what they were doing. It's a sobering thought that God can reject the way we worship.

Sinful Leaders Harm Everyone
HOSEA 4:4-6; 5:1,10

In chapter 4, God says through Hosea that he had a contention with the priests (vv. 4-6). In chapter 5 Hosea wrote that God was going to pass judgment against the priests, the king, and the princes (vv. 1,10). The leaders were involved in sin, and their sin was affecting the people they were supposed to be leading. That is necessarily the case: the actions of leaders affect the people they lead. God says, "My people are destroyed for lack of knowledge" (4:6). He was referring to ignorance of his word. Why did the people lack knowledge of God's word? God says to the priests, "You have rejected knowledge" and "You have forgotten the law of your God." The people did not know God's word because the priests who were supposed to teach God's word were not doing so. In fact, they were doing the opposite: they "rejected knowledge" and forgot the law of God.

Leaders among God's people are not to neglect God's words—not in the period of the old covenant and not today. New Testament Christians are to live according to the Bible, God's Word. But they will not live what they do not know. Multiple surveys reveal that Christians today do not know the Bible. In the postmodern, secularized culture in which we live, we assume ignorance of the Bible in the populace. The scandal is biblical ignorance among Christians. No wonder Christians show a growing tendency to compromise on all kinds of moral issues: many of us don't know what God says in his Word. Christians who lack biblical knowledge are the products of churches that do not teach the Bible. Why spend a lot of time and effort studying the book of Hosea, for example? We do it because Hosea is in the Bible, and God's people need to know the Bible—all of it. Therefore, somebody should teach it—all of it. Perhaps to apply this message about God's word in Hosea, we all should ask about our own study of the Bible. How are we doing with that? Are we devoted to learning and living all of God's Word, or is our faith built on just a few selected verses? We don't want to live like the sinful leaders of Hosea's day. They had forgotten God's law, and their neglect of God's word was hurting themselves as well as the people they were supposed to be leading.

God Punishes Sin
HOSEA 4:9-10; 5:6,10,12,14-15

God's righteous wrath against sin is described throughout the Bible, including these chapters in Hosea. In 4:9 God says he will pass judgment on both the priests and the people: "I will punish them for their ways / and repay them for their deeds." He also says he will withhold their prosperity (v. 10). In 5:12 God says he was going to be like a moth to Israel and like dry rot. God's judgment does not have to come as a sudden explosion. It can come as the quiet process of decay, as corruption gradually disintegrates a life—a person's life or a nation's life. But God's judgment would soon come to Israel in a more dramatic way as Assyria invaded and conquered Israel. So in 5:14 God compares his judgment to the violent attack of a lion.

God punishes sin. God stated from the beginning of creation that sin leads to death, and that has not changed. In God's Word he has told us what is right and what is wrong, and that has not changed either. From the beginning people have been sinners. So sin could have been the end of any possibility of relating to the holy God who hates sin, the end of any possibility of knowing him now and forever, except for his grace and love. Even in a section of Scripture like Hosea 4–5 that is so filled with descriptions of the awfulness of sin, God still holds out hope. In the final verse of chapter 5, God says he is going to withdraw from Israel. He would not continue to contend with them and would do nothing to intervene in the destruction that was coming: "until they recognize their guilt and seek my face; / they will search for me in their distress" (5:15; cf. 5:6). Because of God's grace and love, he always holds out a way of salvation.

This section began with the story of a hurricane—Hurricane Camille of 1969. But Gulfport has seen other hurricanes. One of the most memorable was Hurricane Katrina that made landfall on August 29, 2005. I will never forget watching the evening news and seeing the footage of the destruction of the area where we had lived and ministered. Obviously, we were concerned about the status of the people we knew and loved there. We couldn't reach anybody on the phone. I went down there with a group of people to try to help. I worked to "mud out" the sanctuary of the church I had pastored. Even though that building was well north of the coast, it had been six feet under Katrina's floodwaters.

A flood is another image God uses to describe his judgment. In 5:10 God says, "I will pour out my fury on them like water." Surely nobody wants God to pour out his wrath on them. God always punishes sin. But praise his name he has provided a way for our sin to be forgiven. God expressed his righteous wrath against sin when he poured out his wrath on Jesus who became our substitute, the sacrifice for our sin. We deserved God's righteous judgment, but Jesus took God's judgment for our sin on himself when he died in our place on the cross. Jesus's death on the cross was the perfect expression of God's love and his wrath. I have heard that great demonstration of love and wrath described as a flood. It was as if a reservoir of water ten thousand miles wide and ten thousand miles deep were being held back by a dam. Then the dam breaks, and all of that water is about to fall on us. That's what it would be like for God's judgment to come like a flood. But just before the flood crashes down on us, an enormous pit opens and swallows all that water and saves us. That's what Jesus's death on the cross did for us. God has provided a way of salvation in Jesus. Praise God for his outrageous, lavish grace offered to undeserving sinners! When we put our faith in Jesus and confess and turn from our sin, God forgives our sin, reconciles us to him, and restores us.

After our reconciliation to God, our salvation, how do we avoid sin, live pure lives, and grow in Christlikeness? One way we avoid sin is by doing the same thing we do when a hurricane is coming. We run! We heed warnings like those in Hosea 4–5, so when temptation is coming we evacuate the area. Second Timothy 2:22 says, "Flee from youthful passions." First Timothy 6 refers to the love of money, and it says, "Flee from these things, and pursue righteousness" (1 Tim 6:10-11). First Corinthians 10:14 says, "Flee from idolatry," and Paul wrote in 1 Corinthians 6:18, "Flee sexual immorality!" Flee. When the possibility of sin approaches, staying where we are is foolhardy. Evacuate.

To avoid sin, we also pray. Jesus taught us to pray, "Forgive us our debts, / as we also have forgiven our debtors" (Matt 6:12). God gives us pardon for past sin. He also gives us power over present sin. Jesus taught us to ask God, "Do not bring us into temptation, / but deliver us from the evil one" (Matt 6:13). So always, every day, we turn to God—to express love for him and gratitude to him and to ask him for help in avoiding sin. We love God and hate sin.

Reflect and Discuss

1. How do sin and separation from God compare and contrast with a natural disaster like a hurricane?
2. Is it inevitable that what is in our hearts will be expressed in our deeds and words? Why or why not?
3. How can you control what is in your heart?
4. How does sin break fellowship with God—in your life or in the lives of people you know? How may fellowship with God be restored?
5. In what ways does committing sin change us and hurt us?

6. What are some worship practices in the world today that are actually manifestations of sin?
7. To whom are you a leader? Who is watching your life? How is your lifestyle affecting them spiritually?
8. How would you assess your recent reading and study of the Bible? What is your plan to grow?
9. What can you say to people to communicate the certainty of God's judgment and the greatness of his grace in offering to take that judgment on himself?
10. What are some practical ways to avoid sin?

God and Oscillation

HOSEA 6–7

Main Idea: Partial faithfulness to God is unfaithfulness, and it renders us spiritually useless; God rejects unfaithfulness as sin, and he calls us to reject it as well.

I.   **What Does God Say about Spiritual Oscillation?**
  A. It involves unfaithfulness (6:7).
  B. It manipulates the truth about God (6:1-3).
  C. It often includes religion (6:6).
  D. It sometimes includes slavery to fleshly pursuits (7:4-5).
  E. It makes people pathetic and useless in serving God (7:8-16).
    1. A flawed cake (7:8)
    2. The first gray hairs (7:9-10)
    3. A flustered bird (7:11-12)
    4. A faulty weapon (7:16)
II. **How Does God Respond to Spiritual Oscillation?**
  A. God sees our sin (7:2).
  B. God sends his truth (6:5).
  C. God is ready to heal and redeem (6:4; 7:1,13).

Years ago, I was reading the sixth chapter of Hosea and a memory from my childhood came to mind. I remembered my grandmother's oscillating fan. When I was a boy, during a few summers my parents drove me about an hour from our house to my grandmother's home in Luverne, Alabama, and I stayed with her for a week. Luverne is in south Alabama, and in those days her place was not air-conditioned. People who are saved by putting their faith in Jesus will never experience how hot hell is, but should they ever want a sample, they could drive to Luverne, Alabama, in July and stay there for a week without air-conditioning. My dear grandmother did not have air-conditioning, but she did have an oscillating fan. It was black with shiny silver blades, and it oscillated—rotating from one side to the other. I would position myself at the end of its rotation because it would pause for a second or two and blow on me, until it oscillated back to the other side. I hated that fan.

I wanted it to blow continuously on me. I guess the idea was that it was supposed to cool the whole room by blowing in every direction, but it succeeded only in rearranging the sweltering air around the room.

I thought of that oscillating fan when I read this part of Hosea because people in Israel were oscillating—back and forth, hot and cold, one direction and then the other. It was *spiritual* oscillation—committed to God, then not committed, saying they wanted to seek God, then not seeking him. A few statements in these verses powerfully express their oscillating spiritual condition. Chapter 6 begins with, "Come, let's return to the LORD." They sound ready to be right with God, to leave sin and return to God. The statement that closes chapter 7 uses the same Hebrew word, but in an entirely different way—translated "turn." That repetition creates an inclusio, which means this extended passage begins and ends in the same way. In this case, the two chapters begin and end with the same key term, and that repetition amplifies the central meaning of the passage. Hosea 7:16 says, "They turn, but not to what is above." The word translated "what is above" is the Hebrew word *al*. "Al" is a proper name in English; it's short for "Allan," "Albert," and other names. In Canaan, *al* was the word for "upward"; it was also the name of a pagan deity worshiped by Canaanites. I think Hosea was referring to that deity in this verse, but he added the word *not*. They were calling *al* a god, but Hosea called him "not god" (Moseley, *Critical Evaluation*, 47–51, 58–59). So Hosea said that one day they say, "Come, let us return to the LORD," and the next day, "They return, but to 'not God.'" Spiritually, they were oscillating from the one true God to pagan gods.

In 6:4 the Lord says to them, "Your love is like the morning mist / and like the early dew that vanishes." The images of mist and dew signify impermanence. We see mist, or fog, in the morning, but when we look again a little later, it's gone. And we know if we walk on the grass early in the morning in our sandals, our feet will get wet with dew. But in a few hours the grass will be dry. God was saying Israel's love for him was like that. It's here, then it's gone. They were wet, then they were dry.

Have you witnessed spiritual oscillation in someone else, or in yourself? A teenager attends a youth camp or retreat and commits completely to love Jesus and live for Jesus. But over time that commitment wanes, and she swings back to living for other things. In church on Sunday, a believer's emotions are stirred by the music, and his mind is impacted by the truth of the Bible; and when he leaves worship, he knows nothing is as important to him as glorifying God, loving God, and pleasing God. But Monday morning comes, then Tuesday, and priorities shift. Spiritual oscillation is so common.

What Does God Say about Spiritual Oscillation?

In Hosea 6–7 we can see five facts about spiritual oscillation and the way it is manifested in our lives. First, it always **involves unfaithfulness**. Of course it does. It's faithfulness and unfaithfulness, back and forth. That's the nature of spiritual oscillation, and it's exactly what Israel was doing. In 6:7 God says, "They, like Adam, have violated the covenant; / there they have betrayed me." Interpretations of the meaning of "Adam" differ, but I think that word is most likely a reference to the town by that name at the mouth of the Jabbok River (Andersen and Freedman, *Hosea*, 435–36). At some point, possibly in Israel's recent past, the people of that town had become known for doing something noticeably unfaithful to Israel's God. Through Hosea, God was saying that the entire nation was now as unfaithful as that town. They "violated the covenant," and they "betrayed" God. The latter verb is sometimes translated, "dealt faithlessly" (RSV, ESV).

Israel was in a covenant relationship with God, as we are in a new covenant relationship with God through Christ. They were vacillating, wavering in the most important relationship, the relationship that was to define them as individuals and as a nation—their covenant relationship with God. The idea of a covenant was to bind two parties together in a contractual bond that neither party was to break. But Israel *was* breaking that covenant. They were faithful to God. Sometimes. Then they would swing back to unfaithfulness. But 99 percent faithfulness is still unfaithfulness. Can you imagine a young man saying to his fiancée during their engagement, "Honey, I promise I'll be completely faithful to you 99 percent of the time." No sane woman is going to sign up for that because 99 percent faithfulness is 100 percent unfaithfulness. To think that a little vacillation is OK is a complete misunderstanding of the nature of a covenant commitment, and it's what Israel was doing in their relationship with God. People still do it, and it's a wicked betrayal of the God who loves us and is always faithful to us.

Spiritual oscillation also **manipulates the truth about God**. God is gracious, merciful, and forgiving. That's the truth. But some people presume on the grace of God and interpret it as God's permission to do whatever they want to do because he'll forgive in the end.

In the first two verses of chapter 6, Hosea quotes the Israelites as citing the grace and mercy of God: "He has torn us, / and he will heal us; / he has wounded us, / and he will bind up our wounds. He will revive us after two days, / . . . and on the third day he will raise us up." Those statements reflect the truth about God's character. He heals, helps, and gives life. Furthermore, God is consistent; we can count on him. "His appearance is as sure as the dawn. / He will come to us like the rain, / like the spring showers that water the land" (v. 3).

No matter what we may do, God's character is constant: he forgives, heals, and revives. That's true, but spiritual oscillation manipulates that truth to mean *we* can be inconsistent with no consequences—counting on the grace of God while forgetting the holiness and wrath of God, manipulating the truth to our own advantage, selecting the biblical truths best suited to serve our spiritual oscillation while ignoring the rest of the Bible.

Catherine the Great was a Russian empress who perpetuated the medieval system of serfdom in Russia in the eighteenth century. She owned more than five hundred thousand serfs, and even when serfs were abused by their masters, she did not allow them to appeal to her for help. She was a law unto herself, a despot. She famously said, "I shall be an autocrat: that's my trade. And the good Lord will forgive me: that's his" (Kidner, *Love to the Loveless*, 64). She was taking God's forgiveness to mean that she could do whatever she wanted and then face no accountability or judgment before God. She manipulated the truth to her own advantage. So do a lot of people who vacillate spiritually.

Spiritual oscillation **often includes religion**—not right religion, but religion nonetheless. In 6:6 God says, "I desire faithful love and not sacrifice, / the knowledge of God rather than burnt offerings." Sacrifices and burnt offerings were part of the religious experience of the Israelites. The people of Israel were involved in all kinds of sinful behavior, but they were also involved in religion. They presented their sacrifices and burnt offerings. Priests are mentioned in 6:9, and even they were committing all sorts of heinous acts of wickedness.

We have seen this happen. People come to church to assure themselves and others that they're good people, and once convinced of that, they go out and do what they want to do, even if what they want to do includes sin. Then, they return to church with the assumption that their

presence in the sacred precincts compensates for the sins they committed outside of worship. But what does God desire from us? He tells us he
desires steadfast love from us, and he wants us to know him. He does *not*
want mere religious formalities like sacrifices and offerings.

Jesus quoted Hosea 6:6 twice, and on both occasions he quoted it
to religious people. On one occasion, some Pharisees criticized Jesus
for eating dinner with tax collectors and sinners (Matt 9:10-13). On the
other occasion, some Pharisees criticized Jesus for breaking one of their
fussy rules about observing the Sabbath (Matt 12:1-7). On both occasions, Jesus told them that they should go and learn Hosea 6:6: "I desire
mercy and not sacrifice." Jesus wants a transformed life in which we treat
people with mercy. Jesus is not satisfied with mere religious ritual. When
religion degenerates into mere ritual, it becomes another form of spiritual oscillation—participating in holy worship, then leaving to live an
unholy life, then again gladly entering the presence of God in worship,
and then leaving to live independent of God's presence.

Spiritual oscillation **sometimes includes slavery to fleshly pursuits**.
Hosea 7:4 says of the Israelites, "All of them commit adultery; / they are
like an oven heated by a baker / who stops stirring the fire / from the
kneading of the dough until it is leavened." The baker doesn't need to
stir the fire anymore; it's already hot enough. We refer to being on fire
with passion, or enflamed with lust. That's the idea here. The heat refers
to the heat of their passion, and they were so hot they could not be any
hotter. Verse 5 says that on a day of public celebration, like honoring
the king, "the princes are sick with the heat of wine." They were hot,
but they were not on fire for God. They were on fire with the sins of the
flesh—adultery and drunkenness. Who could ever read the Bible and
continue to think sins like that are OK with God? They're so clearly condemned in the Bible. Yet even people who turn to God also turn away
from God as they turn to the sinful ways of the world. They go back and
forth. God condemns that way of living.

Spiritual oscillation also **makes people pathetic and useless in serving God**. "Pathetic" and "useless" are insulting words, but those words
summarize verses 8 through 16 of Hosea 7. In those verses Hosea uses
four insulting illustrations to describe Israel's spiritual compromise.
The first illustration is *a flawed cake*. God calls Israel "unturned bread
baked on a griddle" in verse 8. That clause refers to a flat cake, flatbread, cooked over a fire. You don't have to be a baker to know what
happens to flatbread when it's over a fire and the baker doesn't turn it.

The side next to the fire is burned, and the other side is not cooked at all; it's what we call half-baked. Israel's commitment to God was half-hearted, the requirements of their covenant with God were half-lived, so Hosea said they were half-baked (Smith, *Twelve Prophets*, 1:293–95).

Second, the oscillating Israelites were like someone's *first gray hairs*. I began serving as an interim pastor for churches when I was a young man. As an older man, I saw a member of one of the first churches where I had served years earlier. After we greeted each other, he said, "You were our interim pastor when your hair was black!" It happens. Black hair becomes gray. And how delusional would I be to deny that reality. But Israel was just that delusional. Verse 9 says, "Foreigners consume his strength, / but he does not notice. / Even his hair is streaked with gray, / but he does not notice." So a guy's hair is starting to gray. A few people kid him and say, "I see a little gray up there." He replies, "Actually, my hair is black." And people respond, "Is it though?" Verse 10 mentions "the pride of Israel" (ESV). Maybe it was pride or vanity that caused them to say, "What gray hair?" Somebody has to be clueless, pathetic, to deny the appearance of gray hair when it is as plain as . . . the hair on your head. Hosea used that illustration to describe Israel: they were clueless, pathetic.

The statement "he knows it not" appears twice in verse 9 in the ESV. A similar statement is made in reference to Samson, in what may be one of the saddest statements in the Bible. The Spirit of God had come upon Samson multiple times to enable him to accomplish God's will. But after Samson committed sin after sin, the Spirit of God did not come upon him to help him, and Judges 16:20 says, "He did not know that the LORD had left him." Spiritual oscillation produces a pathetic cluelessness that renders us useless in serving God.

First a flawed cake, then the first gray hairs, and the next insulting illustration is *a flustered bird*. Verse 11 says, "Ephraim has become like a silly, senseless dove; / they call to Egypt, and they go to Assyria." They were trying to establish diplomatic relations with countries that might be able to help them. Instead of going to God for help, they went from one nation to another. They went to a nation they thought would be politically expedient, and the next year when the political winds changed, they went to another, "like a silly, senseless dove." Some people have seen that kind of behavior while dove hunting, especially if they were in a field where several of the hunters were not good shots. As a dove flies into the field, a hunter shoots at him and misses. So the dove swerves away from that hunter, only to fly near another hunter who shoots and misses. So the dove flies away from him, too, only to be shot at again. Now the dove doesn't know where to fly; he's swerving back and forth confused, wondering why these hunters are in the field when obviously they can't shoot anything, and he's frightened, flustered. Hosea said that oscillating Israel is that dove—a silly, clueless bird. It was insulting, but it's an accurate picture of a life of unfaithfulness to God.

Hosea's final illustration is *a faulty weapon*—the "faulty bow" in verse 16. The people of Israel were not trusting fully in God; Hosea said they were like a bow, a weapon we cannot trust. A soldier is in a battle facing the enemy. It's a life-or-death situation. He pulls back his bow to shoot. At that moment, he has to be able to trust his bow. Will it work? Maybe, maybe not (cf. Ps 78:57). That was Israel. Were they trusting in God? Sometimes. And sometimes they were trusting in themselves or the help of other countries or some pagan god. In their relationship to God, they were inconsistent, uncommitted, oscillating.

A flawed cake, denial of the first gray hairs, a flustered bird, a faulty weapon—God said those are what unfaithful Israel was like. It's an insulting picture, but it's what God thinks of spiritual vacillation, unfaithfulness to him, inconsistent obedience to his word. God's words about Israel's unfaithfulness should motivate us to faithfulness. Spiritual inconsistency, oscillation, renders us pathetic and useless. It also dishonors God and dishonors our relationship with him.

How Does God Respond to Spiritual Oscillation?

The ways God responds to spiritual oscillation should provide further motivation to be faithful to God. First, **God sees our sin**. Israel's sin was not hidden from God. He saw it and described it in these verses and elsewhere through Hosea and other prophets. Amazingly, people in Israel forgot that God sees everything. In 7:2 God says, "They never consider that I remember all their evil. / Now their actions are all around them; / they are right in front of my face." What we do is in front of God's face. He sees it all. Surely the Israelites knew that, but they weren't thinking about it: "They never consider that I remember all their evil." The Hebrew is colloquial: "They do not say to their heart that I remember all their evil." They likely would have acknowledged God's omniscience as a fact, but they did not speak about it to their hearts. They did not consciously think about the fact that everything they were doing was before God and he remembers.

Do we think about God's constant presence with us and his complete knowledge of all we do? Sometimes when I'm wondering whether I should write the note I want to write or say the words I'm about to say, I think of Jesus sitting next to me. He's looking at what I'm doing and listening to what I'm saying. Would I want to do this or say this if Jesus were right here? Try that exercise sometime. When we do that, we're not just exercising our imagination because it's the truth. God really is with us, and he really does see what we do and hear what we say. God said of Israel's deeds, they "are right in front of my face." Sadly, God also said, "They never consider that I remember all their evil." We should consider that God sees our sin.

Also, when he sees spiritual oscillation, **God sends his truth**. In 6:5 God says, "I have used the prophets / to cut them down; / I have killed them with the words from my mouth. / My judgment strikes like lightning." Israel was unfaithful to God, and he responded by sending prophets to preach his truth to them and call them to faithfulness.

Here in Hosea, God vividly portrays his word and its effects: "I have . . . cut them down." How? With the swords of the Assyrians? No, with "the prophets." "I have killed them." By sending hurricanes or drought? No, "I have killed them with the words from my mouth." God portrays his word as a weapon that attacks sin. God's word denounces sin; it confronts and rebukes the sinner. God said to Jeremiah that his word is "like fire" and "like a hammer that pulverizes rock" (Jer 23:29). God's word is powerful, so the rebuke of God's word is often painful, like being burned with fire, cut by a sword, or struck by a hammer.

We should not marvel that the sinful culture in which we live opposes the Bible and vilifies people who believe the Bible and preach the Bible. The Bible exposes the sins of this culture and rebukes that sin. Then, when people are confronted with God's truth about their sin, they face a choice. They can turn from their sin and submit to God, or they can continue down the road of rebellion against God and his truth. Western culture has gone so far down the road of rebellion that it mocks the truth of God's Word and ridicules those who believe it. It's tragic to argue with the God of the universe about what is true and what is false, what is right and what is wrong. It is foolish to argue with the God of truth who made us and to whom we will give an account.

Finally, **God is ready to heal and redeem**. God was ready to heal and redeem sinful Israel. But they did not want God's healing and redemption. They wanted their sin. God says in 7:1, "When I heal Israel, / the iniquity of Ephraim and the crimes of Samaria / will be exposed." God was ready to heal, but Israel/Ephraim was not ready to turn from sin. In verse 13 God said, "Though I want to redeem them, / they speak lies against me." God wants to heal, save, restore, forgive, redeem. But he will not force his redemption on people who do not want it. Israel did not want it.

I think I would enjoy preaching a sermon only from chapter 6, verse 4.

"What am I going to do with you, Ephraim?
What am I going to do with you, Judah?
Your love is like the morning mist
and like the early dew that vanishes."

G. Campbell Morgan preached a sermon on that verse. He called it "The Difficulty of God." God's difficulty, his dilemma, is that he sees people committing sin and caught in the consequences of sin, and God wants to set people free from the bondage of sin and heal the effects of their sin, but people reject his offer of freedom and healing. In his sermon Morgan called this dilemma "the struggle . . . between the passion of the Divine heart and the perversity of the human will" (*Heart and Holiness*, 57).

Morgan was right. It is indeed perverse to reject the one true God who loves us and to refuse his offer of forgiveness, freedom, healing, and eternal life in order to cling to the bondage and pain of sin only to face the wrath of God against sin. God did not want to send his judgment on Israel. Hear the pathos in God's heart when he asks, "What am I going to do with you, Ephraim?" He sounds like a father whose child has lived in sin for so long and keeps suffering for it, and the father has told his child over and over again to forsake the sin and come to God, but the child refuses. The father desperately wants the child he loves to be healthy and holy, and he asks, "What am I going to do with you?" This is God's dilemma. He has told us that he hates sin and will express his righteous wrath against sin, so his wrath is coming to us because we are sinners. But he offers a way for our sin to be forgiven so that we can be saved and reconciled to him. But people refuse God's offer and prefer their sin, so God knows his judgment must come, but he wants to heal instead, so he asks, "What am I going to do with you?"

Don't live so that God asks that question about you. God offers us a way to be forgiven of sin, saved from sin and from the wrath of God against sin. That way is Jesus the Savior. All people who have never put their faith in Jesus as Savior should do it today. People who look to Jesus as Savior and Lord have a covenant relationship with God himself, and those people should never oscillate—sometimes faithful to God and sometimes unfaithful. They should never allow their love for God to become "like the morning mist and like the early dew that vanishes" (6:4). He has told us what he desires: steadfast love and the knowledge of God.

Reflect and Discuss

1. Recall moments in your life in which you oscillated spiritually. What caused that oscillation?
2. Is it possible to distinguish between major oscillation and minor oscillation?
3. Why is it so easy to assume a little oscillation/unfaithfulness in our relationship with God is acceptable?
4. In what ways do people today manipulate the truth about God?
5. What is the difference between faithfulness to God and participation in religion?
6. Consider again Hosea's insulting illustrations of oscillating Israel. Perhaps you know someone who became spiritually clueless and useless in serving God because of unfaithfulness. How will you prevent that from happening in your life?
7. As you review your words and actions over the last few days, would you have changed anything if you had stopped to think that God was watching or that Jesus was sitting right next to you?
8. Explain how God's Word proves to be a sword, a fire, a hammer, and lightning in your life and in the lives of other people.
9. When you read that God asks, "What am I going to do with you, Ephraim?," what feelings and thoughts do you have about God?

Who, or What, Is Your God?

HOSEA 8–9

Main Idea: Worshiping other gods was common in Israel, as it has been in every nation and age, but idolatry is harmful; it leads to other sins, and it is unacceptable to the one true God who loves us.

I.   Idolatry Is More Common Than We May Think (8:5-6,11; 9:7,10,15).
II.   Our Worship Cannot Be Right if an Idol Is in Our Hearts (8:2,11,13).
III.   Idolatry Leads to Other Forms of Sin (8:3-4,9-10,12; 9:10).
IV.   Idolatry Results in the Judgment of the One True God (8:4; 9:3,7, 9,11,14).
    A. God's punishment of sin follows patient waiting.
    B. God's punishment of sin follows a warning.
V.   The Real God Offers a Love Relationship and Will Restore Us (8:9; 9:10).

"Man must have an idol." That statement was made not by a theologian, a Bible teacher, or a preacher but by the businessman Andrew Carnegie, who went on to describe his own worship of the god of more money (Wall, *Andrew Carnegie*, 224–25). I think Carnegie was on the right track in what he wrote, but I would amend it by saying, "Man must have a *god*." The god may be either the real God or a false god, but people will worship a god. An often-quoted statement by theologian John Calvin is that the human heart is "a perpetual factory of idols"—a "*factory* of idols." Only one true God exists; therefore, only one legitimate object of worship exists, but we *make* other things and people into gods. We treat them as if they were God and worship them though they are not God. So we invent, we manufacture, gods. And Calvin said the human heart is a *perpetual* factory of idols. Idolatry was an ancient problem, and it's a modern problem. To one degree or another, idolatry is a problem virtually every day of our lives. In chapters 8–9 of Hosea's prophecy, we can learn about idolatry, but we don't learn anything good about it.

Idolatry Is More Common Than We May Think
HOSEA 8:5-6,11; 9:7,10,15

In 8:5-6 Hosea referred to a calf idol the people were worshiping. The people of Israel had made and worshiped a golden calf in the wilderness after God delivered them from slavery in Egypt (Exod 32:1-8). Calves and bulls were common images of gods in the world of the Old Testament; they represented fertility. So the people were worshiping false gods, but as for the true prophets of the Lord, the people of Israel were regarding them as fools, crazy men (9:7). That should sound familiar to us since in contemporary Western culture people who believe, live by, and preach the Bible are regularly belittled as backward, hateful, or stuck in the past. The people of Hosea's time had gone far down the road of idolatry. They were giving their allegiance to paganism while maligning God's servants.

In every era of Old Testament history, the Hebrews demonstrated susceptibility to idolatry. Abraham's father worshiped the gods of Mesopotamia (Josh 24:2). Jacob's wife Rachel "stole her father's household idols" (Gen 31:19). Jacob had to tell the people in his household, "Get rid of the foreign gods that are among you" (Gen 35:2). While in Egypt, the Hebrews worshiped other gods (Josh 24:14). After the exodus from Egypt, the people of Israel worshiped a golden calf and said, "Israel, these are your gods, who brought you up from the land of Egypt!" (Exod 32:4). That false claim was a foretaste of Israel's future idolatry: when the Lord would bless them, they would attribute his blessings to another god, typically Baal (Hos 2:5-8). Furthermore, throughout the history of Israel, Israelites participated in idolatrous practices like cult prostitution (Deut 23:17; 1 Kgs 14:23-24; 15:12; 22:46; 2 Kgs 23:7; Hos 4:14), child sacrifice (2 Kgs 17:31; Ezek 16:21; 20:31), worship of idols on high places (1 Kgs 14:22-23; 2 Kgs 17:9-11; 21:1-3; 2 Chr 11:14-15; 28:1-4), and divination (2 Kgs 17:17). Ahab and Jezebel actively promoted the worship of the false god Baal in Israel, and they even tried to purge the land of prophets of the one true God (1 Kgs 16:31-33; 18:4,19). During that time, through the prophets Elijah and Elisha, the one true God demonstrated his superiority over Baal (for example, 1 Kgs 18) (Bronner, *Stories and Elijah and Elisha*, 35–138). The Lord God of Israel, the Creator of all that exists, reigns forever as Sovereign over all. Baal doesn't reign, nor any other imagined deity.

For centuries, no extrabiblical attestation of Baalism existed. Then in 1929 archaeologists began excavating a site in Syria called Ras Shamra. They discovered that the site had been the city of Ugarit, a large and important city that reached its zenith during the time the Hebrews were in Egypt. Ugarit was conquered about 1200 BC, during the biblical period of the judges. Archaeologists also unearthed thousands of tablets written in the previously unknown language of Ugaritic. Many of those tablets contain stories about the gods worshiped by the Syrians, Canaanites, and Phoenicians. Most of those gods are mentioned in the Old Testament, including Baal. So, when the Hebrews entered Canaan, they encountered a pagan religion that had been entrenched in the area for centuries (see Moseley, "Baalism," 22–25; Young, *Ugarit in Retrospect*).

False ideas and pagan practices have always attracted God's people and corrupted the worship of the one true God. Throughout the Old Testament period, prophets called Abraham's descendants to put aside idolatrous worship, and Hosea was one of the prophets God used. Hosea described the Israelites as so theologically compromised that they called Yahweh by Baal's name (2:16). Hosea prophesied against cult prostitution (4:14), and he denounced Canaanite deities by using titles for them like "Shame" (9:10). He condemned the implements of illicit worship like jewelry (2:13), sacred pillars, ephods, and household idols (3:4; 10:1-2). Hosea also singled out certain places for judgment because of their association with Baal worship, such as high places (10:8), illicit altars (8:11; 10:1,2,8; 12:11), and even cities like Samaria (8:5-6; 10:5), Gilgal (9:15), and Beth-Aven (4:14-17).

Many modern people think of idolatry as a thing of the past. The word *idol* conjures images of stone statues or clay figurines before which people in antiquity bowed and offered worship. Of course, idols *were* common in the ancient world, and specifically in the Canaanite culture the Israelites only partially displaced. Anat was the goddess of warfare, Baal was the god of the storm and fertility, and Asherah was the goddess of fertility. We do not bow before deities by those names today, but we still elevate wealth, beauty, romance, shrewdness, power, sex, and strength—that is the modern pantheon to which people offer their devotion and commitment. The new shrines are theaters, spas, office buildings, televisions, banks, computer screens, and stadiums. What is an idol, after all? Tim Keller wrote that an idol is "anything more important to you than God, anything that absorbs your heart and imagination more than God, anything you seek to give you what only God can give" (*Counterfeit Gods*, 19).

Ezekiel 14:3 refers to people who had "set up idols in their hearts." Idols do not have to be made of wood, clay, or stone. They can be in our hearts. We make idols out of our career, body image, knowledge, success, hobbies, wealth, or any person to whom we give greater devotion than we give to God. And since idolatry occurs in our hearts, we have to monitor our hearts constantly and rid our hearts of idols. When we see, for example, a greater commitment to diet and exercise than to time spent with God, we have to decide whether a new idol has risen in our hearts. When we spend more time participating in a hobby than worshiping and serving God, we should consider the possibility that God has been displaced as the one Ruler of our hearts. Idols capture our affection and distract our attention from the one true God who is to be our one object of worship, our one glorious obsession.

Our Worship Cannot Be Right if an Idol Is in Our Hearts
HOSEA 8:2,11,13

In Hosea 8:11 God refers to a multiplication of altars. Evidently, religion was booming in Israel at that time. But the religion was not an expression of obedience to the one true God and his law, so the religion was sinful. Therefore, the multiplication of altars was only the multiplication of sin. Verse 13 says the people were sacrificing meat; that sounds orthodox since God's law directed his people to sacrifice animals. But it says, "The Lord does not accept them." Why not? Because the Israelites were also worshiping idols, and our worship cannot be right if idols are in our hearts.

Amazingly, at least some of the idolatrous Israelites claimed to know God. Hosea 8:2 quotes them as saying, "My God, we know you!" God had said that there was "no knowledge of God in the land!" (4:1). The people were presuming to know God, but they did not know God. First John 2:4 says, "The one who says, 'I have come to know him,' and yet doesn't keep his commands, is a liar, and the truth is not in him." The Israelites were definitely not keeping God's commands, so they did not know God in any meaningful way. The truth was not in them.

"My God, we know you." They did not know God. They knew *a* god, the gods they were making and worshiping, the gods they were imagining to be gods though they were only idols. Such theological delusion happens all the time. People invent their own gods by choosing certain attributes of God they like, then combining those attributes to construct a deity that is to their liking. They proceed to worship that idol instead of the one true God in all of his glory, greatness, and holiness. So people say things like, "My god is not a god of wrath," or "My god is accepting and affirming," meaning he accepts and affirms whatever *they* think is right. Christians are not immune to this kind of god manufacture. Some Christians build their conception of God on a few verses in the Bible while ignoring the rest of the Bible. But that limited god is not the real God. It's only our idol, and the idols of our imagination are always less than the one true God.

In the second of the Ten Commandments, God tells us not to make any image of God and worship it (Exod 20:4-5), but that is exactly what we do when we imagine God as we like and worship that image. In J. I. Packer's book *Knowing God*, Packer wrote about how our imaginations lead to idolatry.

> How often do we hear this sort of thing: "I *like to think* of God as the great Architect (or, Mathematician; or Artist)." "I don't think of God as a Judge; I *like to think* of him simply as a Father." We know from experience how often remarks of this kind serve as the prelude to a denial of something that the Bible tells us about God. . . . Those who hold themselves free to think of God *as they like* are breaking the second commandment. (*Knowing God*, 42)

We are not free to think of God as we like. When we think of God as we like, we always create something less than God, an idol. Teachers often encourage young people in school to think creatively and to use their imaginations. When it comes to knowing and worshiping God, our imaginations distort God. The only way to know God well is to be as uncreative as possible, to listen to God's Word, and to conform our thinking to the way God has revealed himself in Scripture. Our worship and our knowledge of God cannot be right as long as we have an idol in our hearts.

Idolatry Leads to Other Forms of Sin
HOSEA 8:3-4,9-10,12; 9:10

We create idols in our imagination; we set them up in our hearts. And our behavior flows from what is in our hearts. Jesus said, "From the heart come evil thoughts, murders, adulteries, sexual immoralities, thefts, false testimonies, slander" (Matt 15:19). What we do arises from what happens in our hearts—what we feel, think, and believe. Proverbs 4:23 says, "Guard your heart above all else, / for it is the source of life." We are not what we appear to be; we are what is in our hearts. How important, then, to guard our hearts, to ensure that our hearts continually submit to God as our King.

The people of Hosea's Israel were guilty of committing numerous forms of sin. Hosea 8:3 says they had "rejected what is good." Verses 4, 9, and 10 refer to their failure to consult or include God in major decisions in their country and its direction. Verse 12 says they had even lost the capacity to understand God's law as from God. Here God says, "Though I were to write out for him / ten thousand points of my instruction, / they would be regarded as something strange." To paraphrase, God could fill not one Bible but one hundred Bibles with his truth, and people would still say, "How weird, how out of step with the times." The Israelites of Hosea's lifetime were not ready to receive God's word. In the same way, many people today regard the truth of God's Word as strange. Like the Israelites, they have a prior and greater commitment to their own lifestyles and their own ideas because they have made a god and they imagine that he affirms whatever they want to do.

In Hosea 9:10 God cites a historical fact that reflects a reality people have always faced. God says of the Israelites, "They went to Baal-peor, / consecrated themselves to Shame, / and became abhorrent, / like the thing they loved." That statement refers to an incident that occurred when the Israelites were in the wilderness, specifically in the area of Peor, which was in Moab. The opening verses of Numbers 25 describe two sins of the Israelites: idolatry and immorality. They worshiped the god of Moabites ("Baal of Peor"; Num 25:3), and they committed the sins of the Moabites. The Moabites imagined a god who did not prohibit immorality. Such idolatrous imagination, God said through Hosea, is "abhorrent." They worshiped an abhorrent god, and their behavior became abhorrent. They "became abhorrent, / like the thing they loved." Idolatry leads to other forms of sin.

Idolatry inevitably encourages the development of sinful lifestyle patterns. The development may occur gradually or quickly, but it will occur. We will be transformed by what we worship. In C. S. Lewis's children's book *The Voyage of the Dawn Treader*, one of the main characters is a boy named Eustace Scrubb. Eustace had a great desire for wealth and power. He expressed those sinful desires in the petty ways schoolboys typically do—teasing, bullying, tattling, and ingratiating adult authorities. One night, Eustace found an enormous pile of treasure in a cave. It was a dragon's hoard of gold, silver, and jewels. That night he slept in that cave and dreamed of all the wealth and power that would be his now that he had found such a vast treasure. When he woke, however, he discovered to his horror that he had become a dragon himself. Now he did indeed have power, but he was also hideous, hated, and utterly lonely. Lewis was making the point that we become like what we worship. Eustace had thought like a greedy, hoarding dragon, so he became a dragon (*Voyage*, 462–69). Since we become like what we worship, idolatry leads to other forms of sin.

Idolatry Results in the Judgment of the One True God
HOSEA 8:4; 9:3,7,9,11-15

God announces his punishment numerous times and in various ways in Hosea 8–9. In 8:4 God refers to Israel's coming destruction. In 9:3 he refers to their future exile from the land. Also in chapter 9, God says, "The days of punishment have come," and, "He will punish their sins" (vv. 7,9).

Maybe the most ominous announcement of God's judgment of sin in the entire book is in the final verses of chapter 9. God says he is going to limit the birth of children (vv. 11-14). That could be one consequence of the physical hardship of exile—being bound and dragged by the Assyrian army halfway across the Near East. God even says in verse 15, "at Gilgal / . . . I began to hate them. / I will drive them from my house / because of their evil, wicked actions. / I will no longer love them." We should not interpret that statement to mean God felt animosity or hostility for them. In the book of Hosea, God stated clearly his love for Israel and his anguish over their waywardness. In the Old Testament, using the language of hate is one way God expresses his rejection. In the latter verses of Hosea 9, God was announcing that the people had turned away from him, and he was turning away from them. To use the marriage picture of the book of Hosea, God was suspending the marriage relationship with the people who had broken off relations with him. Let's note two Bible truths about God's punishment of sin. First, **God's punishment of sin follows patient waiting**. The book of Nehemiah was written after God's judgment had already come on Israel. They had been conquered by Assyria, and Judah was later conquered by Babylon. The ninth chapter of Nehemiah records a prayer in which the people of Israel look back on their history and confess their sins to God. They recite that throughout their history they had repeated a recurring pattern of unfaithfulness: they would turn away from God and fall into sin, then God would call them to repentance, then they would call out to God for deliverance, then God would deliver them, but then they would return to sin. During all those years, time after time, God was waiting before he sent his punishment for sin. He could have kept his promise to punish sin at any point, but he was waiting. Waiting for what? He was waiting for people to turn to him in faith and enter the love relationship he offers people. His grace and mercy caused him to wait.

During the early decades of the first-century church, some people wondered why Jesus was delaying his return. He had said he would return to condemn sin, vindicate righteousness, and rescue his people forever. People were asking why he was delaying. Will his final judgment never come? The apostle Peter answered that question in 2 Peter 3:9. He wrote, "The Lord does not delay his promise, as some understand delay, but is patient with you, not wanting any to perish but all to come to repentance." Today, God is delaying his final judgment to allow people time to repent, to give them another opportunity to repent, and another, and another.

Still, God's patience does not negate God's judgment. God's judgment is coming. Peter wrote in the next verse,

> But the day of the Lord will come like a thief; on that day the
> heavens will pass away with a loud noise, the elements will burn
> and be dissolved, and the earth and the works on it will be disclosed.
(2 Pet 3:10)

God's final judgment is coming on this earth, on every person on the earth—either at death or at the coming of Christ. Because of God's mercy, he waits for repentance before his judgment comes.

Second, **God's punishment of sin follows a warning**. A few paragraphs above, we considered the cycle of sin recited in Nehemiah 9—rebelling against God, then calling out to God, then God's gracious deliverance, then return to sin. Nehemiah was looking back on that cycle in the history of Israel. Hosea was living in the middle of that cycle. He was witnessing covenant unfaithfulness all around him. He saw extreme forms of sinfulness in Israel, and he was issuing a call from God to Israel to return to God before it was too late and his punishment of sin arrived. God was using Hosea to warn people to turn to him before his judgment came.

How do we know the judgment of God is coming? God has promised that he will punish wickedness, and he keeps his promises. And we have evidence that God keeps his promise to judge; he kept his promise to pass judgment against Israel. God's judgment of Israel stands as a warning to our generation that God always keeps his promises, including his promise to condemn sin.

The Real God Offers a Love Relationship and Will Restore Us
HOSEA 8:9; 9:10

Israel was rejecting the love relationship God was offering. They turned away from God's love and were loving other things—their false gods and their sin. In 8:9 God says, "Ephraim has paid for love." The people of Israel were expending resources to purchase love. How tragic when they could have received God's love for free. Yet they were giving their love to others, not to God. Their love was disordered; loving other gods and loving their sin were more important to them than loving God. In fact, that's one way we can determine whether something is an idol in our lives. We ask, "Does this thing or person cause me to love God more or less? Does it push me closer to God, or does it pull me away from God?"

In 9:10 God says, "I discovered Israel / like grapes in the wilderness. / I saw your ancestors / like the first fruit of the fig tree in its first season." What a beautiful statement of God's love. God was reminding them that the reason he chose Abraham and the reason he delivered Israel from slavery in Egypt was because they were precious to him, "like grapes in the wilderness." How beautiful, how valuable! That's how God saw Israel! God had always wanted a love relationship with Israel, and he had always wanted to use Israel to call all the nations to a love relationship with him.

Living in a love relationship with God is a privilege and joy. It's also a necessity. We *need* a love relationship with God. We need the one true God because only he can take away our sin. Only he has come as the God-man Jesus to atone for our sin by dying as our sacrifice. Only he can give us eternal life because he *made* eternity, and he defeated death by rising from the dead. Only God can transform us. He takes away our sin and makes us clean. He gives us new and abundant life, and no false god can do that.

So, how do we become the kind of persons who are no longer attracted to false gods? How does that happen? What do we do? Do we look at our failures and try to do better? Do we listen to a sermon or read a book and try to follow good advice? We saw earlier in this section that we become like what we worship. When we worship abhorrent idols, our behavior becomes abhorrent. But the opposite is also true. When we worship the one true God in Christ, we become more like him, and we enjoy his strength, his purity, his joy, his peace, even his glory.

Second Corinthians 3:18 says, "We all, with unveiled faces, are looking as in a mirror at the glory of the Lord and are being transformed into the same image from glory to glory." How are we transformed into the image of Jesus? How are we transformed from people who are seduced by the false gods of this world to people who are captivated only by Jesus and consumed with love for Jesus? "We all, with unveiled faces, are looking as in a mirror at the glory of the Lord and are being transformed into the same image." We're transformed into the image of Jesus by beholding the glory of Jesus. Every day, behold his glory. Every day, think of Jesus. Behold his perfection, how he faced every temptation we face, yet without sin. Behold his holiness, close to sinners yet never sullied by sin. Behold his compassion, healing the sick, seeking and saving the lost. Behold his righteous indignation at the self-righteous religion of the Pharisees. Behold him in the garden, praying in agony yet yielding his will to the will of the Father. Behold him on the cross, suffering and dying not for his sin, because he had none, but for my sin and for yours, that we might be reconciled to God. Behold the empty tomb and the resurrected Jesus appearing to his disciples victorious over death. Every day, behold the glory of the Lord until his glory takes hold of you, dominates your mind, emotions, and will, and you are transformed by his glory. Every day let's turn away from the idols of this world and the idols of our minds until we are fully enthralled with the glory of the one true God.

Reflect and Discuss

1. What things, persons, ideas, or activities compete with God for preeminence in your heart? Why?
2. Why do you think idolatry is so common? Why is it a temptation for you?
3. Why is the connection between knowing God and obeying God inevitable (1 John 2:4)? How does that connection apply to your life?
4. What are some common but inadequate or false images of God today? Why are they false? How do you ensure that they are not temptations for you?
5. Do people today regard God's Word as "something strange" (Hos 8:12)? How so? How can we help people be open to God's truth?
6. Why do we become like what we worship?
7. God's judgment of sin is coming. How should that fact change the way we live?
8. How are you doing with "looking . . . at the glory of the Lord" (2 Cor 3:18) day by day? How can you make beholding the glory of Jesus more common and significant in your life?

A Watershed Moment

HOSEA 10–11

Main Idea: When we stand at crossroads where we will choose between God's way and ours, God helps us by confronting us with the realities of his judgment of sin and his compassionate offer of salvation.

I.   **Understand Our Crucial Choices (10:1-4; 11:12).**
    A.   Our hearts can be false or true (10:2).
    B.   We can fear God or something else (10:3).
    C.   We can have a fake or a real relationship with God (10:4; 11:12).
II. **Face the Clear Consequences of Sin (10:5-13).**
III. **Hear God's Compassionate Call (11:8-9).**

A watershed is typically defined as a dividing mountain ridge, a crest in a mountain range from which all the rain or melting snow flows in two opposite directions. In the Rocky Mountains, for example, all along the peaks of that mountain range are places where rain falls and flows east into creeks, onto the South Platte River, and ultimately to the Mississippi River and the Gulf of Mexico. But the rain that falls on those mountain peaks just a foot or two to the west will flow in the opposite direction to the Colorado River and ultimately to the Pacific Ocean. The watershed is the dividing line. Water that falls to the east of that dividing line will never flow west, and water that falls to the west of that dividing line will never flow east.

In the church we speak of watershed issues. Possibly the best example is the issue of the inerrancy of Scripture. That's a watershed issue. When people claim the Bible has errors, that assertion will lead them down a path that will flow eventually into the acceptance of all sorts of man-made ideas instead of the acceptance of the authority of Scripture. If, on the other hand, people assert that the Bible is inerrant, that belief will lead them down the path of submitting to the truth of Scripture on every issue. So where people stand on a host of issues is determined by where they stand on the one issue of the inerrancy of Scripture. Why are people hundreds of miles apart from one another in their conclusions about what is true and false, what is right and wrong, what is eternal and what is negotiable? The reason for the vast difference is that they started on different sides of the one issue of the truth of the Bible. It's a watershed issue.

We also face watershed *moments*—moments that are critical turning points when everything changes and things will never be the same. I was once in Cuba for a week to teach the Old Testament. Before I left, an older Cuban believer took me on a tour of some sites in the area, including San Juan Hill, the site of the famous battle where Teddy Roosevelt and the Rough Riders fought in the Spanish-American War. In the late nineteenth century, the relationship between the United States and Spain was tense, and a major issue was Spain's rule in Cuba. Both countries applied diplomatic pressure to influence each other; the outcome was uncertain, and tensions were high. Then, on the night of February 15, 1898, a great explosion sank the *U.S.S. Maine* in Havana Harbor, killing more than 260 crew members. The result was a U.S. declaration of war against Spain and the Spanish-American War, with the American battle cry, "Remember the *Maine!*" The sinking of that ship was a watershed event and a watershed moment.

Hosea lived during a watershed moment for Israel, and he preached that it was a watershed moment. He preached that if Israel repented of sin and turned to God, they would experience God's blessing and life, but if Israel continued in sin and turned away from God, they would soon experience God's judgment and death. That message should sound familiar since it's repeated throughout the Bible. Faith in the one true God, knowing God, and obeying God lead to God's blessing and life. But faith in ourselves, turning away from God, and disobeying God lead to God's judgment and death.

Understand Our Crucial Choices
HOSEA 10:1-4; 11:12

Hosea preached to a particular group of people during a particular period of time, but he also preached a universal and timeless message. People of every age should understand our crucial choices. Hosea began chapter 10 of his prophecy with a reference to God's blessing on Israel: "Israel is a lush vine; / it yields fruit for itself" (v. 1). This is not the only time God refers to Israel as a vine (e.g., Ps 80:8-14; Jer 2:21; Ezek 17:2-10;

19:10-14). In Isaiah 5, for example, God describes how he planted a vine. He prepared the field, cleared it of stones, planted the vine, built a watchtower to protect it and a wine vat for the harvest. Then, God says that his vine is Israel, but the only harvest he saw from Israel was sin, injustice, and violence (Isa 5:1-7).

God gave Israel many blessings. But what did they do with those blessings? Hosea 10:1 says, "The more his fruit increased, / the more he increased the altars. / The better his land produced, / the better they made the sacred pillars." They used God's blessings for their own selfish purposes. They even worshiped false gods because they thought that could help them be more prosperous. That was their fruit—sin, selfishness, and self-centered religion.

God blesses us, too, and the greatest blessing he offers us is a relationship with himself. He offers himself! How will we respond to God's offer of blessing? We have some crucial choices to make, choices the Israelites faced and Hosea described. First, **our hearts can be false or true**. Verse 2 says, "Their hearts are devious." It's difficult to translate the Hebrew word behind "devious." It may mean something like either "divided" or "smooth" (Brown et al., *BDB*, 323–25), but the meaning in this context is clear: Israel's heart was not right before God. Hosea has preached before that the root of sin is the condition of the heart. Are our hearts true before God, faithful, honest? Or are our hearts deceitful, false, divided?

A second choice we face is that **we can fear God or something else**. In verse 3 Hosea quotes Israel as saying, "We do not fear the LORD." That was an amazing statement, since God had commanded them to fear him. They were declaring their disobedience. Deuteronomy 10:12 says, "What does the LORD your God ask of you except to fear the LORD your God by walking in all his ways, to love him, and to worship the LORD your God with all your heart and all your soul?" That is only one of many verses in the Bible that tell us to fear God.

Everybody is afraid of something. A major choice in life is whether to fear God or to fear people. When we fear God, we respect his holiness, his power, his word, and his judgment. When we fear God, we want to obey God and give him our wholehearted worship and reverence. But when we fear people, we're concerned with what they think of us, and we want to live to please them, to believe what they believe, to say what they want to hear because we're afraid of their rejection or displeasure. Usually when we fear people, we don't fear God, but when we fear God, we have little or no fear of people. This is actually a major life choice: who or what are we going to fear?

Third, here's another crucial choice: **we can have a fake or a real relationship with God**. Hosea wrote in 10:4 that Israelites "speak mere words, / taking false oaths while making covenants." Their covenant with God was empty, meaningless. In 11:12 God says, "Ephraim surrounds me with lies, / the house of Israel, with deceit." The people of Israel had no real love for God or commitment to God. Rather, they had "mere words" about commitment, but those words were untrue and empty—false oaths.

Years ago, for a period of time, the speed limit was fifty-five miles per hour on all highways in the United States. During the time when that law was in force, one day I was driving on a major highway, admittedly a little over the speed limit. A big eighteen-wheeler blew past me like I was standing still. As he passed, I saw the bumper sticker on the back of that truck. It read, "For Safety and Fuel Economy, I'm Committed to Speed Limit 55." Obviously, the driver was not abiding by those words, so they were only words, "mere words." How often do we claim a commitment to God that we don't keep? How often do we sing words of commitment to God that are "mere words," "false oaths"? Some people claim a commitment to God when they don't even know God; they have never put their faith in Jesus as Savior and Lord. Don't have a fake relationship with God. Have a real relationship with God. Don't merely say words; give your heart and life to God.

Face the Clear Consequences of Sin
HOSEA 10:5-13

People in Israel were making the wrong choices, turning away from God instead of turning to God. People who choose sin over submission to God have to face the consequences of that choice. The Israelites were about to face God's punishment as the consequence of their sin, and Hosea preached that God's punishment was imminent. In 10:5-10 Hosea referred to the loss of their idols, the death of their king, the destruction of their pagan worship sites, and even war as foreign nations invaded Israel. God's judgment was coming; all those hardships would be the consequences of their sin. History records that all those events came to pass in Israel in the final quarter of the eighth century BC. Before God's punishment came, he used his prophet Hosea to warn the people to turn away from sin before it was too late.

Galatians 6 says,

> *Don't be deceived: God is not mocked. For whatever a person sows*
> *he will also reap, because the one who sows to his flesh will reap*
> *destruction from the flesh, but the one who sows to the Spirit will reap*
> *eternal life from the Spirit.* (Gal 6:7-8)

It is an eternal law that God states in his Word multiple times: we reap what we sow. God stated that principle through Hosea too. In 10:12 he wrote,

> *Sow righteousness for yourselves*
> *and reap faithful love;*
> *break up your unplowed ground.*
> *It is time to seek the Lord*
> *until he comes and sends righteousness*
> *on you like the rain.*

Verse 13 states the same principle: "You have plowed wickedness and reaped injustice; / you have eaten the fruit of lies."

God works in the lives of people according to the law of the harvest. Harvest is an agricultural reality that God has chosen to signify a spiritual reality. When we sow seeds, we reap a harvest. We reap only after we sow, and the type of harvest we reap is determined by the type of seeds we sow. That's a physical law that operates in the natural realm; it's also a spiritual law that operates in the spiritual realm. When we commit sin, we're sowing fleshly, sinful seeds in our lives, and we'll reap corruption and judgment. But when we submit to the Spirit of God, we're sowing spiritual, holy seeds in our lives, and we'll reap a life that is blessed and eternal. Our choices have consequences. When we sow righteousness, we reap God's blessing. When we sow sin, we reap suffering.

God will give justice. He will punish evil, either immediately or eventually. The second chapter of Romans says that God always rewards righteousness and punishes sin. "He will repay each one according to his works" (Rom 2:6). Every sin will be punished. God is a just judge. When someone is guilty, he will find him or her guilty. And we're all guilty of sin. Furthermore, God will justly apply his eternal law that sin leads to death. That penalty will be paid for every sin. The question is, Who will pay the penalty? Without a Savior, we will pay for our own sin.

Those without Jesus will pay eternally for their sin in hell. But Jesus died on the cross as our sacrifice to pay the penalty for our sin. When we receive him, he takes the penalty for us. Someone will pay for our sin: either we will pay the penalty for our sin, or Jesus will pay the penalty for us when we put our faith in him. When people are presented with that choice, surely they will not choose to pay their own penalty for sin with their death. If they understand the choice, most people will choose for the Savior to pay the penalty for their sin. If they comprehend fully Jesus's gift to them, it's likely they will be so grateful to their Savior that they will want to worship and serve him now and forever. Yes, God is holy and just; he is also gracious and merciful. And we praise him for all his glorious and perfect attributes.

Hear God's Compassionate Call
HOSEA 11:8-9

Hosea preached about God's coming judgment. He also preached about God's grace and mercy. Hosea made abundantly clear that the people of Israel had gone far down the road of sin. He wrote of sexual sin, idolatry and participation in pagan worship practices, abuse, the corruption of the worship of God, and marital unfaithfulness. Government leaders were corrupt, religious leaders were corrupt, and the people in general were corrupt. It's important that we see the depth of sin in Israel, and it's important that we understand how offensive that sin was to the holiness of God. When we comprehend those facts, we can begin to see that *our* sin is also offensive to God. Only then can we comprehend how deep is the mercy and grace of God that he would offer atonement and forgiveness for our sin.

We see God's mercy and grace in chapter 11 of Hosea. In spite of the depth of Israel's sin, God was not yet giving up on the people of Israel. In the book of Hosea, God allows us to see the conflict in his own heart regarding his holy response to sin. He says in Hosea 6:4,

> *"What am I going to do with you, Ephraim?*
> *What am I going to do with you, Judah?*
> *Your love is like the morning mist*
> *and like the early dew that vanishes."*

God knew his people were unfaithful to him and had earned his holy judgment. But he did not want to send judgment; he wanted to bless.

So, "What am I going to do with you, Ephraim?" Similarly, in chapter 11 God reveals a struggle in his heart. He asks,

> *"How can I give you up, Ephraim?*
> *How can I surrender you, Israel?*
> *How can I make you like Admah?*
> *How can I treat you like Zeboiim?*
> *I have had a change of heart;*
> *my compassion is stirred!*
> *I will not vent the full fury of my anger;*
> *I will not turn back to destroy Ephraim.*
> *For I am God and not man,*
> *the Holy One among you;*
> *I will not come in rage."* (vv. 8-9)

"Admah" and "Zeboiim" were cities of the plain in the area of Sodom and Gomorrah that were destroyed with those cities. "I have had a change of heart" translates a word that also had a physical sense, meaning to turn over or to turn around. God's heart was in upheaval; it's possible to render the statement as "My heart recoils within me," or "My heart is turning over within me."

Such a statement about what is happening in God's heart is rare in the Bible, and it's precious. God opens his heart to us, as it were, and allows us to see his internal struggle over punishing people he loves. Using anthropomorphic language, God portrays for us the conflict in the Godhead between wrath and mercy. Throughout the book of Hosea, indeed throughout the prophetic corpus, God affirms that his judgment will fall on Israel and Judah. But here, at this watershed moment in Israel's history, lest we think God is a robot or a principle or a theological system, he shows us that before judgment he asked, "How can I give you up, Ephraim? / How can I surrender you, Israel? . . . / My compassion is stirred." God was feeling conflict in his heart. Perhaps we could say that the conflict was partially resolved by the survival of a remnant of Israelites or a delay in God's judgment. But Hosea doesn't resolve the conflict. He merely quotes God as testifying to the struggle in his heart between justice and compassion. Before God sent his judgment, he waited for Israel to turn to him because he loved them. We can be sure God does not want to give up on us; he did not want to give up even on the people of Israel who had turned from him to sin again and again.

In Florida, in 1986, the *Gainesville Sun* reported of a twelve-year-old boy snorkeling in a tributary of Crystal River. An alligator attacked him in the head, ripping off his mask and snorkel. The boy started swimming frantically to the bank. Other kids saw it and started screaming. His mother heard the screaming and looked to see her son swimming hard to shore, with an alligator behind him chasing. Immediately, she ran to the water, screaming to her son, "Swim!" By the time she arrived at the water's edge, her son was approaching the bank. She waded into the water, grabbed his arm, and began to pull. That's when the gator bit down on the boy's leg. As his mom pulled on his arm, she felt the alligator pulling back on his leg. The boy's mother pulled with all her might and kept pulling, and she won the tug-of-war as she pulled her son to safety. The boy had to spend some time in the hospital, but he survived. The alligator broke one of the boy's legs, and both legs were badly scarred from the alligator's teeth. But one report said his arm was also scarred because his mother's fingernails had dug into his arm in her determination not to let her son go ("Mom Rescues Son").

God does not want to let us go. "How can I give you up, Ephraim? How can I surrender you, Israel?" You and I have scars too. We have the scars of past sin and pain. Some of those scars are ugly, and some of them still hurt. The sins of the world, the flesh, and the devil pull us from God and leave their scars. But God did not let go of us, and we remember how strongly God pulled us to himself. This is the heart of God. "How can I give you up, Ephraim? How can I surrender you, Israel? . . . My compassion is stirred." God did not want to give up on Israel, and he does not want to give up on us. Even though Israel had gone far down the road of sin, God continued to love them. That's how God loves us.

Remember that God told Hosea to love his unfaithful wife in the same way God loves. Do we love sinful people the way God loves them? Do we relate to people who are headed for judgment in the same way God relates to them? Billions of people in our world are bound for eternity in hell. Do our hearts recoil within us? Is our compassion stirred? Are we disturbed, distressed by that? Do we say with God, "How can I let you go into eternity without Christ? My heart is repulsed by the fact that judgment awaits you." God calls his church to love and pursue lost sinners in the same way he loves and pursues us. He pursues us in outrageous grace based on nothing but his infinite love for undeserving sinners. He poured out that love on the cross, taking our sin and its penalty on himself as our sacrifice. Then he rose again, showing that he has the power to give life. When we put our faith in him, he takes away our sin, makes us new, and gives us eternal life. This is the gospel. Praise his name! As we read Hosea, may we be warned by the reality of God's holy judgment and welcomed by God's love and grace. May we embrace the God who pursues us, feel compassion for those under wrath today, and run to the world with the gospel while there is still time.

Reflect and Discuss

1. What are some of the blessings God has given you? What have you been doing with those blessings?
2. What do you fear? Do you fear anything more than you fear God? If so, why?
3. In your worship or service for God, are there ways you offer "mere words"?
4. How do you think the biblical law of the harvest applies and will apply to people and societies today? How will it apply in your life?
5. How is your conception of God affected when you read that God asks, "How can I give you up, Ephraim? . . . My compassion is stirred"? How does such a statement by God affect your relationship with him?
6. Do you have scars from past sin and heartache? How is God pulling you to himself and helping you?
7. How are you doing with loving people the way God loves people?

The Great Chasm

HOSEA 12–13

Main Idea: A chasm stands between people who are sinful and God who is infinitely holy, but in his love, God has come to us in Christ to offer a way to bridge the chasm.

I. **Observe the Extensive Sin of Israel (12:1,7-8,11-12,14,16; 13:1-2,12,14,16).**

II. **Consider the Holy Character of God.**
   A. He is Lord of all, possessing all power and authority (12:5,9; 13:4).
   B. He is the only God (13:4).
   C. God speaks to reveal himself and his truth (12:4,6,10).
   D. God is blameless and just in judgment (12:2,14; 13:6).

III. **View the Bridge God Offers (12:10,12-13).**

On Christmas Eve, 1839, near the town of Lyme Regis on the southern coast of England, William Critchard and his wife attended a Christmas Eve party at a friend's house. On their walk home late that night, they noticed that the cliff path they followed had dropped about a foot since that morning. They also saw some cracks in the walls of their cottage, but they were tired and went to bed. At four a.m., they were awakened by a loud cracking sound, and at five a.m. they went outside and found deep fissures in the ground. They realized that something significant was happening, so they set off to warn their neighbors. Sure enough, the movement of the ground in that area continued over the next twenty-four hours, and by the day after Christmas, the landscape had changed almost beyond recognition. A massive section of cliff, about three-quarters of a mile long and estimated to be eight million tons of rock, had shifted toward the sea by several hundred feet, creating an enormous ravine. The plateau of land that had moved was now a virtual island. The new landscape became a tourist attraction. Queen Victoria arrived on the royal yacht to view the scene. Songs were written about what came to be known as the Great Chasm. The phenomenon that created the chasm was called a "landslip" (Strange, "Goat Island").

During the lifetime of Hosea, a great chasm existed between Israel and God. When did the slip begin that created that great chasm? We could say it began as early as the incident of worshiping the golden calf in the wilderness, but there were plenty of spiritual high points after that. Maybe it was when King David, the sweet psalmist of Israel, committed adultery with Bathsheba or when Solomon married multiple wives outside the faith and they "turned his heart away to follow other gods" (1 Kgs 11:4). The split of Israel into two countries certainly contributed to the slip; that's when Jeroboam, the first king of the northern kingdom, built illicit worship sites at Dan and Bethel, and the practice of idolatry escalated. Then, some two hundred years passed between the construction of those altars and the preaching of Hosea—two hundred years of slipping into more idolatry and more immorality. Throughout Israel's history, paganism and secularism spread like gangrene, and both contributed to the deepening of sin and the widening of the chasm between Israel and God.

Observe the Extensive Sin of Israel
HOSEA 12:1,7-8,11-12,14,16; 13:1-2,12,14,16

In chapters 12 and 13 of Hosea, the prophet clearly depicts the chasm between Israel and God. In this section we'll look at both sides of that chasm. First, we'll consider the side of Israel's sin. To one degree or another, we observe Israel's sin throughout the book of Hosea. In chapters 12 and 13 Hosea again describes that sin in lurid detail to make it abundantly clear that God's coming punishment for their sin was more than justified.

In chapter 12 Hosea mentions cheating in business to make more money, oppression, and idolatry, their practice of pagan religion (vv. 7,11). The first two verses of chapter 13 also describe their idolatry—specifically, worshiping the Canaanite god Baal and making idols. Chapter 12 also refers to their "disgraceful deeds" (v. 14 ESV), and chapter 13 refers to their "guilt," "sin," and rebellion (vv. 12,16). Elsewhere in Hosea we have seen references to adultery. Amos prophesied in Israel during the same time period as Hosea, and he mentioned drunkenness (Amos 6:6).

We could understand 12:1 as an introductory summary of the sins of Israel. It says, "He continually multiplies lies and violence. / He makes a covenant with Assyria, / and olive oil is carried to Egypt." They were making political alliances with Assyria and Egypt because they were not trusting God. They were not turning to God for help; they were turning to people for help. Such misplacement of trust is clear in Hosea and in other prophetic books (e.g., Isa 30; Jer 2:13-19). "Lies" refers to their sins of speech; they were not telling the truth. "Violence" refers to their sinful deeds. God told them that what they were saying was not true and what they were doing was hurting people. So the summary is that they were not trusting God, their words were sinful, and their deeds were sinful. It was like that old poem: "Everybody has their faults; you have only two—everything you say, and everything you do." Israel's sin was comprehensive.

In spite of the outrageously long list of sins Israel was committing, 12:8 reveals that they were also proud: "In all my earnings, / no one can find any iniquity in me." They were so spiritually clueless that they actually claimed they had not committed sin. It's been said that pride is a disease that makes everybody sick except for the one who has it. In other words, everybody can see pride except for the one whose pride ironically blinds him to his pride. But it's also true that pride blinds us to our other sins. Blind pride led sinful Israel to say, "No one can find any iniquity in me." These were the sins of Israel: dishonesty in business, oppression, idolatry, disgraceful deeds, rebellion against God, trusting in people instead of God, lying, violence, adultery, drunkenness, and pride. Israel had no legitimate reason to be proud.

How does our beloved country compare with Hosea's Israel? Drunkenness and illicit drug use are widespread and portrayed in the media every day as perfectly legitimate forms of entertainment. Sexual sins like pornography and homosexuality are not only accepted but also celebrated and aggressively promoted. God says that sex outside of marriage is sin, but more and more people are committing such sin and living together outside of marriage. God says such a lifestyle is sinful, but our culture touts it as perfectly normal, even preferred. Our culture is so untethered from God and his design that people commonly argue in public that more than two genders exist and that the idea of gender is fluid. Such an argument is a rejection of God's design, rebellion against his Word, and even irrational. Yet our society is so morally perverse that even such obvious biological realities are distorted. As for followers of Jesus, in both the private sector and the public sector some of them have been fired or dragged into court because of their adherence to moral standards based on God's Word. The public media portray Christians as either mean and hateful or as some sort of strange, alien species whose narrow-mindedness poses a danger to the public's safety and well-being. Compared to other countries, the United States has a large number of people who claim to be Christians, but based on the beliefs and life-styles of the people who attend church, it's clear that even much of the church has been corrupted by compromise with our sinful culture.

If it seems excessively negative to list the sins of our culture, we should remember that we are studying Hosea, and Hosea listed the sins of his culture. Yes, we should also be grateful for our country. We should be grateful for the freedoms we enjoy and grateful for the people who have worked, fought, and died to preserve those freedoms in a world where aggressors would impose tyranny by force. We should be grateful for advances in technology, access to health care, and material abundance, all of which should cause people to give thanks to God for his blessings. Still, we can hardly claim moral superiority to Hosea's Israel. Israel was morally and spiritually decadent, and so is Western culture in the twenty-first century.

Consider the Holy Character of God

In chapters 12 and 13 of his prophecy, Hosea interweaved descriptions of Israel's sin with descriptions of God's character. As we study these two chapters and reflect on these inspired statements about who God is and what he does, the depth, height, and breadth of God's greatness inspire us to worship this God who is so glorious.

Perhaps the chief point about God in these chapters is that **he is the Lord of all, possessing all power and authority**. The repetition of the name of God here underscores his preeminence. In 12:5 Hosea says, "The LORD is the God of Armies; / the LORD is his name." In that statement, "LORD" is the Hebrew *Yahweh*, the covenant name of God, the name God revealed to Moses (Exod 3:14). This God delivered his people from slavery in Egypt by many miracles, demonstrating his power over Pharaoh and all the not-gods of Egypt. Verse 5 says that covenant God is the God of Armies—angelic hosts and the armies of Israel. He is the commanding Ruler of all that exists. *Yahweh* is his "name," and the word translated "name" typically refers to remembering. So *Yahweh* is God's memorial name, the name by which he will be remembered forever. God added further in verse 9, "I have been the LORD [*Yahweh*] your God / ever since the land of Egypt." The same statement is in 13:4.

The repetition of God's name occurs in a similar way in the book of Leviticus. Leviticus is filled with laws God gives as his commands. Throughout Leviticus God repeats, "I am the Lord." Why? God is reminding us of who is speaking (see 2:13,16,21). He is issuing commands. Does he have the authority to command individuals and an entire nation how to live? Yes! How do we know he has that authority? He is the Lord! He is the one true God who spoke the universe into existence. He is the one who sustains the universe and superintends the movement of every subatomic particle by his power and knowledge. He knows everything about everything—past, present, and future. He gives us our every breath. He is the Lord! That fact alone should be enough to move us to bow before him in worship, to submit our lives to him, and to obey his commands. He is the almighty Lord.

Second, **he is the only God.** In 13:4 God says, "You know no God but me, / and no Savior exists besides me." No Savior exists besides God. That is the repeated affirmation of the Bible. Deuteronomy 4:35 says, "The Lord is God; there is no other besides him." Deuteronomy 4:39 likewise says, "The Lord is God in heaven above and on earth below; there is no other." All those statements declare that only one God exists, and they deny the existence of other gods.

Here in the United States, we live in a pluralistic society, where people are legally free to believe in any god and practice any religion they choose. We Christians believe all people should have that freedom; we regard it as a basic human right. Christians have worked, fought, and died to preserve religious freedom for all people. But we also believe that if people do not believe in and worship the one true God, their religion is false and futile, and it is our duty and privilege to tell them of the one true God who has come to us in Christ. We do that knowing that declaring the existence of only one God and denying the existence of any other god will invite criticism from our culture.

Years ago, a man I knew moved to a city to pastor a church. The man is a Bible believer, an inerrantist, and people in the community began to learn that about him. When he was still new in town, a man approached him and said, "I've heard that you're narrow-minded." My friend said, "That depends on the subject. On some subjects I'm narrow-minded, and on other subjects I'm closed-minded." The oneness of God is a subject about which we Christians are closed-minded. The issue is not our personality or our willingness to consider other points of view. The issue is truth. We believe the Bible is God's revelation of himself, we believe his revelation is true, and the Bible states repeatedly that only one God exists. Since that statement is true, every idea that conflicts with that statement is false because two opposing ideas cannot at the same time be true. If one is true, the other must be false. Are we narrow-minded and dogmatic? *We* are not the issue. The issue is *truth*, and absolute truth is "dogmatic" by definition since everything that conflicts with the truth is necessarily false.

So let us believe in the right of all people to hold their own beliefs and practice their own religion. Let us defend their right to do so. But let us also proclaim the truth that only one God exists—the God who created the universe, who called Abraham and his descendants, and who came to us in Jesus the Christ. Through Hosea, God said to sinful Israel, "No Savior exists besides me."

Third, **God speaks to reveal himself and his truth**. Hosea 12:4 refers to Jacob's encounter with God at the Jabbok River (Gen 32). Some translations have, "There he spoke with him," to refer to God speaking to Jacob. The Hebrew text of verse 4 reads, "There he spoke with *us*." It's true that God spoke with Jacob at the Jabbok River, but when God spoke with Jacob, that conversation was recorded in the scriptural record so that what God said to Jacob became God's word to us. That is true for every part of the Bible. God speaks to us from his Word. Verse 10 also affirms God's verbal revelation: "I will speak through the prophets / and grant many visions; / I will give parables through the prophets." God spoke through the prophets and revealed the truth by means of visions and parables. Through God's words in the Bible, God reveals himself. He reveals the truth about reality, and he reveals what he expects from us. Verse 6 states plainly what God expected from Israel: "You must return to your God. / Maintain love and justice, / and always put your hope in God." God wants from us love, justice, and faith in him.

Thank God that he tells us who he is and what he wants. Throughout history, humans have asked questions of ultimate meaning, like these: Who is God, and what is he like? How do we find God, and what does he want from us? What is the origin of the universe and the nature of reality? God in his grace and love has answered those questions for us in his Word. We don't have to speculate as to what God is like; God tells us what he is like in his Word. And he tells us how to know him, how he expects us to live, and how to enjoy life in this world he created. Thank God that what Hosea wrote is true: God has spoken to us.

Fourth, **God is blameless and just in judgment**. Hosea announced repeatedly that God's judgment was coming to Israel. Not many years after Hosea prophesied, God's judgment *did* come. But unlike the punishment from the gods described in ancient mythology, the punishment from the one true God is not the result of a temper tantrum, jealousy, or revenge. God's punishment is based on his revealed word. Hosea 12:2 says, "He is about to punish Jacob according to his conduct; / he will repay him based on his actions." God had given his law to his people. He had made his standards clear. Furthermore, God made the consequences clear. If Israel was faithful to God and obeyed his commands, they would enjoy his blessing. If Israel was unfaithful to God and disobeyed his commands, they would suffer his judgment (Lev 26; Deut 28). The choice was Israel's. They could choose obedience and blessing or disobedience and judgment. God's judgment of Israel was neither arbitrary nor surprising. It was based on God's word given centuries earlier. The people chose to disobey God, and thereby they earned God's punishment. That's what verse 14 says: God will "repay him for his contempt." In fact, in the original, that line literally means that God would cause Israel's contempt, or evil deeds, to return to him, or turn back on him. It's clear that the cause of the coming judgment would be Israel's sin. Their sin was returning to them; they were reaping what they had sown.

God gave Israel opportunity after opportunity to put their faith in him and live in a love relationship with him. He was turning away from them because they had repeatedly turned away from him already. God's love for people, even sinful people, is communicated multiple times in the book of Hosea. He offers restoration and a love relationship with him. He sends his punishment because people choose it by setting themselves against God, by refusing to worship and obey him. It has been said that hell is God's great compliment to human free will. If people choose to live without worshiping and serving God, God will honor that choice and allow people to live in this life and the next life without him. But that is no life; it is only suffering and death.

This is our God as he revealed himself through this part of Hosea's prophecy. He is the Lord of all, the ultimate authority, the only God. He speaks to reveal himself and his truth, he is blameless and just in judgment, and he is loving and gracious. Stop to think about the greatness of God. When we understand how great he is, how loving and gracious he is, how powerful and holy he is, how could anyone turn away from the one true God? Yet Israel stooped so low as to rebel against him. Hosea 13:6 says they forgot the Lord. They forgot him! What does it mean to forget God? Forgetting God involves forgetting his glorious character—his greatness, holiness, incomparability, unlimited power, and infinite knowledge. Israel forgot all he had done for them. They forgot his law and its demands on their lives. A repeated theme in God's law is to remember (e.g., Deut 5:15; 7:18; 8:2,18). But Israel forgot.

View the Bridge God Offers
HOSEA 12:10,12-13

The result of Israel's rebellion was alienation from God. Sin always leads to spiritual separation (Isa 59:2). That is the great chasm that stands between people and God. The chasm divides people who have sinned from God who is perfectly holy and condemns sin. How can that chasm be crossed? How can people be reconciled to God whose holiness they have offended by their sin? Consider one more attribute of God expressed in these verses. God is also loving and gracious. God did not send his judgment right away. He waited and warned. Hosea 12:10 reminds us that he used the prophets, like Hosea, to call people to turn from sin and turn to God. He is blameless and just in his judgment, but God delays his judgment because of his grace and love.

In verse 12 Hosea referred to the patriarch Jacob serving for a wife. Jacob moved to Syria where he chose Rachel as a wife. Rachel's father, Laban, told Jacob he had to work for seven years to earn Rachel as a wife. Jacob loved Rachel, so he worked seven years for the privilege of marrying the woman he loved. But Laban tricked him and gave him Rachel's sister Leah instead. Jacob then worked seven more years to earn Rachel as his wife. Who could doubt Jacob's love for Rachel? He worked for her father, the man who tricked him, for fourteen years in order to be married to Rachel.

In the next verse Hosea makes a parallel statement regarding how God had related to Israel: he brought Israel up by a prophet, and as Jacob guarded sheep, God guarded Israel by a prophet. Hosea wrote that God's relationship with Israel was parallel to Jacob's working for Rachel. His point is that nobody could doubt Jacob's love for Rachel, and nobody could doubt God's love for Israel. Just look at all he had done for Israel through the centuries. What a beautiful portrayal of God's love and grace.

Since God is loving and gracious, he offers a bridge over the great chasm between himself and sinful people. He offers a way to be reconciled to him. As you have read about the great chasm in this section, have you recalled another place in the Bible where a great chasm is mentioned? Luke 16 records a parable Jesus told about a rich man and a poor man named Lazarus. Lazarus dies and goes to heaven, and the rich man dies and goes to hell. The rich man is suffering in hell and desperate. He looks up and sees Abraham and Lazarus far off in heaven. He calls out to Abraham and asks him for comfort. Abraham replies by saying, "A great chasm has been fixed between us and you, so that those who want to pass over from here to you cannot; neither can those from there cross over to us" (Luke 16:26). The rich man received no help because between heaven and hell is a great chasm, and it is fixed. Jesus's parable is a grim story. It's also an urgent story because it's a story about time running out. Jesus did not mince words about what's at stake. He did not pretend that our years are limitless and our options infinite. A day will come when our alternatives shut down, and the great chasm will be fixed, uncrossable.

We don't know when our final day will come; it may be tomorrow. But today it is not too late to turn to God in faith and receive his offer of reconciliation. God's greatest and final revelation of his offer of reconciliation was when he came to us himself incarnated in human flesh as the God-man Jesus. Jesus came in fulfillment of Old Testament prophecy, was born of a virgin, lived a sinless life, performed many miracles, taught of the kingdom of God, then died as the once-for-all sacrifice for our sins, and rose again on the third day. Now he offers abundant and eternal life to all who put their faith in him. When Thomas asked Jesus how to get to heaven, how to bridge the chasm between us and God, Jesus told him, "I am the way, the truth, and the life. No one comes to the Father except through me" (John 14:6). Jesus himself is our Savior, the one and only bridge over the great chasm between sinners like us and the holy God. Praise his name.

Reflect and Discuss

1. What similarities or contrasts can you see between Israel in Hosea's time and Western culture today?
2. Why do you think Israel strayed so far from God and his law? How does Israel's story serve as a warning to people and cultures today?
3. Why is it important to remember God's greatness, authority, and holiness? What do Hosea's statements about God's greatness and authority have to do with the way you live?
4. How do we communicate the truth about the one true God and his way of salvation in a pluralistic society?
5. How does God communicate himself and his truth today?
6. What does it mean to forget God, what are the possible consequences of forgetting him, and how do we remember him?
7. Why does God bridge the chasm between himself and sinful people, and how does he accomplish that?

The Place of Beginning Again

HOSEA 14:1-7

Main Idea: When we obey the call to return to God, God's anger will turn from us, he will heal our turning hearts, and his blessing will return to us.

I. **Return to God and His Way (14:1-2).**
   A. Realize what God wants (14:1).
   B. Request forgiveness (14:1-2).
   C. Reach out to others to offer God's call (14:1-2).
II. **Renounce Substitutes for God (14:2-3).**
   A. We reject mere rituals in worship (14:2).
   B. We reject trust in humanity (14:3).
   C. We reject faith in our gods (14:3).
III. **Rejoice in God's Blessings (14:4-7).**
   A. God is consistent (14:5).
   B. God will give beauty (14:5).
   C. God will give stability (14:5).
   D. God will give bounty (14:6).

We humans seem to like new beginnings. We mark the beginning of each new year, hoping to experience or accomplish new things in the year ahead. Cultures in virtually every place on earth and in every era of history have marked the occasion of the new year with celebrations of various kinds. We see every birthday as the introduction to a new year of our lives and fresh opportunities for the future. And our lives are full of new beginnings—starting a new school or a new school year, changing jobs or getting a promotion, moving to a new city, getting married, joining a new church, having a baby. In fact, every Monday is a new beginning, introducing a new week with new possibilities.

In the final chapter of his prophecy, Hosea called for a new beginning with God. During Hosea's lifetime, God's people were not being faithful to God. God compared their unfaithfulness to him to the unfaithfulness of Hosea's wife to Hosea. Just as a husband and wife share a covenant relationship, God and his people shared a covenant relationship. At some point Hosea's wife worked as a prostitute, and just as Hosea's wife was unfaithful to Hosea, God's people were unfaithful to God when they prostituted themselves with other gods. They strayed from God and worshiped idols, they established alliances with other countries instead of trusting God, and they observed religious rituals instead of offering heartfelt worship to God.

God sent Hosea to call Israel back to God. So Hosea exposed their sin and implored them to return to God, to begin again. Some of *us* would like to begin again with God—maybe all of us. We know we're not all we should be with God and for God. Have you ever thought of every time of worship, whether public or private, as a place of beginning again? Worship is always a potential place of starting over for us. Think about Louisa Fletcher's words in her poem called "The Land of Beginning Again":

> I wish that there were some wonderful place
>   Called the Land of Beginning Again,
> Where all our mistakes and all our heartaches
>   And all of our poor, selfish grief
> Could be dropped, like a shabby old coat, at the door,
>   And never put on again. . . .
>
> It wouldn't be possible not to be kind
>   In the Land of Beginning Again;
> And the ones we misjudged and the ones whom we grudged
>   Their moments of victory here
> Would feel in the grasp of our loving handclasp
>   More than penitent lips could explain. . . .
>
> So I wish that there were some wonderful place
>   Called the Land of Beginning Again,
> Where all our mistakes and all our heartaches
>   And all of our poor, selfish grief
> Could be dropped, like a shabby old coat, at the door,
>   And never put on again. (*The Land*, 3–4)

It's a beautiful thought—to have a place of beginning again, a place where we can leave past sins and hurts, never to pick them up again. All of us have spoken words we regret; we've thought things and done things that were not pleasing to God. We need a place of beginning

again. Do you feel that need? What will it take to get there? Hosea helps
us with that.

Return to God and His Way
HOSEA 14:1-2

In the first verse of Hosea's final chapter, Hosea gave a command:
"Israel, return to the LORD your God." What does it mean to return to
God? Answering that question is the first step to beginning again. We
have to **realize what God wants**. The Hebrew word translated "return" is
often translated "repent" or "turn." The word means to turn and go in
a different direction. Repentance is returning to God, beginning again.
Repentance is more than changing our minds; it's changing the way we
live, behaving in a different way. Repentance is different from a New
Year's resolution. We may keep our resolutions, but most of the time we
don't. Repentance, by definition, is different from that. If our behavior is not altered, then we have not repented. In Acts 26:20 Paul said
that he preached to people "that they should repent and turn to God,
and do works worthy of repentance." "Works worthy of repentance."
Some works are worthy of repentance; they indicate that repentance
has occurred. In a worship service, when someone walks forward at the
time of invitation to make a spiritual commitment, or goes to a pastor
or Christian friend to share some kind of decision for Christ, we rejoice
in that, but we won't know if repentance has taken place until we see
changes in thinking and acting. Repentance means turning and walking
in a different direction. That's what God wants.

Some people live as if God accepted a certain amount of sin in our
lives. He does not. God has gone on record concerning his expecta-
tion of our holiness. First Peter 1:15 says, "As the one who called you
is holy, you also are to be holy in all your conduct." Holiness is not
sin management, making sure our sin remains at an acceptable level,
or making sure our sin remains private. No, holiness is the eradication
of sin, separation from sin. Jesus said, "Be perfect, therefore, as your
heavenly Father is perfect" (Matt 5:48). Holiness, perfection, is God's
standard for us. The question is, How are we going to respond to his
standard? We humble ourselves before God, confess our sin, and repent
of it. That's what God wants: "Return to the LORD your God" (Hos 14:1).

We turn from sin and turn to God, and we **request forgiveness**.
Throughout Hosea's prophecy, he pointed to the sins of the people. In

verse 1 again he said, "You have stumbled in your iniquity." For people to be motivated to turn and go in a different direction, they have to recognize they're going in the wrong direction. A lot of people don't recognize that. They know they're not perfect, but they think that's not a big deal because, after all, who is perfect? In the church, however, we who have God's Holy Spirit in us ought to have a constant and acute awareness of our need to confess sin and repent. We don't ever want to be blind to our sin or impressed with our goodness so that we don't see our need to change and grow.

So Hosea pointed out their sin: "You have stumbled in your iniquity." In verse 2 he told them to say to God, "Forgive all our iniquity." Hosea told them to request forgiveness. Maybe the sin in your life is a nasty temper, a gossiping or critical tongue, a bitter spirit, a failure to forgive, greed, lust, pride, not obeying parents, not honoring God with possessions, prejudice, or laziness in serving God. You name it. Maybe it's something that's obvious, and everybody knows about it; maybe your spouse nudges you whenever a preacher mentions it. But maybe nobody knows about it. You have hidden it from your friends, from your pastor, from your spouse or parents, but you know about it and God knows about it, and you know God doesn't want it in your life.

What are you going to do about sin? "Return to the Lord your God" and say to him, "Forgive all our iniquity." Don't be guilty of being satisfied with the way things are in your walk with God. Don't make the terrible mistake of saying, "This is just the way I am. It's the way I was raised; it's the way I always have been and the way I always will be." Instead, return to God, request forgiveness. Say to God, "Forgive all our iniquity." God will forgive, and you can be at the place of beginning again where things can be different, *you* can be different. Today can be that place of beginning again.

We can also follow Hosea's example and **reach out to others to offer God's call**. The verbs Hosea used are imperatives. "Return" and "say to him" are commands. Hosea was not indifferent about Israel's decision to turn from sin and to God. He didn't say, "I'm just offering you some options. Continue in sin, or turn to God." Hosea exhorted the people; he urged them to return to God. In verse 2 he even told the people the words to say to God. "Take words of repentance with you / and return to the Lord. / Say to him, 'Forgive all our iniquity / and accept what is good.'"

Hosea was like a pastor at the time of the invitation in worship. Sometimes the pastor will say to people, "Pray this prayer," or "Say this to God." That's what Hosea was doing. He told the people to say to God, "Forgive all our iniquity." Hosea was *exhorting* them to say that to God. Maybe some Christians reading this should say to God, "God, help me have what Hosea had—a sense of urgency about calling people to turn to you." Maybe some Christians need to repent of their cool-heartedness regarding the lostness of people who are headed for an eternity in hell. God help us reach out to people and exhort them to turn to God.

Renounce Substitutes for God
HOSEA 14:2-3

Hosea described the sins of the people specifically in verses 2–3, and people practice the same sins today. We seek substitutes for God, and to begin again we have to renounce any such substitute. So we follow Hosea's direction, and **we reject mere rituals in worship.** In verse 2 Hosea told them they should say to God that they would "repay you / with praise from our lips." Various translations render that clause differently. Literally, the Hebrew reads, "We will give the bulls of our lips." Bulls were used as sacrifices, so Hosea was saying, "Say to God, 'God, we will offer the sacrifice, or offering, of our lips.'" Hosea was urging them not to be satisfied merely to present a sacrificial animal on the altar in worship. He told them to present to God the bulls of their lips, *words* that expressed their hearts' devotion to God, the praise of their lips. If we're going to begin again with God, shouldn't that be our commitment to God? "God, I don't want merely to *attend* worship. I don't want merely to *critique* worship. I want to *worship* you—to sing heartfelt words of praise and to speak heartfelt words of devotion." Hebrews 13:15 gives the same message to followers of Jesus that Hosea gave to Israel. It says, "Let us continually offer up to God a sacrifice of praise, that is, the fruit of lips that confess his name."

Also, **we reject trust in humanity** as a substitute for trust in God. In verse 3 Hosea told the people to say to God, "Assyria will not save us." He was referring to Israel's alliance with Assyria in which Israel paid tribute so Assyria would protect them from their enemies. Hosea told the people to say, "We will not ride on horses." He was referring to their cavalry. They were trusting in their military to save them. Israel was not a secular nation like nations today. They were God's chosen people, a kingdom of priests with a special covenant with God in which they were to trust only him, but they were trusting in their military and in other people. God's people today are people who have put their faith in Jesus; we, too, are to trust in God, not humanity. Human solutions, whether to our personal problems or to societal problems, are superficial and temporary. God's solution is Jesus—salvation and sanctification accomplished by his saving and sanctifying power. That solution is neither superficial nor temporary; he changes our hearts and gives us eternal life. Therefore, we put our trust in God and reject substitutes for him.

Likewise, **we reject faith in our gods**. In verse 3 Hosea told the people to say to God, "We will no longer proclaim, 'Our gods!' / to the work of our hands." Hosea was referring to idolatry—offering worship to idols they had manufactured. If they wanted to be right with God, they had to commit themselves to worship only the one true God, not idols. Earlier in this book, as part of an explanation of Hosea's polemic against wrong belief and practice, we sought to define and describe idolatry. In short, an idol is a god we make. Throughout human history, people have made idols with their hands, but we also make idols with our minds. We imagine something to be paramount when it is not. We treat someone as preeminent when he or she is not. Our belief and worship are right only when God is first above all. If we want to renew our relationship with God, we will have to renounce all the gods of our own making and worship only the one true God.

Empty religious rituals, trusting people instead of God, and making idols—those sins were manifestations of unfaithfulness in Israel's relationship with God. Israelites wanted to be able to *say* they trusted God, while really trusting themselves and others. But if we're going to begin again with God, we renounce substitutes for God, and we put our trust in God.

In Charles Spurgeon's book *Morning and Evening*, he wrote a devotional on 1 Samuel 7:12, where these familiar words are found: "The Lord has helped us to this point" ("Hitherto"). Spurgeon used the King James Version, which reads, "Hitherto hath the Lord helped us." Or, as we sing in that hymn, "Here I raise my Ebenezer," a word that means "stone of help." We raise our stone of help because "hither by thy help I'm come." We tell God that we have come this far by his help. We look back on God's help in our past, and we look forward to his help in our future. Spurgeon's words are appropriate for a place of beginning again. He wrote,

The word "hitherto" seems like a hand pointing in the
direction of the *past*. . . . "hitherto the Lord hath helped"!
Through poverty, through wealth, through sickness, through
health, at home, abroad . . . , in perplexity, in joy, in trial, in
triumph, in prayer, in temptation, "hitherto hath the Lord
helped us"! . . . But the word also points *forward*. For when a
man gets up to a certain mark and writes "hitherto," he is not
yet at the end, there is still a distance to be traversed. More
trials, more joys; more temptations, more triumphs; more
prayers, more answers; more toils, more strengths . . . ; and
then come sickness, old age . . . , death. Is it over now? No!
There is more yet—awakening in Jesus' likeness . . . , the glory
of God, the fullness of eternity. . . . O be of good courage,
believer, and with grateful confidence raise thy "Ebenezer"
for: He who hath helped thee hitherto will help thee all thy
journey through. (Spurgeon, "Hitherto hath the Lord helped
us. 1 Samuel 7:12")

The place of beginning again is where we can look back and remember
our past and look forward with hope to our future. God has brought us
this far, and we trust him to carry us forward. Let's raise our Ebenezer,
our stone of help, thanking God for his help in the past and trusting
God for the future. Our trust is in him; we renounce substitutes, and we
trust in God.

Rejoice in God's Blessings
HOSEA 14:4-7

Verses 4-7 of Hosea 14 address the wonderful results of returning to
God. The results are blessings. In verse 4, as a result of the repentance
of the people, God said, "I will heal their apostasy; / I will freely love
them." The word translated "apostasy" or "waywardness" is related to the
word translated "return" in verse 1. In verse 4 it refers to turning *away*
from God instead of turning to him. So God said that when they turned
to him, he was going to heal their turning *away*. Then in the second part
of verse 4, God said, "My anger will have turned from him." That's the
same Hebrew word again; now it refers to God's anger turning away
from Israel. So Hosea preached that when we turn from our sin, God's
anger turns from us, and God heals our turning hearts. Then, verse 7

says, "The people will return and live beneath his shade. / They will grow grain / and blossom like the vine." The word translated "return" ("again" in the NASB) is the same Hebrew word Hosea used now for the fourth time in these verses. Verse 7 says that prosperity, or fertility, will return to God's people. By means of four uses of the same Hebrew word, Hosea used wordplay to highlight what happens when we turn to God. When we return to God, his anger turns from us, he heals our turning hearts, and his blessing returns to us.

To illustrate God's blessing as a consequence of our repentance, in verse 5 God said, "I will be like the dew to Israel." That's a picture of how **God is consistent**. The dew is present every morning. God said to his people that when they returned to him, they would not have to worry about whether he was going to be there for them. He would be with them like the dew is on the grass every morning (cf. 6:4).

Moreover, **God will give beauty**. In verse 5 God said Israel "will blossom like the lily." The lily is a beautiful flower. When we return to God, the ugliness of our sin is replaced by the beauty of righteousness.

Dew comes every morning, but it soon disappears; lilies are beautiful, but they don't have deep roots, and their blooms don't last long. So in verse 5 God added another illustration of what his people will be like when they return to him. God said they will "take root like the cedars of Lebanon." **God will give stability**. Lebanon was well-known for its cedar trees. In fact, today the flag of the modern country of Lebanon bears a picture of a cedar tree. That's what God's people are like when they return to him—strong, stable, and beautiful.

God added another illustration in verse 6: "His new branches will spread, / and his splendor will be like the olive tree." **God will give bounty**. The olive was a source of food; olives are still a staple in the Israeli diet. The olive was the source of olive oil, which was burned in lamps to provide light, and the olive was used for numerous other things. The olive tree is also an evergreen—the same all year long. So this is an illustration of constant bounty.

God was telling his people what they will be like when they return to him. We will have abundant bounty. We'll be the picture of beauty and stability. And we can count on God's consistency. God was going to be like the dew, and his people were going to be like a beautiful flower, a mighty tree, and fruit providing bountiful help. God invites people to turn to him, request his forgiveness for past sins, renounce all substitutes and trust God only, and reach out to others with his offer of restoration. When we turn to him, he pours out his blessings on us as we enjoy the new life he gives us. There *is* a place of beginning again, and it is a wonderful place. We can have it when we "return to the LORD [our] God." That exhortation was Hosea's consistent message to the people of Israel. The one true God who loved Israel and loves the world still wants people to turn to him.

Reflect and Discuss

1. When have you been at the point of needing or wanting to begin again with God? What happened?
2. What is it like to feel sorrow over sin but fail to repent? Have you witnessed that happen in someone's life?
3. How have you been doing at calling other people to turn to God as Hosea did?
4. Why are we tempted to merely attend worship or critique worship instead of offering heartfelt worship to God? What motivates us to turn from mere ritualism?
5. Make a list of people or things people trust instead of trusting God. Which are temptations for you?
6. In what ways could you say, "The LORD has helped us to this point"? Spend some time expressing thanks to God for his past help and expressing trust in him for his future help.
7. What are some blessings you can anticipate when you turn to the Lord fully and walk with him closely?

Joel

How to Respond to Tragedy

JOEL 1

Main Idea: Judgment and tragedy should cause you to run to God, not away from him.

I. **Judgment and Tragedy Will Come into Our Lives (1:1-4).**
II. **Run to God, Not Away (1:5-20).**

Years ago, one Friday night my wife, Ashley, and I hired a babysitter for our two daughters and went on a date. Our girls and the babysitter had been playing with makeup and doing makeovers while we were gone, and our older daughter, Maddy, accidentally spilled some blue eyeshadow on our white carpet. When we got back to the house, we talked with the babysitter about how the night had gone, paid her, and got ready to send her on her way. Unbeknown to us, Maddy had gone away from us to the other room and tried to clean up the blue eyeshadow so we would not see it. She got a wet paper towel and tried to wipe up the mess but instead smeared the blue eye shadow all over our white carpet. She tried to cover up what had happened, but it just made things worse. So Ashley and I had a conversation with her about telling us first when bad things happen instead of trying to cover them up or fix them herself. We probably could have vacuumed up the blue dust easily, but now we had a blue stain on the carpet. We tried to explain to her that she would not have gotten into trouble for an accident, and even if she had done something wrong, we would have been more lenient if she had come to us and let us help fix it.

The same is true in our relationship with God. When problems and challenges arise in our life, we must run *to* God and not *away from* him. One of the main themes of the book of Joel is "return to the LORD" (e.g., 2:12-13). It is repeated throughout the book as a reminder to the people to give the Lord priority in their lives. Running away from him makes things worse, which is what Joel was telling the people of God—in this case probably Judah in the southern kingdom of Israel. The problems going on in the nation should have driven them to God in response. Judgment and tragedy should cause you to run to God and not away from him.

Judgment and Tragedy Will Come into Our Lives
JOEL 1:1-4

God speaks to his people through his prophet Joel. When it comes to Joel, we know hardly anything about him except his father's name (Pethuel) and his own name, which means "the LORD is God." Joel's biography is not needed because the focus of the book is on the message, not the man (Robertson, *Joel*, 18).

A locust plague has devastated the land. Joel is sent by God to explain how to respond. He does not spend time explaining why this has happened. In plenty of Old Testament books, the whys of national tragedy are given. Here the focus is on what to do now and what might be coming down the pike. Joel "both interprets the disaster for the prophet's generation and looks ahead to the end of the age" (Garrett, *Hosea, Joel*, 312). What has happened may be a portent of what is to come, so learning how to respond is imperative.

Nothing this severe has happened in any of their lifetimes. Even the senior adults, who have been around the block a time or two, have not seen anything like this. But there is a lesson to be learned. God does not want them to miss this teachable moment. He wants them to pass it down to future generations so they will be prepared. The parents in Judah had to read the Israelite version of *The Hungry Caterpillar* to their children ("caterpillar" is the Septuagint translation for "locust"), except in this version it's a horror story.

This is a teachable moment for us as well. In Joel, no specific sin is given. No specific cause is given. One is not needed. That is not the point of the book. The focus is not on the question "Why?" but rather "What now?" As such, it is a message for every generation. He wants to teach them what God is doing through calamity. And perhaps that's why we have no date for the book. Maybe he's trying to teach us in every generation what to do when calamity strikes (Ferguson, "Day of the Locusts"). And how should we respond? By running *to* God, not away from him.

These successive locust plagues have devastated all the produce. And as we will see later in the passage, it is not just economic destruction but religious as well. They were no longer able to worship God or relate to him in the way to which he had called them. It was absolutely crushing.

Since few of us live in an agrarian culture where a failed harvest means months of destitution and possibly starvation, these locust plagues may not immediately sound horrific to us. It is difficult for people who have fast-food restaurants with an abundance of "value" menus on every corner to understand food shortage. But from time to time, we might get a taste of this due to some natural disaster. Imagine prolonged rolling blackouts or sustained gas shortages. Imagine government embargoes on gathering to worship. If our fuel, our food, our power, and our money were in short supply, and we were unable to worship God in places we normally would, how disturbing would that be? How would you respond?

This is what was happening to the people of Judah as God poured out his wrath on them with plagues as he had done with the Egyptians in the exodus. They were not going to escape this judgment simply because they were his chosen people. And if the people thought this was merely a natural disaster and not God's direct judgment, then they would think that all they needed to do was shelter in place and ride this out until things went back to normal. But then they would miss the lesson God wanted them to learn (Robertson, *Joel*, 23).

The idea that this plague is from God's hand comes directly from Deuteronomy 28 (see vv. 38-51,64). These verses informed God's people centuries before that unfaithfulness, sin, and an unrepentant heart would lead to locusts coming in—and if the lesson was not learned, then eventually human armies would show up as well.

Yes, the book of Joel and other books talk about a final judgment with God at the end of time, but God also acts in history and in real time to drive us closer to him. God chastens us to wake us up and bring us back to him. Also, the faithful are suffering alongside the unfaithful. In Joel, at the very least, the innocent plants and animals are suffering and crying out to the Lord alongside the people. Although those creatures are not making a conscious effort to sin against God, the decision to do so by the people in general is affecting them.

Sometimes in our own lives, tragedy can be a direct consequence of the sins we commit. From this, God wants you to wake up, confess, repent, and come back to him. But even if the tragedy you experience is not the direct result of your sin, your response should be the same: run to him. If you experience tragedy, you must run to God. God may allow or cause those things to happen in your life, and it may seem harsh, but it is the love of the heavenly Father.

About fifteen years ago I was able to go on a mission trip to central Asia where the basketball team I was on would play against different universities and semipro teams in the area. After the games, we would take the teams out to dinner and would share the gospel with them, which prompted different conversations. One of my teammates on that trip was an athlete who had played football at a Division I Power Five university. His testimony of being saved was a testimony to the love and goodness of God's discipline. After his career in football, he got into a marriage where he had been consistently cheating on his wife. This man was going to a church where his sin was eventually found out. The pastors and the deacons began to do church discipline whereby they confronted him and began the process of potentially removing him from church membership. Through these conversations, the man realized that he was lost and that he needed a Savior, so he gave his life to Jesus. Later, when he gave his testimony before being baptized, he said, "I thank God for church discipline because it saved my life." This is what the book of Joel has for us, as it calls us to run to God in faith during times of calamity.

First Peter 4:17 says, "For the time has come for judgment to begin with God's household, and if it begins with us, what will the outcome be for those who disobey the gospel of God?" Yes, judgment will certainly come against unbelievers, but God says he is not going to allow *anyone* to continue in sin against him without correction. This message is one contemporary Western Christianity needs to hear. Some leaders have become so upbeat in their teaching that they almost never call sin "sin." Many tend to want to highlight God's love and acceptance without also clearly communicating the truth that Jesus did not drown in his own blood on the cross for us to say that our sin is no big deal and to remain in it. We need to be told when we are in sin, and we need to be told when we need to repent.

New terms are being used about church life such as "spiritual trauma" or "religious trauma." Let me be clear: people who have been abused by spiritual leaders in their life have my deepest sympathy. Jesus would never treat you like that, and there is healing in him. At the same time, simply because a pastor calls your sin "sin" does not mean he is causing you trauma. Leaders who lovingly show you what the Bible says and how your life is departing from God's design are showing the utmost care for you. John the Baptist boldly told Herod regarding his affair with his sister-in-law that it was not lawful for him to have her. Today he might get canceled for such an act, but grace does not mean sin is ignored. It means being told of your sin and being informed that forgiveness is available if you will run to Christ.

Run to God, Not Away
JOEL 1:5-20

Starting in verse 5, Joel switches the perspective from what is happening to them to what their response should be: run to God. How? Godly sorrow that leads to repentance. You do this by mourning your sin and asking the Lord to rescue you from it. Joel summons multiple groups to participate in this: drunkards, the general public, the priests, and the farmers (Stuart, *Hosea–Jonah*, 2014, 240).

The first group Joel addresses is one immediately affected by the locusts' devastation: the "drunkards" (v. 5). With no vineyards, these men and women would be without the thing they crave. Joel's point in mentioning them here is not primarily to condemn their drunkenness, although drunkenness is clearly a sin. After all, he mentions how the priests are also affected by lack of wine and the inability to make their offerings (v. 9; Allen, *Joel*, 29). The emphasis here is on what has been cut off (their supply is gone) and how the group affected should respond. He calls on the drunkards to weep and wail—signs of repentance.

The next group Joel addresses is the public. He explains how the locusts were affecting "my grapevine" and "my fig tree" (v. 7). This image is both a literal one, where the plants and trees in the area were affected, and a spiritual image of God's people, whom God has called his vine, vineyard, or fig tree (Ps 80:8-11; Isa 5:1-2; Hos 9:10). The locusts are described as a nation and a beast that is ravaging Israel (v. 6). How should the people respond? With godly sorrow. This sorrow is described in vivid terms of a would-be bride wearing a black funeral gown instead of a white wedding dress (v. 8). A young woman is getting ready for her wedding day. The makeup is done. The hair is just right. But her groom dies suddenly. She must attend a funeral instead of a wedding. The prospects of a future husband and family and provision are all gone with him. The way that young woman would sob is how we should respond to our sin when calamity strikes.

The "priests" are the next group addressed because they were no longer able to offer wine as a drink offering in the house of the Lord (v. 9). The damage is more than economic; it is spiritual. Field and vineyard harvests allowed the people to give glory to the one who gave them the gifts. It was also the way they approached God in worship. This plague has broken their relationship with God (Patterson, "Joel," 240). Therefore, priests must mourn. The fields mirror how the people should respond. The fields are mourning (v. 10).

Finally, Joel addresses the "farmers" (vv. 11-12). They have lost their income and livelihood. Things that brought joy to the nation are gone, so weeping should follow.

Joel 1:13-20 gives the prophet's instructions to the priests to call for a solemn assembly for the nation. People of all ages would come to the temple fasting, weeping, and calling out to God in repentance and prayer. In so doing, they were obeying God's word. When Solomon built the temple, there was a dedication service where Solomon's prayer foretold the future. Solomon explained in his prayer that in the future, when locusts destroyed the crops or armies conquered the nation, then the people should turn their eyes to the temple and pray for deliverance from God. Then the Lord would hear their cries, forgive their sins, and restore the people (1 Kgs 8:37-40).

As New Testament Christians, we do not have a building that we point our eyes to; rather, we have something better: a person. Jesus says in John 2 that he is the temple of the living God. He says that if people want to destroy the temple, then he will build it back up in three days (referring to his resurrection). If we want to have God hear us, forgive us, stay his hand of judgment, and restore what has been taken from us, we must run to Jesus and pour out our hearts to him, and he will hear and act. When tragedy strikes, we must realize that there is a heavenly Father who loves us, who wants what is best for us, and who is calling us to run to him. He has his arms open wide, and even when he disciplines us, it is because he loves us and wants our good.

Why should the people consecrate this national assembly of solemnity? Because the day of the Lord is near, and it will come like the "shattering" from El Shaddai.[1] The day of the Lord is a constant theme in Joel and is mentioned four times in the book. It does not just refer to

---

[1] The words in Hebrew sound similar (Patterson, "Joel," 243).

the last day. It refers to any time in history that God shows up to judge or to save. It is a type or pattern that occurs in history until the end. All the "days" in history are previews or trailers of the final day. This locust plague is an example, since we will see locusts again in the book of Revelation (Rev 9).

The fullness of God's wrath has not yet been poured out and may be averted if the people will repent. But the ruin is enormous. Not only has this harvest been ruined, but the storehouses are empty (v. 17), so the next planting and harvest are in jeopardy. The animals give the people an example of how to respond: they are groaning and panting for God (vv. 18,20). God calls for us to run to him in godly sorrow that leads to true repentance. Often, like Israel, we can play the game of acting like we are sorry for our sin when we are just sorry about the consequences. We should sorrow and repent because our sin breaks fellowship with God, not because it shuts off his blessing. We should pant for God like the animals.

Conclusion

This will not be the last time God's vine is devoured by the beasts (vv. 6-7). Psalm 80 tells of the exile of Israel when once again the vine of Israel is being ravaged by the beasts of the field (Ps 80:8-13; cf. Dan 7). How will this be remedied? How will restoration occur? It will happen when the "son of man" is made strong (Ps 80:14-17). Salvation will come to God's people through the Son of Man, Jesus Christ. Then they will not turn away from him anymore (Ps 80:18). Jesus, the Son of Man, took on the plagues of God's judgment so we could be free to run to him for restoration.

As has been said, there are two ways you can view your relationship with your dad when things go sideways and life is messed up. Option one is "I messed up. I hope my dad doesn't find out." Option two is "I messed up. I have to tell my dad." Option two is the gospel way to live life. Judgment and tragedy should cause you to run *to* God, not *away from* him.

Reflect and Discuss

1. Describe a time when you or your children tried to cover something up and made it worse. How could things have worked out differently?

2. Why do you think we are tempted to run away from God instead of to him when things go bad?

3. What is the value in discussing what to do next rather than trying to figure out why something happened or where to place the blame?

4. What are some modern calamities that would be similar for us to what the locust plague was for Israel? How would these make us feel? How would we be prone to act?

5. Give examples of tragedies that occur because of our sin. Give examples of tragedies that occur that are not necessarily due to our sin.

6. How can discipline be loving? How does God discipline us?

7. The Bible says that godly sorrow leads to repentance. What does fake repentance look like? What does genuine repentance look like?

8. Joel here calls the people to obey earlier Scripture from 1 Kings 8. How can we obey God's Word in times of tragedy?

9. Name some examples of a "day of the Lord" in history. What was God trying to teach through them?

10. How does our relationship with God the Father through Jesus cause us to respond differently in trying times than we would if we didn't have that relationship?

Return to the Lord

JOEL 2:1-17

Main Idea: You must turn to or return to the Lord.

I. You Turn to or Return to the Lord by Taking His Warnings Seriously (2:1-11).

II. You Turn to or Return to the Lord Genuinely (from the Inside), Not as an Act (from the Outside) (2:12-13a).

III. You Turn to or Return to the Lord Based on His Gospel Character (2:13b-14).

IV. You Turn to or Return to the Lord through Intercessory Prayer (2:15-17).

When I was a sophomore in high school, unfortunately I fell into the habit of cheating on vocabulary quizzes in French class rather than studying for them. During this time in school, we had TI-82 calculators that could store information, not just do arithmetic. My friends and I discovered that we could key the vocabulary words and their translations into the calculators, leave the calculators on our desks, and tell the teacher that we were simply preparing to do some "math homework" when we finished our quizzes early.

On one occasion I got caught. My teacher took the paper and informed me that we were going to have a chat after class. My biggest concern at that point was not the grade or anything test related but that the teacher would tell the office, who would then tell my father. That was bad news! I sat in her office and begged my teacher not to tell the office, trying to convince her that a zero would be the "worst punishment" I could get, but I didn't really care if my parents were notified. Thankfully, she bought my bluff. She said that she would pray about how to respond and inform me in the morning. That whole night and into the morning I was scared to death over what punishment she would ultimately inflict upon me.

When I met with her before school the next day, she saw me sobbing and said, "Jon, I think there is just a little boy inside of you crying out for help, and I'll tell you what I am going to do for that little boy: I am going to forgive you. I am going to give you another chance to take the quiz, you will not get a zero, and I will not tell your parents." I then took the quiz and got a perfect score on it (I suppose because all my efforts plugging the words into my calculator had helped me actually learn them). The waterworks and show of remorse were an act I had turned on, but it looked like I was genuinely repentant, and so I was rewarded in the end. But I did not learn the lesson I should have learned that day.

We see something similar in the book of Joel. We may be able to fool men, but we can never fool God. God always knows the intentions and the truth behind the show and the tears. If there is a pattern of sin in your life that has broken your relationship with God, then you must truly repent. The Bible says, "Blessed are the pure in heart, for they will see God" (Matt 5:8). If you are not pure in heart and in relationship with him, then you are not seeing God. Even if you are a believer, that relationship can be fractured, and that fellowship can be skewed. Restoration does not come by acting like everything is OK or by crying tears because you want the consequences to go away but only by genuinely repenting of your sin.

This is what is happening in the lives of the people of Israel. We are not told what the sin is because Joel's purpose is not to indict specific sins but rather to show what we should do when we are in sin, no matter what the sin may be. When God's judgment is poured out because of sin, what do we do next? We saw in the last sermon that the people of Judah were affected by the devastating locust plague, and they were on the verge of starvation, so the prophet called them to express godly sorrow and genuine repentance. This response was necessary because the locust plague was only a preview of what was to come. In chapter 2, this response is described as returning to the Lord (v. 12). But *how* can we return to the Lord or turn to him for the first time? Joel 2:1-17 gives us four answers.

You Turn to or Return to the Lord
by Taking His Warnings Seriously
JOEL 2:1-11

God warns his people through a ram's horn blast that the day of the Lord is coming, which calls for trembling (v. 1). The judgment that began with the locusts will progress to an army (ch. 2) and is also a portent of the judgment at the last days (ch. 3). Deuteronomy 28:38-51 has already warned the people of this type of progressive judgment. God gives this warning to his people and to us through the Spirit so we can be prepared ahead of the final judgment. The day of the Lord is a pattern for any time in human history that God shows up to judge or rescue sinners.[2] The holy Lord steps in and intervenes in a special way to judge his people.

What he warns them about specifically is a foreign and unstoppable army that was going to destroy their land and their livestock, leaving them like a desert without color (vv. 2-11). The locusts were described like an invincible army in chapter 1; now an actual army is in view but described in locust-like terms (Garrett, *Hosea, Joel*, 334). The devastation is described as uncreation; Eden is turned into a wasteland (v. 3). This army is inevitable and inescapable. They climb city walls, they march in line, and they enter through windows (vv. 7-9). "Arrows shot at them make no difference—they just keep coming" (Stuart, *Hosea–Jonah*, 2014, 251). They would eventually break through, destroy the walls, decimate the soldiers, rape the women, kill the children, brutalize the remainder, maim and pillage, burn and ravage (Allen, *Joel*, 61).

Joel uses apocalyptic language of "darkness," "gloom," "clouds," and "total darkness" (v. 2) as well as the earth quaking and heavenly lights darkened (v. 10) to signal that it will be like the end of the world. "Their world came to an end" (Garrett, *Hosea, Joel*, 342). All this is caused by the Lord's army (v. 11). As children, we used to sing about being in the Lord's army and shooting the artillery. This army is unaware that they are the Lord's, being used by God, yet they are nevertheless. Their actions are God's judgment and should cause the people to see their sin and change their ways. People must take this warning seriously.

You Turn to or Return to the Lord Genuinely (from the Inside), Not as an Act (from the Outside)
JOEL 2:12-13A

The irony of the situation in Joel is that God is both the general of the army that will chasten them and the refuge they are to run to (Stuart, *Hosea–Jonah*, 2014, 249). Even now, amid this horrible judgment, Israel

---

[2] See Duane Garrett's incredibly helpful excursus, "Joel as a Paradigm for the Prophetic Method," in *Hosea, Joel*, 387–91.

should return to the Lord. They must do this genuinely from the inside (their heart) and not as an act from the outside. God wants his people to realize that this judgment should drive them to him with their whole heart. This theme runs through the entire Old Testament from the Torah to the Prophets.

Deuteronomy 4:29-30 explains what the people of Israel should do when they are under the hand of judgment:

> But from there, you will search for the LORD your God, and you will find him when you seek him with all your heart and all your soul. When you are in distress and all these things have happened to you, in the future you will return to the LORD your God and obey him.

Concerning a situation after the time of Joel, Jeremiah 29:11-14 says something similar. This passage is so often misused as a motto at Christian school graduations for some triumphal future successes because that is in God's "plans." Readers miss the context of Jeremiah 29:11. These verses are about returning to the Lord with all your heart and receiving restoration, which is a thousand times better promise than getting a law degree or succeeding in business.

God's restoration comes when we seek him with all our heart. This first happens when we accept the Lord as Savior, and then it is cultivated into a habit in our daily walk with him. Godly sorrow, true repentance, is to be the habit of the Christian life. It is not the regret of getting caught doing something wrong; rather, it is being sorry for the specific sin that was committed. God knows that people can put on dramatic displays of sorrow—like tearing clothes and putting ashes on the head—but not mean anything in their hearts. The weeping, the mourning, and the fasting (v. 12) should be signs of an inward reality (v. 13a), not a pretense. Religious rituals can be good if they are outward displays of a heart turned toward God; they can be empty if they are just a show. God wants people to tear their hearts, not their clothes. He wants genuine penitence over what you did, not an act of contrition because you do not like what has happened as a result of your actions.

We can do the same as the people of the Old Testament. We can go through the motions while our hearts remain far from God. Do you clear your Internet history on your phone and cry to God for forgiveness with no real intent to stop? Do you cry to your parents and tell them you are sorry for lying to them when really you just wish they had not found out? Do you tell your teacher that you feel bad for cheating, but when the discomfort of being caught goes away, you return to the habit? Do you shed crocodile tears to your spouse when you do not treat her right, but as soon as the ice thaws, you act that way again? God desires inward-out heart change, not dramatic gestures with no real substance.

You Turn to or Return to the Lord Based on His Gospel Character
JOEL 2:13B-14

Another way we return to the Lord is through his eternal, gospel character. The only hope we have of restoration is to throw ourselves on the mercy of God and to bank on the fact that his character is one of grace, love, and patience. The Bible says that graciousness, mercy, and steadfast love describe God's character. God reveals himself as this kind of Lord repeatedly throughout the Old Testament, beginning with his revelation of himself to Moses in Exodus 34:6-7. He is loving and gracious, slow to anger, and forgiving, and yet he will by no means clear the guilty.

How can God be gracious, loving, and merciful and still be just, by no means clearing the guilty? The world asks how a loving God can send people to hell, but the Bible asks how a just God brings anyone to heaven. This is resolved by the cross of Jesus Christ, where God pours out both his wrath on sin and his love to sinners. God is both just and the justifier of the one who has faith in Jesus (Rom 3:26). We turn to the Lord or return to him based on that gospel character.

Joel asks, Who knows whether God will "relent" from doing what he threatened (v. 14)? When the Bible talks about how God relents from doing something he previously said he was going to do, we need to be clear about what is happening. God didn't change; the situation changed: people repented and found God's grace. When we humans repent or change, it impacts our character, not God's. He does not change. He always forgives the repentant, and he is always wrathful toward the unrighteous. The change is in our experience of God, not in God himself. Just as the sun does not actually rise at sunrise but our view of the sun does, so God is consistently holy no matter what, but our experience of his holiness can change based on whether we repent.

Joel says that perhaps God will "leave a blessing" to the people that they can then turn around and use to glorify him as an offering (v. 14). When it comes to blessing in our lives, we need to ask ourselves what we want most out of having a relationship with God. Do we mainly want him or the blessings he gives us? If you were offered a mansion that was paid for next to a crystal lake, on streets paved with gold, but Jesus was not there, would you take it? Your honest answer to that question says a lot about whether you love the gifts or the Giver more. We are meant to use the gifts God gives to us to honor him and bless others out of gratitude for the Giver! O. Palmer Robertson writes,

> This is what you want, isn't it? If by a feigned repentance you actually are after something for yourself, then you can expect bitter disappointment. God cannot be deceived by man's connivings. But if by repentance you hope to have the opportunity to give greater glory to God, you may see your heart's desire fulfilled. (*Joel*, 52)

You Turn to or Return to the Lord through Intercessory Prayer
JOEL 2:15-17

Yet again, in Joel 2:15, the people are told to consecrate a solemn assembly. This echoes what Solomon said to do in his prayer of dedication for the temple (1 Kgs 8). This is urgent, and everyone needs to be there, even if newlyweds are in the middle of honeymooning (Joel 2:16).[3] The priests will wail to God in prayer on behalf of the people, urging him to spare his people and keep his covenant promises so the nations know that the God of Israel is among his people (v. 17). The priests are standing in the gap between the people and God, praying to God for them. "The idea behind this is that God's name would be disgraced before the nations if he allowed his own people to fall. More than that, this was an appeal for mercy" (Garrett, *Hosea, Joel*, 349).

The New Testament says there is one mediator between man and God, Jesus Christ (1 Tim 2:5). It also says he is praying for you (Rom 8:34). In life, there are times when you want access to something, and in order to get it, you need someone to act as a go-between. When I was younger, we had this famous preacher stay with us as he was speaking at my dad's school, and he mentioned something about going to the upcoming Super Bowl. The game was three days away, so I told him I was

---

[3] "Even the newlyweds who might otherwise be legitimately exempted from such duties (Deut 24:5) were to be in attendance" (Patterson, "Joel," 251).

jealous that he had tickets. He said that he in fact did not have tickets yet, but he would have them secured by the weekend. I asked him how this was possible. He told me that you are only three people away from anything you want in the world. He knew someone who knew someone who knew someone who could get him tickets.

The Bible tells us that we are only one person away from the thing we need most, which is forgiveness of sins and a right relationship with God. That person is Jesus Christ. He is our High Priest who can bring us back to God. When he died on the cross, the curtain separating humanity from God in the most holy place was torn in two from top to bottom (Mark 15:38). We are no longer separated from God, and Jesus ever lives to make intercession for us (Heb 7:25). He is actively advocating for us in prayer at God's right hand. We can come boldly to the throne of grace and ask for help in our time of need (Heb 4:16). We can turn back to God through the intercessory prayer of our Lord Jesus. If you are not experiencing the peace of God that you want, and if you know you need it, then you need to turn to the Lord, for Jesus has given us access to him.

Conclusion

How can we turn to or return to God and expect him to receive us? How can we escape the judgment and the wrath to come? We can escape what Joel 2 talks about because something like it has already happened. The earth already quaked. The sun went down at midday. The peoples wagged their tongues and said, "Where is your God?" when Jesus suffocated to death on the cross. He took the inevitable and inescapable wrath of God so that we could return to the Lord.

Reflect and Discuss

1. Was there ever a time in your childhood when you were caught doing something you should not? How did the consequences or lack thereof affect that behavior in the future?

2. Discuss a time in your life when you fooled someone into thinking you were sorry when you really were not. What effect did this have on the relationship?

3. Have you ever gone through the motions of a religious ritual, but your heart was not in it? How did this affect your relationship with God?

4. What are some tangible ways to take God's warnings in the Bible seriously?

5. What does genuine repentance look like as opposed to going through the motions?

6. In the past, what have you thought Jeremiah 29:11 was teaching? How does the truth of what it actually means help even more?

7. How does the good news of grace in Jesus Christ motivate you to turn back to God?

8. God doesn't change, but our experience of him can. How does that truth encourage you?

9. What are some ways we can determine which we love more: God or his gifts?

10. How does the truth that Jesus is praying for you impact your life right now? How can it impact your prayer life?

The Restorer

JOEL 2:18-32

Main Idea: God can restore what has been lost.

I. **He Can Restore Physically (2:18-25).**
II. **He Can Restore Relationally (2:26-27).**
III. **He Can Restore Spiritually (2:28-32).**

As a society, we have become fascinated with restoring old things. Television shows that take old homes and fix them up are popular. In the past, calling something a "fixer-upper" was not a compliment, but now it is seen as a great opportunity. The same is true with restoring old cars, repurposing antiques, and even retooling storylines from 1980s movies and sitcoms.

A friend told me a story recently about how his son came up to him excitedly saying, "Dad, Dad, you'll never guess what I found! They made a prequel to *Cobra Kai*. It's called *The Karate Kid*, and it's awesome."

As a culture, we love repurposing old things to make them relevant for new use. Stories of redemption and restoration are everywhere. In fact, the whole premise of the Netflix show *Cobra Kai* is that the antagonist from *The Karate Kid*, Johnny Lawrence, can have restored the years of his life that he lost. But the question remains: Can this be done in real life with real people? We can do it with cars and homes and storylines, but is it different with people? The Bible says God can restore what has been lost. He is the great Reverser and the great Restorer. In Joel 2:18-32 we see the Lord's power to restore in three ways.

He Can Restore Physically

JOEL 2:18-25

God has the power to restore your life physically. After Joel has called the people to repentance, in the near future God will work to restore Judah. He is motivated to be compassionate toward his people because of his holy jealousy and zeal for the exclusive devotion that belongs to

him. We know this is a godly jealousy because of the parallel line in
2:18b (Stuart, *Hosea–Jonah*, 2014, 258). Hebrew poetic lines that are parallel modify or help explain the full meaning of the verse. The Lord's
jealousy is shown in sparing his people. This is not sinful jealousy that
wants what you do not have but rather godly zeal for what is yours, like
the jealousy of wanting exclusive devotion in marriage.

This zeal moves God in love and pity to intervene for his people.
The mention of sparing (v. 18) is exodus language that recalls when
God's people were slaves in Egypt and he acted on their behalf and
spared them any more distress because he was moved to compassion
by their plight. The answer to Judah's prayers of repentance will be the
physical restoration of the harvest. They had been a reproach among the
nations, but God will spare them from further embarrassment (v. 19) by
removing the foreign army who has harassed them (v. 20).

God will comfort three who had been sorrowful with renewed joy:
the land (v. 21), the animals (v. 22), and the people (v. 23). Previously,
Joel discussed how the land, animals, and humans were to suffer, and
now they will all be restored in the order of their suffering (Garrett,
Hosea, Joel, 360). The land was to have a harvest and a plentiful growth
season after the destruction of the locusts. This will be God's doing.
The animals who were starving will now have fruit to eat again because
the fig tree and grapevine that were previously devastated will now be
renewed (v. 22). The same will be true for the people.

Joel asks the people to go from mourning to partying because of
the blessing of rain that God will provide for them. Some think the
reference to rain in verse 23 might be a double entendre: (1) referring
to the early and late rains that will bring the promised restoration and
(2) a play on words reference to the "teacher of righteousness." I agree
with Garrett that Joel is giving a double meaning with an obvious point
and an underlying point.[4] In the context, the idea of rain is a natural
one. The people will go from a drought, a famine, and locust plagues to
God's sending them rain. He will send the early rain of autumn to cause
the seed to germinate, and then he will send the late rain of the spring
to cause the crops to come to full growth as a sign of his grace and mercy
to vindicate his people (Garrett, *Hosea, Joel*, 361). This vindication will

---

[4] I am dependent on Garrett's notion of a wordplay and double entendre. See his
discussion in *Hosea–Joel*, 362–63.

be in the near future. There will be plenty of food and wine as God blesses his people agriculturally by bringing back the physical provision that had been taken (v. 24).

The idea of the "teacher of righteousness" is a prophecy of what will happen in the not-so-near future of the Messianic Age. This will be final restoration, a lasting and full blessing, and the abundant life that comes only from the Messiah's presence. The phrase *teacher of righteousness* was used by different Jewish communities as a promise of and hope for the coming Messiah. We have a different vantage point from the first hearers. We know that as great as rain and a renewed crop are, they pale in comparison to the joy and the wiping away of tears that happen at the arrival of the Messiah. Joel explains that rains will come, but ultimately the Messiah is coming to grant us righteousness. Restoration was to happen through the rain soon and through the Messiah in the distant future.

Joel 2:25 is one of the most encouraging verses in the entire Bible about the potential for restoration. God assures that he will restore the years the locust swarms have eaten. We know that literally speaking you cannot get years back. But what the Lord promises is the ability to take what was lost and give it back, plus more!

For Judah it will look like a plentiful harvest and storage of agricultural goods, but for us it looks a little different. When you experience regret over poor choices and wish you could go back and get back the time you lost, the good news of Jesus Christ tells you that God can give you certain things back. There are time and opportunity for God to restore what has been lost. As a pastor, I have had the blessing of seeing this happen over and over.

People with addictions who have lost so much have been freed by the gospel and provided a new opportunity to make an impact. My mother was born into an alcoholic family, which caused her parents to break up and my mother to live ten years of her life in a Baptist children's home. However, through this experience she was taken to church weekly, was saved by the gospel of Jesus Christ, and made a commitment that when she had a family in the future it would be different from her past. She was determined that her family would not experience what she had, and by the life-changing power of the gospel, that has been true. The family years stolen by the locusts of alcoholism have been given back and more!

God can restore the years the locusts have eaten in your marriage. I have heard testimony after testimony of people in unhappy marriages and broken relationships who have reconciled. Sometimes couples joke, "We have been married for twenty-seven years, and they have been twenty-three of the happiest of my life." The sentiment expresses the fact that marriage is not always easy, that sometimes there are years of challenges, and that the latter years can be better than the former.

Restoration is seen everywhere. I know a family who raised their daughter in a Christian home and sent her to college where she played on a soccer team. The daughter came home one day and told her parents she was a lesbian and was moving in with her girlfriend. The parents were devastated and pleaded with God, and today that same daughter is happily married to a man with several children and a strong walk with the Lord. God restored to that family what the locusts threatened to eat.

I know a wonderful Christian young lady who was born to a drug-dealing father and a prostitute mother. Her mom would take her on the job and make her stay in the car because they were homeless and had no one else to help. As a teenager, she began to stay with friends from school and just "happened" to stay with a Christian family. They began taking her to church. She heard the gospel and got saved. Today she is training for ministry and making a huge impact for the kingdom of God. The years have been restored that the locusts have eaten.

No matter what you have been through, restoration is possible. I love the evangelism method called "3 Circles" (NAMB). It explains that when we depart from God's design for our lives (i.e., when we sin), it leads to brokenness, but the good news of Jesus Christ brings us forgiveness and a new opportunity to recover and pursue God's design for our lives. We cannot go back and untangle the webs of our past actions, but we can from this point forward pursue what God wants for our lives. We serve a God of second chances who knows what is best for our lives. He can restore what the locusts have eaten.

He Can Restore Relationally
JOEL 2:26-27

Not only can the Lord restore physically, but he can restore relationally. Joel 2:26-27 references how the renewed harvest will lead to eating plenty and therefore praising the name of the Lord. God's people will praise him for what he has done for them. Their bountiful harvest and satisfied appetite are evidence of divine favor being restored (Garrett, *Hosea, Joel*, 364).

This is not just economic blessing; it is relational. Food and resources had been withheld, but they would now be restored, which is a sign that the relationship between God and his people had been mended. The fact that they had an abundance of grain and wine now meant that they were finally able to give grain and wine offerings again at the temple. The broken relationship with their God would be fixed. Through this restoration, they will praise his name, and they will no longer be ashamed as if God had abandoned them (Garrett, *Hosea, Joel*, 364). Sacrifices bridge the gap between sinful humanity and holy God.

All the Old Testament sacrifices point to Jesus's death on the cross. Through his sacrifice for our sins, no matter what you have done or where you have been, you can be brought back into right relationship with God. He loves you and wants a relationship with you. Through confession and faith, it can be restored! And a restored relationship means a renewed sense of the presence of God.

The Lord also promises his presence among his people, which is a sign that the covenant relationship has been reestablished. He refers to them as "my people" (v. 27; Patterson, "Joel," 254). He is their God and no one else (Stuart, *Hosea–Jonah*, 2014, 260). They belong to him and he belongs to them.

One of the main concerns in the Old Testament is the presence of the Lord. What was lost in Eden is promised to humanity again in the exodus. God wants to dwell amid his people. He rescued them from slavery in Egypt so he could live with them in the tabernacle and they could worship him. There is a time in the history of Israel when the shekinah glory of God leaves Judah during the exile (Ezek 10), and it does not return when the new temple is built (Hag 2). But there is a promise that one day every eyeball will see the return of the Lord to Zion (Isa 52:8). And John says of the Lord Jesus Christ that he dwelt or "tabernacled" (TLV, AMPC) among us, and we beheld his glory (John 1:14). Through Jesus Christ, we can have the presence of God live with us (John 14:16). That's where Joel turns next. God did not want his people to come to a building to encounter him anymore but wanted to live with and in us, as Joel promises the people.

He Can Restore Spiritually
JOEL 2:28-32

Joel 2:28-32 makes a promise to God's people about the last days. In the distant future or the "last days," God will pour out his spirit on every believer and for all time.[5] As one of my preacher friends once illustrated, in the Old Testament the Holy Spirit operated kind of like the star power in Super Mario Bros. When one of the main characters, like Mario or Luigi, gets the star, they become invincible for about twenty seconds. That is how the Holy Spirit functioned in the Old Testament: only the main characters and only temporarily. So kings, judges, priests, and prophets might have the Spirit rush on them for a specific task or for a season, but the indwelling of the Spirit was not permanent and was not for everyone in Israel. The Spirit was operational part of the time with some of the people.[6] But Joel points to a day when the Spirit is poured out on everyone regardless of gender (male or female), class (king to slave), or age distinction (young to old), and he would be poured out permanently. The evidence of the Spirit's outpouring would be prophecy, visions, and dreams. God would restore Judah spiritually. Everyone would have the same access and experience with God. And the other evidence that this was taking place would be apocalyptic signs like the sun going dark at midday and the moon turning to blood (vv. 30-31). These are symbols for the end of the world—the day of the Lord.

When was this prophecy fulfilled? Unfortunately, from time to time people try to do mental gymnastics to answer that question when the Bible gives a clear answer. They try to say it's the millennial kingdom or some other time, but I would rather go with Peter and the apostles than some Bible scholars. When are the end times Joel talks about? Clearly the New Testament answer is the events surrounding the passion of the Christ and the inauguration of the church. When Jesus breathed his last breath on the cross and then walked out of the borrowed tomb, we entered the last days. Clearly these apocalyptic symbols accompany

---

[5] "After this" is eschatological language. Garrett points this out when he says that "Peter appears to have interpreted the gift of the Holy Spirit as the inauguration of the eschatological age" (*Hosea, Joel*, 370ff).

[6] "In the new age, *all* of God's people will have *all* they need of God's Spirit. The old era was characterized by the Spirit's selective, limited influence on *some* individuals" (Stuart, *Hosea–Jonah*, 2014, 260; emphasis in original).

Jesus's death, resurrection, and the establishment of the church. When he died, the sun went dark at midday. When he ascended, he poured out his Spirit on all believers at Pentecost. When the Spirit was given to the Gentiles, Peter and Cornelius saw visions and dreamed dreams.

It should not be controversial to agree with Peter about all that happened around the passion of Jesus and the launching of the church. Every generation of Christians has said or thought they were in the end times, and there is a reason for that. We have been living in the last days since the grave opened on Easter. In history, everything after the cross is the end times. The church is not plan B; it is plan A, which is what the apostles were repeatedly preaching in Acts. That is why they were urging all people everywhere to call on the name of the Lord and be saved (Joel 2:32; cf. Acts 2:21). The end-time judgment of God had fallen in the middle of history on the cross of Jesus Christ, and those who wanted to avoid the judgment to come needed to call on the name of the Lord Jesus Christ.

We are living in the "already-not yet" because we are already in the last days, but they have not yet been fully consummated. That achievement will wait for the second coming. But as we have seen throughout the book of Joel, the "day of the Lord" shows up ahead of the end in human history as a preview of the full consummation. It can show up as a locust plague of judgment (ch. 1), an invading army (ch. 2), the cross and gift of the Spirit (ch. 2), or the final judgment (ch. 3). God intervenes in human history to judge and to save, and when he placed the sins of the world on his Son and then raised him from the dead, he brought the world into the end times. All someone must do to be rescued instead of condemned is to call on the name of the Lord (Joel 2:32; Rom 10:13).

Conclusion

The people of Judah heard prophecy after prophecy about the end of the age. They were told that at the end of the age a new David would appear (Ezek 34). They were told the dead would be raised (Ezek 37). They were told the Spirit would be poured out on all flesh (Joel 2). So at Pentecost, Peter and the other apostles were preaching the fulfillment of eschatology (Acts 2:14-36). In essence they were saying, "You have been waiting for the end of the world when the Messiah would show up. Well, look at what is happening around you. David's son showed up, and he is the one you handed over to some pagan Romans and made fun of with a sign above his cross that said, 'King of the Jews.' You have been waiting for the last day when the graves would open. Guess what? About a month ago the graves opened, and one man walked out, and it was not you. It was Jesus of Nazareth. You have been waiting for the end times when the Spirit would be poured out. Look around, the Spirit has been poured out on your sons and daughters who are speaking to you right now, but he has not been poured out on you. He has been poured out on the followers of Jesus." The people are cut to the heart and reply, "What must we do to be saved?" The answer is given: "Call on the name of the Lord. Repent. Be baptized every one of you!"

If you do, then you can be restored to a right relationship with God. If you do, then you can be restored spiritually as God's Spirit comes to live inside you. If you do, then you can have the years the locusts have eaten given back to you.

I am reminded of a friend who is a church planter in a major northern city. He was born and raised in the Northeast where he was a drug dealer. At one point, he and some friends went to rob another drug dealer, and it turned violent. One of his friends shot and killed the other drug dealer. My friend was arrested and put in jail for murder. In solitary confinement, he asked a guard for something to read and was given a Bible. He read voraciously and called on the name of Jesus for salvation. Today, he is out of prison, married with children, and even reconciled to an estranged son from his former life. He has planted a thriving church in the heart of a great American city. There is nothing the locusts can take from you that Jesus cannot give back. Do not let them eat another second of your life. Call on the name of the Lord.

Reflect and Discuss

1. Discuss things you like to restore or see restored. Why do you enjoy it?
2. Name some of examples of "bad" jealousy and some examples of "good" jealousy. How does good jealousy help us understand how God relates to us?
3. What are some examples of what physical restoration might look like in the life of an individual, a family, or a church?
4. Restoration does not mean everything from your past just goes away. What does it mean for God to restore the years the locusts have eaten if you cannot really get time back?

5. Make a list of blessings and gifts God has given you. How does making a list help your relationship with him?
6. How does the promise of God's presence with you give you encouragement and endurance during difficult times?
7. Why is it important for every believer to receive the Holy Spirit?
8. How does the idea that we are already living in the end times impact your daily walk as a Christian?
9. How can someone "call on the name of the Lord"?
10. .Make a list of people in your life who might need to hear about the good news that restoration is possible. Pray for them.

What Do the End Times Have to Do with My Life?

JOEL 3

Main Idea: The end times should cause me to forgive, to praise, to believe, and to share.

I.   **Forgive (3:1-8)**
II. **Praise (3:9-15)**
III. **Believe (3:16-18)**
IV. **Share (3:19-21)**

When I was a kid, the movie *Back to the Future 2* was a favorite for my brothers and me. It came out in 1989, and the main character, Marty, goes twenty-five years into the future to 2015. He saw things like flying cars, hoverboards, laces that tied themselves, clothes that dried themselves, and many more things that were mind-blowing to an eight-year-old who lived in a world where the Internet had not yet been experienced. The movie was so captivating, and we wanted so badly to be part of that future world, that rumors started to swirl around elementary schools all over the country. "You know they have actually invented hoverboards, but the 'Parent Safety Board' will not allow the patent to go through because they think hoverboards are too dangerous for kids." "That darn parent safety board!"

The movie was captivating because humans are intrigued with the future. We want to know what the future may hold. That is why sermon series on the end times are extremely popular. The joke I was told in seminary was, "If you want to build a crowd in church, preach on sex or preach on the end times. And if you really want to build a big crowd, preach on sex in the end times."

People want to know the future because they want to know what is coming down the pike. If you know what is coming, then it gives you an advantage in the present. If I could go back and talk to myself in 2018 or 2019, I would say to buy stock in N95 masks, hand sanitizer, and Zoom! If you can know the future, then you can know how to prepare in the present and be ready.

The problem is that every human vision of the future is wrong. We do not have flying cars yet, though we are several years past 2015. We have hoverboards, but they have wheels and hover over nothing. I want my self-drying jacket but will have to wait. We do not know what is coming. We cannot perfectly predict the future. And yet, for my entire life I have heard preachers who know what the Bible says about no one knowing when the Lord will come back, and still they try to predict the coming of the Lord.

The only person who knows the future is God! Thankfully he gives us a picture of what the future will look like at the conclusion to the book of Joel. God does tell us through the prophet what is coming down the pike. But why does he tell us thousands of years in advance? What do the end times have to do with me right now? What do the end times have to do with my life? Joel 3 gives a vision of the future and implies four different responses from humanity.

Forgive
JOEL 3:1-8

The first response is to forgive. The Bible clearly commands us to forgive those we hold grudges against and to forgive those who have wronged us. In the Bible one of the main motivations for forgiving is that God will judge human evil, and he does not need our help. Vengeance belongs to God. He will repay, so we love and forgive our enemies (Deut 32:35; Rom 12:19-21).

Joel begins chapter 3 with "those days," again referring to the end times (the restoration of Judah he mentioned in ch. 2). The end of chapter 2 revealed that the last days are inaugurated by the resurrection of Jesus and the establishment of the church at Pentecost.[7] The last days extend to the end of the age when God pours out his final judgment on the earth. Joel 3 gives the reader a glimpse of that final judgment at the end of the world.

During this time—the time of the last days—God will gather all the people in the Valley of Jehoshaphat for final judgment and pour out his vengeance on the nations because of what they have done to God's

---

[7] "After the gift of the Holy Spirit at Pentecost, the early Christians correctly viewed themselves as having entered the 'eschatological age'" (Garrett, *Hosea, Joel,* 378).

people (v. 2). He brings specific charges against these nations, such as exiling his people, dividing up his land, and selling his people into slavery (vv. 2-3). Garrett writes, "The fact that the price of these slaves only bought a night with a prostitute or a little wine shows how cheaply they were regarded" (*Hosea, Joel*, 380). Selling slaves was a capital crime in the Sinai covenant (Exod 21:16), so this is a serious charge (Stuart, *Hosea–Jonah*, 2014, 267).

God was not going to allow his people to be treated like this forever. Judgment was bound to arrive. In talking about this coming judgment, God mentions specifically the people along the Mediterranean coast who have done these things (vv. 4-6). The people who did this on a small scale are types of all nations who sinned against God's people (Garrett, *Hosea, Joel*, 381–82). Joel establishes the pattern for the way the nations had treated Israel and would therefore treat God's people throughout history. The Lord says he will give these nations "a taste of their own medicine" (vv. 7-8; Patterson, "Joel," 261). I do not believe this is to be taken as a literal warning that God will cause their people to be sold into slavery. It is symbolic of the fact that God will hold them accountable for what they have done.

This text is clear that God is the one who gets even. God is the one who pours out judgment. He does not need his people's help. One thing that can empower us to let go of our anger is knowing God will set all things right. We are called to forgive because we trust in the justice and vengeance of God (Rom 12:19-21).

Tim Keller in his preaching lectures with Ed Clowney explained that some may take the perspective that confidence in a God of vengeance will make us vengeful and unkind people. He then quotes Croatian theologian Miroslav Volf, who says,

> Only those that believe in divine wrath can forgive. Refusing
> to retaliate requires a belief in divine vengeance. This
> idea may be unpopular in the West, but imagine talking to
> people whose cities have been pillaged, whose wives and
> daughters have been raped, whose fathers and sons have
> been slaughtered. The only way to prevent violence by us is to
> insist violence is only legitimate when it comes from God. It
> takes the quiet of the suburbs to birth the idea that the only
> way humans will be nonviolent is if they believe in a God who
> refuses to judge. In a land soaked by innocent blood, that idea

would die. If God were not angry at injustice and did not make an end of violence, he would not be worthy of our worship.

Keller clarifies that skeptics think belief in a God who judges will make us judgmental and violent people when the opposite is true. If we have truly been wronged, the only way we will refuse to pay someone back is if we have a strong conviction that God will eventually sort all of that out ("Preaching Christ").

When it comes to anyone who has really wronged you, only two options exist. Either the person who hurt you is an unbeliever who will pay for that sin against you for eternity in hell, or the person who wronged you is a believer, and that sin has been taken care of by Jesus's death on the cross (Piper, "Future Grace"). After all, Jesus took this exact judgment on himself (cf. lots cast, Joel 3:3, with what the nations did at the cross, Matt 27:35).

Bitterness and unforgiveness are failures to believe the gospel fully. When you hold a grudge, you are saying that the cross of Jesus Christ is enough to forgive the sins you have committed against God, but it is not enough to forgive the sins committed against you. That is a failure to believe in the sufficiency of the cross. The cross is enough. Forgive as you have been forgiven because God has poured out his vengeance at the cross or will at the end of the age, and he does not need your help.

Praise
JOEL 3:9-15

The second response to what God will do at the end of the age is to praise him. Joel 3:9-10 explains how everyone was to gather in this valley for war and bring what they had available to them to use as weapons. This call included everyone from the soldiers down to the weaklings, and they were to bring with them agricultural tools to use for battle. Every segment of society and of the economy will be on a "wartime footing" (Patterson, "Joel," 262). Then they will line up for war like a scene out of the movie *Braveheart*. They will "stir themselves up" (v. 12 ESV), which is a picture used in the New Testament of people being awakened from the dead to face final judgment (cf. Rev 20; Garrett, *Hosea, Joel*, 387). They will rally against the Lord, but they have no shot. They will be crushed underfoot like grapes in a wine press (v. 13). This is the day of the Lord, when the final sentence of judgment will be carried out and apocalyptic signs of the end of the world will accompany it in the heavens (vv. 14-15). This was God's verdict to hold humanity accountable for their sin.

Commentators ask about the location of this valley, but I do not think the place is as important to Joel as the pattern being referenced. How does God judge his enemies? The battle waged by King Jehoshaphat against the enemies of God in a valley shows what is being referred to here. After all, *Jehoshaphat* means "the LORD judges." In 2 Chronicles 20 a coalition of armies arrays itself against Judah and Jehoshaphat in events similar to the ones described in Joel 3. The king puts the choir in front of the army, and they sing Psalm 118. As they worship, God routs the enemy, and the human soldiers do not lift a sword. I believe that is what Joel is referencing here. God does not need the help of his people to pour out judgment, but he is enthroned on their praises as they appear before him for battle, and as they worship, the enemy is crushed.

So one of our responses to the final judgment in the Valley of Jehoshaphat is to do what King Jehoshaphat instructed the people to do: sing! We are to sing the praises of our God. Even if you are tone deaf, sing. It is maddening to see men who fold their arms and keep their mouths shut on Sunday mornings gathered with the church when on Saturday night they sing their school's fight song at the top of their lungs. Some ball players tear up at the singing of the national anthem, and yet many are not moved to emotion on Sunday morning when they sing of the empty tomb. Sports are great, and I am grateful to be an American, but those things pale in comparison to King Jesus. We are to worship God in song because as we sing the demons shudder!

Peter Leithart says the Old Testament describes worship as "appearing before God," which is the picture of an assembled army. "Praise allows us to participate in the cosmic battle against evil. Christ enthroned on our praises is a terror to our enemies" (*Kingdom and Power*, 98). Think about it. The walls of Jericho tumble to the ground as the priests play the instruments (Josh 6). The armies of Moab and Ammon perish as the choir sings (2 Chron 20). The jail doors fling open as Paul and Silas sing (Acts 16), and judgment falls as the saints sing and play instruments in heaven (Rev 14; 19). There are many ways for Christians to engage in spiritual warfare, but let us not neglect the singing of praises because as we do it, we are the Lord's army appearing before him ready for battle.

Believe

JOEL 3:16-18

The third response to final judgment is to believe in the Lord. Joel describes the Lord as a lion roaring from Zion. He is frightening to those against him. He shakes the foundation of the world (v. 16). But he is a refuge to his people. "The very manifestation of his coming, so fearful for the unbelieving nations . . . , gives assurance of protection and strength for God's own" (Patterson, "Joel," 263). Our Lord is both terrifying and tender. He is Judge and Savior. God is Judge. He poured out judgment on his own house (cf. Joel 1–2), and then he poured it out on his Son at the cross, so do not think you can somehow escape the wrath of God. If he did not spare his own Son, what makes you think you are exempt? The only hope you have is to find refuge in him by believing in what Jesus did for you at the cross.

Joel explains that God will be a refuge for his people (v. 16), that he will live with them, sanctify them, and protect them from any enemy (v. 17), and that he will restore the land so that it is once again like Eden (v. 18). If you find refuge in the Lord Jesus Christ, no enemies will defeat you (including sin, Satan, and death), and you will get to return to paradise with every tear wiped away from your eyes. A spring and streams will flow out of the house of the Lord (v. 18). This image comes up again and again in the Bible. Ezekiel 47 speaks of a river that flows out of the temple and brings life to everything it touches, including resurrecting life in the Dead Sea (cf. 47:8). Jesus says that whoever believes in him is like the temple that has the river of life flowing out of him or her. That river refers to the Holy Spirit who lives in every believer (John 7:38-39). When Jesus was crucified, and the spear put into his side, blood and water flowed out signifying the river of life that flows out of him to all who believe. And the church, as his temple on earth, should bring living waters to those around them (Garrett, *Hosea, Joel*, 395).

Share

JOEL 3:19-21

The fourth response is to share this news with the world—again, to bring living water to those in need. Egypt and Edom are the last nations mentioned in the book of Joel because they are types of the pagan enemies that harassed Israel throughout her history.[8] They will become desolate (as Judah was in the first half of Joel), while Judah enjoys continual habitation. God will cause this great reversal as his vengeance.

The promises of God to Abraham are never far in the background in the Old Testament. But the promises of God to Abraham with reference to the relationship between his offspring and the nations presents a tension. God says he will bless those who bless Abraham's offspring, and he will curse those who curse them, and in Abraham he will bless all the families of the earth (Gen 12:1-3). This promise is the answer to the problem of the tower of Babylon when people were spread all over the world. And yet, not only will Abraham's offspring bless all the nations, but his offspring will also curse them and even "possess the gate of his enemies" (Gen 22:17 ESV). So there is a tension: God's people will both bless the nations and dominate them.

How can we square this? The tension is resolved in the gospel of Jesus Christ. We are told at the Jerusalem Council that pagan Gentiles voluntarily bowing the knee to Jesus as King and Savior is a glimpse at the fulfillment of these two promises (Acts 15:6-21). As the nations bow and confess Jesus as Lord, they both come into subjection to Abraham's offspring and receive the blessing. Every Sunday morning in churches around the world, a multitude of bacon-eating Gentiles gather together to bow their knees to a Jew and confess him as their King. The promises to Abraham have come true.

The great reversal that ends Joel should call us to evangelism and mission. God will keep his promises to Abraham through Abraham's offspring, Jesus Christ (cf. Gal 3). That means those who bless Christ will be blessed and those who curse him will be cursed. The only hope Edomites or Egyptians or Americans have is to be joined to Christ by faith. So final judgment should be a motivation for us to share the news of what God has done for us in Jesus Christ. We must go on mission to share with our neighbors and with the nations.

Conclusion

When Jesus came to earth the first time, it looked a lot different than it will look when he returns. That time he allowed himself to be put on

---

[8] Garrett says they serve as a sign for all the nations (*Hosea, Joel*, 396). Stuart says they stand as paradigms for the nations (*Hosea–Jonah*, 2014, 270).

trial, to be bound, to be beaten, and to be nailed to a cross while mockers wagged their tongues. His second coming will be as the Warrior-King arrayed in battle to slay the enemies of God. He will not be bound. He will not be beaten. He will not be on trial. No, he will be putting on the trial, rendering the verdict, and carrying out the sentence.

How should we respond? We should forgive our enemies because Jesus will not need us to lift a finger in the Valley of Jehoshaphat. We should praise because our king is enthroned on our praises and causes our enemies to tremble. We should believe because aligning with Jesus is our only hope. And we should share so that others can escape from the Valley and live forever in a land that flows with milk and honey.

Reflect and Discuss

1. Have you ever wondered what the future would look like? Why were you fascinated with it?
2. What are some ways people try to get a grasp on the future?
3. Why do people consult with horoscopes and fortune tellers?
4. How do the gospel and the truth of final judgment motivate us to forgive others who have wronged us?
5. Have you ever thought about why we sing songs in worship services? Why did you think we do it?
6. How has the cross reference of King Jehoshaphat's choir changed your perspective about why we sing worship songs?
7. A lion can be terrifying to outsiders but a comfort to his cubs. How is God both terrifying and tender? How does this affect how we relate to him?
8. According to what you find in the New Testament—cite actual verses—how can you as a Gentile be included in God's people?
9. How are you involved in sharing the good news with others?
10. List your church's mission efforts in the next year. Which of those efforts would you most like to be involved with and why?

Amos

Introduction to the Book of Amos

Date

Amos 1:1 states that Amos prophesied during the reigns of Uzziah in the southern kingdom of Judah and Jeroboam II in the northern kingdom of Israel. Uzziah reigned from 792 to 740 BC, and Jeroboam II reigned from 793 to 753 BC.[9] Since Amos mentions Uzziah but not the kings following Uzziah, as does Hosea, it is usually concluded that Amos prophesied before Hosea. However, both prophesied roughly during the same era in the northern kingdom.

The book of Amos also dates Amos's ministry relative to a natural disaster. Amos 1:1 states that Amos prophesied "two years before the earthquake." Such a dating should sound familiar since it's common for people today to date events by a well-known calamity. People often say things like, "That happened the year before 9/11," or "That event was two years after Hurricane Katrina." Such dating is called "relative dating"—dating an event not with an absolute date, like 2021, but dating it relative to another event, like "the year after COVID-19 hit."

Probably the earthquake Amos mentioned was significant enough that everyone in his lifetime and perhaps in later generations remembered it, but twenty-eight centuries later that earthquake has been forgotten. Israeli archaeologist Yigael Yadin found evidence of an earthquake during his excavations at Hazor in the 1950s and 1960s, and he dated that earthquake to 763 BC (*Hazor*, 150–57). If that was the earthquake to which Amos referred, we could date Amos's ministry to 765 BC. Today it is not common to provide such a specific date for archaeological remains, but even with a broader range of dates, this earthquake would fit during the reigns of Uzziah and Jeroboam.

Regarding the length of Amos's ministry, it has been suggested that his ministry lasted about thirty minutes—long enough for him to deliver his sermon in Israel before he traveled back home to Judah.

---

[9] Eugene Merrill, *A Kingdom of Priests*, 388–89. Merrill proposes that both kings reigned as coregents with their fathers for a significant number of these years—Uzziah with his father, Amaziah, for twenty-five years, and Jeroboam II with his father, Jehoash, for twelve years.

That scenario cannot be completely accurate, given the information provided in chapter 7. Amaziah, the priest of Bethel, had heard of the preaching of Amos, reported it to King Jeroboam, and confronted Amos about what he had been saying. Amaziah also urged Amos to leave Israel; his message was not welcome to the religious establishment and probably not welcome to other Israelite loyalists. Thus, since the content of his preaching was known to some extent, his ministry extended at least long enough for his message to have circulated around Israel. Amos 7:14 indicates that Amos was not a professional prophet. Since he did not earn his living as a prophet, it is indeed possible that his ministry did not endure for years.

Biographical Information

The prophet Amos is not mentioned outside the book of Amos, so all biographical information derives from this book. The first verse states that Amos was from Tekoa. Tekoa was a small town six miles south of Bethlehem, so twelve miles south of Jerusalem. Therefore, Amos lived in the southern kingdom of Judah, but he prophesied in the northern kingdom of Israel.

Amos 1:1 refers to Amos as "one of the sheep breeders." The meaning and implications of that vocation are discussed in the first section of the exposition to follow. Amos stated to Amaziah that he was "a herdsman, and I took care of sycamore figs" (7:14). So the book of Amos supplies three statements about Amos's profession. He was a sheep breeder, a herdsman, and a dresser of sycamore trees. In Amos 7:14, the term translated "herdsman" is not the customary word for shepherd but a word related to the term for cattle or oxen. So, in addition to breeding sheep (1:1), Amos owned and tended livestock. He also said, "I took care of sycamore figs." The sycamore tree appears elsewhere in the Old Testament (1 Kgs 10:27; 1 Chron 27:28; Ps 78:47), but Amos 7:14 is the only place this verb occurs. Evidently it refers to doing something like gathering or tending sycamore figs, or pruning sycamore trees, or perhaps more specifically, "to *nip* the sycamore fruit to fit it for eating" (Brown et al., "*balas*," *BDB*, 118; emphasis in original). Amos, then, was involved in multiple businesses—raising sheep, breeding livestock, and caring for an orchard or perhaps several orchards. Such roles would have necessitated multiple relationships with people, both poor and rich—employees, customers, neighbors, and fellow businesspersons.

The book that bears Amos's name demonstrates that he was a devoted follower of the one true God. He spent time in the presence of God, and God showed him visions (1:1; 7:1-9; 8:1-3; 9:1). He also had the strength of character to speak boldly against people who were invested with power and money. He delivered scathing words of God's judgment to the wealthy elites in Samaria (4:1-3; 6:1), to the chief religious leader in Bethel (7:10-17), and to merchants who were oppressing the poor as they enriched themselves (2:6-8; 8:4-8).

The book of Amos also exhibits significant literary ability by the author. Many people would not expect a shepherd, herdsman, and fruit farmer to possess rhetorical skills, but Amos defies such preconceptions. Amos used a range of literary forms. The opening salvo announcing God's judgment on the nations is highly structured, includes clever use of repetition, and has an obvious rhetorical strategy (1:3–2:3). In chapter 4, Amos uses sarcasm to call attention to the fact that Israel's religion was corrupt (vv. 4-5). Chapter 5 opens as a lament, or dirge, and some of the vision accounts involve plays on words (8:1-2) or complex parallelism (9:2-4). Amos also used the genre of biographical narrative to describe his encounter with Amaziah the priest (7:10-17). Amos was clearly a complex, industrious, and gifted person. Yet despite his success, he had not sold out to the corrupt economic and religious system. Instead of currying favor with the movers and shakers of society, he walked closely with God, listened to God, and spoke boldly the word of God, even when it was directed at people who had the power to hurt him. He was from a small town, but God gave him a message for all Israel and even for nations beyond Israel.

Historical and Cultural Circumstances

What kind of nation was the Israel to which Amos preached? Jeroboam II was the king, and he reigned for forty-one years (2 Kgs 14:23). The book of 2 Kings summarizes the reign of Jeroboam II as "evil in the Lord's sight" (14:24). Though his reign was evil morally and spiritually, it was a success in other ways. Second Kings 14:25 says that Jeroboam "restored Israel's border from Lebo-hamath as far as the Sea of the Arabah"—that is, from a northern border in Syrian territory to a southern border somewhere in the Negev desert. On the human level, such expansion of Israel's territory was possible for Jeroboam because of a vacuum of power during that historical moment. Adad-Nirari, the king of Assyria, had subdued Damascus, so any threat from Syria was mitigated. Assyria had not yet risen to be a world power (Bright, *History of Israel*, 255–56). Thus, Jeroboam was able to enjoy peace and even to expand Israel's borders.

Jonah served as a prophet during this time, and he preached that Israel's geographical expansion was according to God's will (2 Kgs 14:25). Further, 2 Kings states, "The LORD had not said he would blot out the name of Israel under heaven, so he delivered them by the hand of Jeroboam" (14:27). In the midst of such peace and prosperity, many Israelites surely found it difficult to believe Amos's "doom and gloom" preaching. People believed God was blessing them, and both their circumstances and Jonah's preaching supported that belief. However, though God had been blessing Israel, he also showed Amos the extent of Israel's sin and apostasy and told his prophet of a day in the future when he would pass judgment against Israel for their sin. The political, military, and economic superstructure of Israel looked healthy, but its moral and spiritual foundations were rotten, so the nation was close to collapse. The people could not have seen it then, but in only a few decades the Assyrian Empire would rise, its army would make military incursions into Israel, and finally Assyria would conquer Israel's capital, Samaria, in 722 BC. Thus, the prophetic word of Amos came to pass, and people knew he had been a true prophet of the Lord.

With economic prosperity came the exploitation of that prosperity. Amos referred to people who were exploiting the poor. Merchants were making life more miserable for the poor while seeking every means possible to enrich themselves (2:6-7; 4:1; 5:11-12; 8:4-6). Businesspersons were lying and stealing through the use of false balances—charging people an unfair amount and giving them less produce than promised for their money (8:5-6). The moral corruption in the economy existed in other areas. The book of Amos signals sexual licentiousness with the report that "a man and his father have sexual relations with the same girl" (2:7). Amos also refers to drinking wine from bowls, a description of drunken revelry (6:5-6). He mentions lying on beds of ivory and on couches, an apparent reference to slothfulness (6:4).

With such moral degradation, one might suspect that interest in religion was waning. On the contrary religion was booming. Amos refers to people attending the sanctuaries at Bethel and Gilgal and making pilgrimages to Beersheba (4:4-5; 5:4-5). To some extent at least, the people observed the regulations in God's law regarding offering sacrifices, and they participated in worship music (5:22-23). Even the greed of the merchant class did not prevent the observance of the Sabbath and the cessation of business on the holy days (8:4-6). Thus, the people seem to have possessed some knowledge of God's law, either through reading the law or hearing it from priests and prophets. Such knowledge of God's law only increased their guilt (Barton, *Theology*, 68). They knew what God expected, but they were substituting religious rites for righteousness and justice. Through Amos, God told them he hated ritual observance divorced from righteous living (5:21-24).

An Outline of the Book of Amos

An Epithet for Amos

AMOS 1:1-2

Main Idea: We can learn a lot about Amos and his message by reading the few words of his introduction.

I. **God Uses Laypersons to Do His Work.**
II. **God Reveals Himself.**
III. **God Speaks.**

Sometimes it's possible to say a lot about a person with only a few words. For example, we refer to William Shakespeare as "The Bard," and in a way, that says it all. People often referred to Princess Diana as "the people's princess," and those few words express so much about her. If you could use only a few words to describe your life, what would they be? If God, who knows you best, used only a few words to describe you, what would they be?

We refer to a brief description like that as an epithet. An epithet is a brief description that summarizes at least some of a person's essential qualities. The book of Amos begins with an epithet—a brief, general statement about the man Amos and his message. Commentators refer to the first two verses of the book as a superscription; it's an introduction. And we can learn a lot about Amos and his message by reading the few words of his introduction.

God Uses Laypersons to Do His Work

Verse 1 refers to Amos as "one of the sheep breeders." Most translations render the word as "shepherds," as does the Christian Standard Bible's marginal reading. The Hebrew word is not the common word for "shepherd." This word occurs only once elsewhere in the Old Testament, in 2 Kings 3:4, which says, "King Mesha of Moab was a sheep breeder. He used to pay the king of Israel one hundred thousand lambs and the wool of one hundred thousand rams." That's a lot of lambs and rams! Mesha was clearly wealthy, but after all, Mesha was a king. Amos was not a king, but he and King Mesha are referred to with the same word. We should not jump to the quick conclusion that Amos was as rich as a king, because later in the book he wrote that he "took care of sycamore figs" and he had been "following the flock" (7:14-15). So it's unlikely that Amos was what we call "independently wealthy." He labored. On the other hand, it also seems unlikely that he was a small-time shepherd caring for a family flock. The same word in other Near Eastern languages also referred to a person of status, in charge of a group of shepherds.[10]

We would surely be accurate to refer to Amos as a businessman. He lived in Tekoa (v. 1), a small town about twelve miles south of Jerusalem. But probably he also traveled some, especially since sycamore trees do not typically grow in the area of Tekoa (Andersen and Freedman, *Amos*, 778–79). So Amos worked for a living, but he was also most likely a person of means and position. Amos was probably in the Tekoa Kiwanis club. At the ribbon-cutting ceremony for the new city gate, he probably didn't cut the ribbon, but he was on the podium, maybe to deliver the invocation. Surely Amos was also known for his commitment to the one true God. So people knew Amos—a successful businessman, a man of the land, a deeply spiritual person, and an articulate speaker.

Amos was not a priest or a prophet (see 7:14). And when people in that time and place wanted spiritual leadership, they looked to priests and prophets, not businessmen. "Amos? Go to him if you want to know about raising and selling sheep or how to manage an orchard. But how to know God and live for God? Amos is not your guy." But that's just the point. Amos was God's guy. God uses laypeople to do his work.

Sometimes we create unbiblical distinctions between laypeople and pastors. It's true that God calls some people to roles of leadership in his church. The Bible says those leaders ought to be followed (Heb 13:17). On the other hand, that special calling does not mean spiritual leaders have a monopoly on hearing from God and speaking for God. The Bible states that every Christian is a priest (1 Pet 2:5,9; Rev 1:6). All of us who know Jesus as our Savior can speak to him in prayer, hear what he says to us, and speak to others about him. In Christ's Great Commission, our Lord sends all his people, not just pastors, to make disciples of all nations (Matt 28:18-20).

---

[10] Namely, Akkadian and Ugaritic (Gary Smith, *Hosea, Amos, Micah*, 230). Jeffrey Niehaus points out that the cognate Arabic term refers to one species of sheep—a small breed with excellent wool. Perhaps, then, this type of shepherd bred a different product, so a different word was used for the occupation ("Amos," 336).

We should never believe a message is not from God merely because the messenger has an unexpected occupation. In the 1990s, God used the Promise Keepers movement to call many men to a faithful relationship with himself. To spark and lead that movement, God did not use a professional minister but a football coach named Bill McCartney. In the late twentieth and early twenty-first centuries, God also used a layperson to instruct and inspire people to follow God in their families—a psychologist named James Dobson. America's largest nonprofit organization serving and sharing the gospel with prisoners and their families is Prison Fellowship. The founder and longtime leader of that organization was not an ordained minister but a former attorney and government bureaucrat named Chuck Colson, who was once in prison himself. Growing up, I heard pastors preach the gospel, and I am grateful for them. But God used a Sunday school teacher, a layperson, to stir my heart to trust Christ for salvation. I don't even remember what his occupation was, but I know he loved me, he was burdened for my salvation, and God used him in my life.

Amos's epithet—"one of the sheep breeders from Tekoa"—teaches us that God uses laypersons to do his work. Can people say that about you? Can you insert your name in this sentence? "God is using _____ to do his work." What assignment does God have for you?

God Reveals Himself

Amos's introduction also includes the truth that God reveals himself. The first words of the book are, "The words of Amos," and verse 1 goes on to qualify those words as "what he saw." God showed a message to Amos. The words in the book of Amos are Amos's words because he saw them and preached them. The words are also God's words because he gave them to Amos.

Amos's introduction brings together two important Old Testament words—*words* and *saw*. On the one hand, we use those words all the time in the most casual ways, so they hardly seem significant. But what if, instead of saying, "Last week I saw a good movie," someone said, "Last week I saw words that God showed me"? The latter statement would be a bold claim, but the prophets repeatedly made that claim (e.g., Mic 1:1). The Hebrew word translated "saw" is the verb form of the noun that is typically translated "seer," and *seer* was another word for *prophet* (1 Sam 9:9). It's the word Amaziah used to refer to Amos (7:12).

Another form of the same word is translated "vision," and visions were what prophets saw (Isa 1:1). So prophets were people who saw visions that God showed them, and that's what Amos's introduction tells us about him.

God's self-revelation is an expression of grace and love. God has no need to reveal himself to us, but we need him. We could not know God or know about him if he did not reveal himself. Agnostics claim that we cannot know anything about God. They are correct, *unless* God chooses to reveal himself, and he has done so in his Word, in his creation, and in his incarnation in the person of Jesus. We can know about God and his truth because he reveals himself to us. And praise his name, in addition to knowing *about* him, we can know *him* in a personal relationship, and we may enjoy the eternal blessings that accrue to those who know him. He has revealed himself, so we may "see" his truth just as Amos saw it.

Specifically, Amos's introduction says he heard the Lord roar like a lion. Both those words—*Lord* and *lion*—are ways God reveals himself. "Lord" is the covenant name God revealed to Moses at the burning bush (Exod 3:14). When Moses asked for God's name so he could speak that name to the Israelites in Egypt, God said, "I AM WHO I AM. This is what you are to say to the Israelites: I AM has sent me to you." The Hebrew word translated "I am" became the word translated "Lord."[11] How has God revealed himself? He has revealed himself as the great I AM—the one who exists and is self-existent. His name is not, "I am because I was born," or "I am because I came into existence," or "I am because someone made me." His name is, "I am that I am." The continued existence of human beings is contingent on God's allowing us to exist. The same is true of every entity in the universe, except for God. He is the only noncontingent being in the universe. His continued existence is self-determined: "I am that I am."

The name God revealed—"I AM WHO I AM"—both reveals and conceals. It communicates certain truths about God: he exists, he is self-existent, he is with people, and he speaks to them (such as Moses, Amos, and us). However, it does not tell us everything about God. God is inscrutable—mysterious, difficult to understand—because he is God

---

[11] In many English translations, the English word to render this Hebrew word is set in small caps as "Lord" to differentiate it from a few other Hebrew words that may also be translated "Lord."

and we are mere mortals (Isa 40:28; Rom 11:33-36; Eph 3:19). He is infinite and we are finite. His covenant name—the Lord—preserves that mystery.

Amos 1:2 says God revealed himself to Amos as a roaring lion (see 3:8). Readers of C. S. Lewis are familiar with this image of God, since Lewis presents Jesus allegorically as a lion named Aslan in his seven-volume The Chronicles of Narnia. The best-known passage describing Aslan/Jesus is in *The Lion, the Witch and the Wardrobe,* as Mr. and Mrs. Beaver described him:

> Aslan a man! . . . Certainly not. I tell you he is the King of the
> wood and the son of the great Emperor-Beyond-the-Sea. . . .
> Aslan is a lion—*the* Lion, the great Lion. . . . If there's anyone
> who can appear before Aslan without their knees knocking,
> they're either braver than most or else just silly. . . . Safe? . . .
> 'Course he isn't safe. But he's good. He's the King, I tell you.
> (Lewis, *The Lion, the Witch and the Wardrobe,* 146)

Lewis was using an image for God that God himself uses multiple times in his Word.[12] Since God reveals himself with the metaphor of a lion, we should meditate on that word picture. The image of a lion communicates power, danger, and fear. I was once in Tanzania to preach and visit family members who were serving there as missionaries. While my family and I were there, we went on a wildlife-viewing safari. We were to spend an evening in the bush in some tents, but at the last minute the guides made a change, and we slept in little huts with brick walls. I was happy about the change because the guides knew a pride of lions was in that area, and lions often hunt at night. I had been uneasy about the fact that only a tent wall would be separating those lions from us, and I was happy to be safer. Sure enough, the next morning we saw that the lions had made a kill about a quarter of a mile from where we had slept.

The presence of a lion conjures fear. The lion, then, is an appropriate image for God since he has told us to fear him.[13] After we put our

---

[12] For example, Isa 42:13; Jer 25:30; Hos 11:10; Joel 3:16; Amos 3:8; Rev 5:5.

[13] For example, Lev 25:17; Deut 4:10; 5:29; 10:12,20; Josh 4:24; 1 Sam 12:14; Prov 1:7; 9:10; Jer 32:38-40; Amos 3:8; Luke 12:4-5; 2 Cor 5:11; 7:1; Phil 2:12-13; 1 Pet 1:17; 2:17; Rev 14:7; 15:4.

faith in Jesus and he redeems us and makes us new, our relationship with God is characterized by love, but we continue to fear him. However, many people do not fear God. Perhaps they, more than anyone, need to see Amos's image of God as a roaring lion. They need to know of God's power and certain judgment of sin. That knowledge can motivate them to turn away from sin and self and turn in faith to God and receive his salvation.

Of course, word pictures, like picturing God as a lion, only go so far. No analogy can fully represent God's character. On the one hand, God is indeed powerful and should be feared like a lion. On the other hand, God is loving, patient, and good. In the first two chapters of his prophecy, Amos will point out that God was pouring out his judgment on wicked nations only after their cup of sin was full to the brim. We in the church know that God took his just punishment for our sin on himself when Jesus died as the sacrifice for our sin on the cross. The lion became a sacrificial lamb. In the book of Revelation, the apostle John brought those two images together—the lion and the lamb—and used them both to refer to Jesus. John wrote that Jesus is "the Lion from the tribe of Judah" and "one like a slaughtered lamb standing in the midst of the throne" (Rev 5:5-6). Thus, John used two Old Testament images of the prophesied Messiah—the lion of the tribe of Judah (Gen 49:9-10) and the sacrificial lamb (Isa 53:7)—and he showed that both of them are fulfilled in Jesus. God is loving, gracious, merciful, and good; but Amos reminds us that God is also the roaring lion who announces his holy judgment on wickedness.

God Speaks

As a young man, I served as a student pastor for a few years. During that time, I asked more than one group of teenagers this question: "Does God speak to people today?" It wasn't a trick question. In fact, I thought the answer was easy. But in each case the question was followed by a long silence. I was disappointed because I had wanted to hear the young people say, "Yes! God speaks to people today; he spoke to me this morning when I read his Word!"

The writer of Hebrews wrote that God has spoken "by the prophets at different times and in different ways. In these last days, he has spoken to us by his Son" (Heb 1:1-2). In 2 Timothy 3:16, Paul wrote, "All Scripture is inspired by God." The message of those two passages is

that during the old covenant period God spoke through prophets, his
law, and the writers of the books of wisdom (1 Pet 1:10-12). In this new
covenant age God has spoken finally and redemptively in the person of
Jesus. He also continues to speak through Scripture.

Amos's epithet also includes a reference to God speaking, and
Amos portrayed God's voice as a lion's roar: "The LORD roars from Zion
/ and makes his voice heard from Jerusalem" (v. 2). Jerusalem was the
location of the temple, the place where God had chosen his name to
dwell (Deut 12:1-14). Zion was a hill in Jerusalem, and that term was
often used as a way of referring to the entire city. So Amos pictured
God as speaking from Jerusalem, but his voice did not remain there. It
went beyond the city into "the pastures of the shepherds" that were in
the countryside outside the city walls. God's voice, the lion's roar, even
reached beyond the hill country of Jerusalem, beyond Judah's border,
into the northern kingdom of Israel, over the Jezreel Valley where the
capital city of Samaria was located, and all the way to the northwestern
point of "the summit of Carmel" (v. 2). Here Amos confronts his readers
with the truth that God is no ordinary lion. His voice will not be con-
fined to one locale. His speech is supernatural, reaching far beyond the
range of speech caused by natural means.

When God's roar reaches the pastures of shepherds, the pastures
"mourn." When his voice arrives at the top of Mount Carmel, it "withers." These destructive effects of God's speech foreshadow the fact that
God's words that follow will be words of judgment, not blessing. Also,
this verse portrays God's word as powerful. It creates effects; it causes
pastures to mourn and the top of a mountain to wither.

The power of God's word is stressed by the mention of the with-
ering of Carmel. Mount Carmel was the site of the contest between
the prophet Elijah and hundreds of prophets of Baal and Asherah
(1 Kgs 18:19-46). God caused Elijah to prevail when he sent fire from
heaven. That contest was during a time of drought, a fact that may be
echoed in the word translated "withers" in Amos 1:2, since that word is
typically translated "dries" (Brown et al., "*yabesh*," *BDB*, 386). It's likely
that when people heard Amos speak of God's word reaching Mount
Carmel, they would have remembered that God's word had triumphed
over false deities about a hundred years earlier. It was likely not coinci-
dental that the confrontation between Elijah and the Baalistic prophets
occurred on Mount Carmel since that location had long been regarded

as a sort of holy place and Elijah himself repaired an already-existing altar to the Lord (1 Kgs 18:30; George Smith, *Historical Geography,* 226).

We don't know the extent to which Amos's hearers associated Mount Carmel with the worship of pagan deities, but we know the place had a significant religious history. Thus, it's likely that Amos's mention of God's voice reaching all the way to Mount Carmel had both geographical and theological significance. The word of the one true God reaches all the way across the land of his people, and it is so powerful that it shrivels his competition, which is really no competition at all. His word triumphs over all. Amos's word picture is made explicit in Hebrews 4:12:

> *The word of God is living and effective and sharper than any double-edged sword, penetrating as far as the separation of soul and spirit, joints and marrow. It is able to judge the thoughts and intentions of the heart.*

God has spoken, and his word is powerful.

Since God has spoken, we should listen to him. No message in the world is as important as the message that comes from the one true God himself. Listening to other sources to discover truth, or adding to the words God has given us, will always be a temptation, but we must heed "nothing beyond what is written" (1 Cor 4:6). At the beginning of our study of the prophetic book of Amos, we should remember 2 Peter 1:19-21:

> *We also have the prophetic word strongly confirmed, and you will do well to pay attention to it, as to a lamp shining in a dark place, until the day dawns and the morning star rises in your hearts. Above all, you know this: No prophecy of Scripture comes from the prophet's own interpretation, because no prophecy ever came by the will of man; instead, men spoke from God as they were carried along by the Holy Spirit.*

The first verse of the book of Amos is correct in stating that its contents are "the words of Amos," but it is also true that the words are God's words, since he gave them to Amos. The words are "what he saw."

Thank God that he speaks to us. He spoke to Amos, and Amos was faithful to preach what God gave him. The epithet that opens the book of Amos tells a story about the life and character of the man Amos. Maybe a paraphrase of Amos's epitaph could be, "Amos—God gave him a message, and he preached it." Amos's epithet expressed his faithfulness to God. If people wrote an epithet about your life, would it express faithfulness to God?

Reflect and Discuss

1. What has been your experience with the book of Amos in the past? How has God spoken to you through this part of his Word?
2. God called Amos, a layperson, to proclaim his word. What has God called you to do?
3. In your life, how has God used laypersons to do his work? How have they helped you spiritually?
4. In what ways have you observed God using laypersons, including you, to do his work in the world?
5. How does God reveal his character and attributes in the world today?
6. God has spoken in his Word. Describe the importance of God's Word in your life.
7. How can God's Word be made known to the world today?
8. Write an epithet that accurately reflects your life. Is that the epithet you want? What is the epithet God wants for you?
9. What do you think the metaphor of "lion" expresses about the character of God?
10. Amos portrayed God's words as powerful. How have you witnessed or experienced the power of God's Word?

Crying Out against the Crimes of the Nations

AMOS 1:3–2:3

Main Idea: In every generation wickedness exists among the nations, and in every generation God calls his people to cry out against it and to call people to salvation in Jesus.

I. **What Were the Crimes of the Nations (1:3–2:3)?**
   A. Violence against fellow human beings (1:3-5)
   B. Oppression of people for profit (1:6-8)
   C. Violation of a fraternal relationship (1:9-10)
   D. Persistent anger (1:11-12)
   E. Abuse driven by greedy ambition (1:13-15)
   F. Acts of vengeance (2:1-3)
II. **What Does God's Word Say about the Crimes of the Nations?**
   A. All people are responsible to God.
   B. God has given a sense of right and wrong to all people.
   C. God knows the behavior of all people in all nations.
   D. God reveals truth about himself to all people.
   E. God patiently waits before punishing sin.
   F. God uses his people to call the populations of all nations to himself.
   G. God's prophetic word comes to pass.
III. **What Does Jesus Do about the Crimes of the Nations?**
   A. Jesus is sinless.
   B. Jesus spoke against sin.
   C. Jesus died and rose again for sinners.

Daria was born into a poor family in Moldova. By the time she was a teenager, the unemployment rate in Moldova was the highest in the world. She was another mouth to feed, and she had no idea how to help. Then Alexander introduced himself to Daria. He had the perfect solution—a job that paid well. It was in another country, but she could support herself there and send money home to her family. She jumped at the opportunity. When she arrived, however, she discovered that the "job" was not real employment but slavery in the sex industry. She was held by force in a building in that foreign country and made to serve her "bosses" under the threat of losing her life.

Daria's story is heartbreaking. Multiply that tragedy by over thirty-two million. That's how many women are currently enslaved in the world, more than at any time in human history. Slavery is illegal in most countries, but it is more common and more profitable than ever. Every minute two children are prepared for sexual slavery. It's called human trafficking, and many evils are required to traffic in human beings (United Nations, "Human Trafficking").

Tragically, abuse of human beings has existed in every generation, including Amos's generation. Amos was aware of violence and abuse, and he spoke God's words of judgment against it. In this section we will ask and answer three big questions about human rights violations being committed in Amos's lifetime.

What Were the Crimes of the Nations?
AMOS 1:3–2:3

Before turning to speak of the sins of Judah and Israel, Amos addressed the crimes of the six nations that bordered the promised land on every side. As Amos cataloged the crimes of each people group, he criss-crossed Israel geographically—first Syria in the northeast, then Philistia in the southwest, then Phoenicia in the northwest, then Edom in the southeast. Finally, Amos addressed the sins of Ammon and Moab across the Jordan River to the east before preaching against the sins of the Judahites and Israelites.

Amos arranged his oracles of judgment both geographically and rhetorically. He introduced each of the eight announcements of God's punishment with the words "I will not relent from punishing . . . / for three crimes, even four" (1:3,6,9,11,13; 2:1,4,6). In saying, "For three crimes, even four," Amos was not claiming that each nation had committed only three or four transgressions. He was using a numerical formula as a rhetorical technique that communicates going beyond fullness. The idea is that three is complete and four is too much. Three is full and four is overflowing.[14] Amos preached that "crimes," or trans-

---

[14] Billy K. Smith, *Amos, Obadiah, Jonah*, 47. The author of Proverbs 30 used the same rhetorical technique four times to make the point that the realities of our world are beyond our wisdom (vv. 15-31). Unlike Amos, the writer in each case provides a list of

gressions, were overflowing. In the context of Amos 1–2, the "crimes" were violations of "standards of international morality" (Andersen and Freedman, *Amos*, 231). And "I will not relent" could be translated literally, "I will not cause to turn back." In other words, God had been turning away, or holding back his punishment. He would not do so any longer.

What crimes led to this moment of God's announcement of judgment?

Violence against Fellow Human Beings (1:3-5)

In verse 3 God speaks through Amos to Damascus, the capital of Aram/Syria. The crime God names is that "they threshed Gilead with iron sledges." Gilead was a region in northeastern Israel, just south of the Syrian border, and the "iron sledges" were instruments used to thresh grain. They were wide, flat, heavy wooden sleds with sharp pieces of stone or, in this case, iron embedded in the bottom. Either horses or people would drag the sledges over harvested grain, and the sharp points would help separate the grain from the stalks and chaff. Such was the intended use for the sledges, but the Syrians used these implements to torture the people of Gilead, brutally flaying their bodies with the sharp iron points. Clearly this was unnecessary cruelty. When armies in the ancient Near East committed such barbaric acts, it was typically to make an example of a conquered foe, advertising the armies' callous cruelty so all potential enemies would fear to resist them. Such barbarism had exhausted God's patience. Through Amos he announced that he would send destruction to Damascus. God singled out the royal house for judgment, identifying two kings by name surely because they were personally involved in decisions to commit atrocities. The monumental structures of the capital city would be destroyed and the people exiled (vv. 4-5).

The Syrians were guilty of inhumane treatment of their fellow human beings. They treated people like things. They used an

---

four items (also in vv. 11-14). But the list is not intended to be exhaustive. The items are illustrative, demonstrating that the realities of our world are beyond us, so we should not be lofty in our own eyes (vv. 12-13) or exalt ourselves (v. 32). The purpose of the rhetorical technique is to drill a point into the minds of hearers/readers. Other such numerical sayings, but not involving the numbers three and four, are in Gen 11:2; Job 5:19; 33:14-15 (ESV); Ps 62:11; Prov 6:16-19; Hos 6:2; Mic 5:5.

implement intended for agriculture as an instrument of torture. Such inhumanity has not been uncommon in history. The power released from splitting the atom was an amazing discovery that can be employed in many positive ways to aid humanity. But it has also been used to create nuclear bombs that can devastate entire populations, including noncombatants. Scientists have produced powerful chemicals with helpful uses, but these, too, have been used in chemical warfare to harm people. Like the Syrians who used farm equipment to abuse people, humans have used all sorts of otherwise innocent tools to commit violence against their fellow humans. Such violence is a crime God will punish.

Oppression of People for Profit (1:6-8)

Verse 6 recounts that Gaza, a principal city of the Philistines, "exiled a whole community, / handing them over to Edom." Which community or group of people the Philistines oppressed in this way is not certain. The motive was almost certainly profit. Verse 9 states that the Phoenicians of Tyre committed the same crime. They sold people as slaves to the Edomites. Women and children would have been among the people exiled by the Philistines since they exiled "a whole community." Hence, the Philistines' motive was not merely military; it was mercenary. This was trading in slaves. They raided a town, subdued the people, and sold the entire lot to Edom.

Earlier in this section we referred to the contemporary practice of enslaving people for profit. Through Amos, God condemned such behavior, as he did later through Paul the apostle, who included "slave traders" in a list of sinners along with "those who kill their fathers and mothers," "the sexually immoral," "males who have sex with males," "liars," etc. (1 Tim 1:9-10). In response to the atrocity of selling captives, God announced through Amos that destruction was coming to Philistia. He would send fire on Gaza. God then identified three additional cities that would be punished. The only principal Philistine city not mentioned is Gath, omitted perhaps because it was less prominent when Amos preached. God even said that "the remainder of the Philistines will perish" (Amos 1:8). Indeed, that has come to pass; the Philistines ceased to be a people group.

Violation of a Fraternal Relationship (1:9-10)

Tyre was the largest city of Phoenicia during Amos's lifetime, so Amos named that city as a way of referring to the Phoenicians and their leaders. Amos stated that not only did the Phoenicians hand over exiles to Edom as the Philistines did, but they also "broke a treaty of brotherhood" (v. 9). We do not know which treaty Amos was referring to, but we know Solomon had had a treaty with Hiram, king of Tyre, and Ahab had had a diplomatic marriage with Jezebel, a Phoenician princess (1 Kgs 5:12; 16:31). So it's not difficult to envision a covenant relationship existing during Amos's lifetime between Phoenicia and Israel or another neighboring nation.

The leaders of Phoenicia broke the treaty. Literally, the text reads, "They did not remember a covenant of brothers." They made a promise and broke it because they "forgot." The Bible contains many admonitions to speak the truth and keep our word (e.g., Exod 20:16; Eph 4:25). But even without the Bible, people know the importance of keeping promises. International diplomacy depends on telling the truth and keeping promises. Business contracts are worthless unless the parties honor them; marriage vows are made to be kept, not broken. No two people can trust each other if they don't tell the truth and keep their promises. Once we forge a covenant with a promise, we cannot forget it. God was going to send the fire of his judgment on Phoenicia for forgetting their promise.

Persistent Anger (1:11-12)

In this case the nation was Edom, and Edom "pursued his brother with the sword." Possibly this "brother" was Israel, since Israel descended from Jacob and Edom descended from Esau, and Jacob and Esau were brothers. The people of Edom were guilty of violence since they pursued with the sword, and Amos added their motivation for violence: "His anger tore at him continually, / and he harbored his rage incessantly" (v. 11). The word translated "harbored" is often translated "keep." Adam was to "keep" the garden (Gen 2:15), the Israelites were to "keep" God's commandments (Deut 4:2-6), and wise persons will "keep" their heart (Prov 4:23). The word carried connotations like "nurture," "observe," or "guard." The Edomites were nurturing their anger. Such harbored anger harms the one who is angry, and it results in harming others. God was going to send fire on major cities of Edom—Teman and Bozrah— because of their harbored anger.

Abuse Driven by Greedy Ambition (1:13-15)

The Ammonites were immediately south of the region of Gilead, and the Ammonites "ripped open / the pregnant women of Gilead / in order to enlarge their territory" (v. 13). Their ambition was more land, and they were willing to do anything to obtain what they wanted, even to commit the crime of slashing the bellies of expectant mothers. Such abuse was barbaric, and the violence was done against noncombatants. Neither the pregnant women nor the babies would have served in the military, so the Ammonites were violently abusing unarmed people. Surely they intended their actions to frighten and subdue the Gileadites. Their crime was disgraceful and deplorable. In response, God was going to bring down their capital city and send the people into exile (vv. 14-15).

Acts of Vengeance (2:1-3)

The nation of Edom was immediately south of Moab, and the Moabites disinterred the bones of the king of Edom and burned them to lime. Ancestors were typically highly valued in the ancient Near East; it was the practice to honor them. Therefore, burning the king's bones would have been aimed at disgracing him and his countrymen (Gary Smith, *Hosea, Amos, Micah*, 244). This was no material victory; no land or plunder was won. All that was gained was vengeance by subjecting the former king to humiliation. God announced that he would punish Moab— specifically the leaders and Kerioth, a city that is mentioned elsewhere but it's location in uncertain.

What Does God's Word Say about the Crimes of the Nations?

How could God hold these nations responsible for wrongdoing when he had not given them his law that contains his ethical expectations? That's an important question because the answer speaks to how God relates to the nations in every generation.

All People Are Responsible to God

This truth is clear from the fact that God was holding the pagan nations surrounding Israel accountable for their actions. God addressed each nation personally. He said to them, "I will not relent," "I will send fire," etc. He addressed them himself because they were responsible to him. God has created every person, he reveals himself in some way to every person, he expects every person to worship him and obey the light they have been given, and every person will one day give an account to him. The apostle Paul expressed this truth in Romans 2:9-12:

> *There will be affliction and distress for every human being who does evil, first to the Jew, and also to the Greek; but glory, honor, and peace for everyone who does what is good, first to the Jew, and also to the Greek. For there is no favoritism with God.*
> *For all who sin without the law will also perish without the law, and all who sin under the law will be judged by the law.*

God judges every person—Jews who have the law and Gentiles who do not have the law—and in every case he rewards righteousness and punishes evil. But how can God punish people for evil if they do not have his law? That leads us to the second principle.

God Has Given a Sense of Right and Wrong to All People

The Syrians, Philistines, Phoenicians, Edomites, Ammonites, and Moabites were not in a special covenant relationship with God as were the Jews, so God had not given the Mosaic law to those people groups. But God gives to all people his creation law. From the beginning of creation, God has been communicating his will. God punished Cain for committing murder (Gen 4), and after the flood God gave the command not to commit murder (Gen 9). That command preceded the covenant with Abraham and the covenant with Israel at Mount Sinai, and it was for all humanity. God has made all people in his image, so all have the ability to do what is right (Gen 1:26-27). God has also given all people a conscience, which is a sense of right and wrong that is written on the heart (Rom 2:14-15). God's image and the conscience he gives have always been reflected in the laws humans have written. For example, in Mesopotamia the laws of Ur-Nammu (2100 BC) and the laws of Lipit-Ishtar (1930 BC) were

written in Sumerian, and the laws of Hammurabi (1750 BC) and the laws
of Eshnunna (1780 BC) were written in Akkadian. In Anatolia, a collection of laws has been found in the Hittite language (1650–1500 BC). Such
laws have much in common with biblical law insofar as they prohibit such
things as murder, theft, and dishonesty (Skaist, "Ancient Near Eastern
Law Collections," 305–18). Today, documents like the United Nations'
"Universal Declaration of Human Rights" and the Geneva Conventions
denounce abusing people and condemn barbaric practices in war. All
such laws are evidence that God has made all humans in his image and
gives all humans a sense of right and wrong.

As for Israel's neighbors in the time of Amos, the Syrians may not
have had a copy of God's law, but they knew that threshing people with
iron sledges was wrong. They did it anyway, and God was holding them
responsible for their crime. The Philistines and Phoenicians also knew
that selling an entire group of people into slavery was wrong, but they
did it anyway. God did not give his Mosaic law to the Edomites and
Moabites, but they knew that harboring anger and expressing it in violence was wrong. The Ammonites knew that it was wrong to rip open
pregnant women, but they did it. God was holding all those peoples
responsible for their crimes. They were made in God's image, they had
God's creation law, and God gave them all a conscience. Therefore, they
were without excuse.

God Knows the Behavior of All People in All Nations

When the Syrians threshed people in Gilead with iron sledges, God saw
what they did. When the Philistines and Phoenicians treated people like
commodities to be sold, God saw that too. Nothing escapes his notice
(Ps 139:1-18). We know only partially; God knows all. Our knowledge
of the facts is affected by our fallenness; God's knowledge is perfect
(1 Cor 13:9-12). God sees all people and all deeds simultaneously
(Ps 33:13), and he sees the outcome of righteousness and wickedness
(Pss 1:6; 37:13). God's judgment of the nations surrounding Israel was
based on God's perfect knowledge. No nation is out of God's sight, and
nothing a nation does escapes his notice.

God Reveals Truth about Himself to All People

Sadly, not all people have access to God's perfect truth in the Bible.
Most people in the world do not know about Jesus, God's final revealed

truth (Heb 1:1-3). However, God has revealed some truth about himself to all people. All people can see the heavens, and "the heavens declare the glory of God" (Ps 19:1). God, therefore, will express his wrath against unrighteousness since "what can be known about God is evident" (Rom 1:19). The created order reveals not only God's existence but even his

> *invisible attributes, that is, his eternal power and divine nature, have been clearly seen since the creation of the world, being understood through what he has made. As a result, people are without excuse.*
> (Rom 1:20; cf. Gen 26:10; Acts 14:17)

The nations surrounding Amos's Israel knew enough about God to worship him and to refrain from sin. They did neither, so they were "without excuse." God was judging them on the basis of their sin against the light he had given to them.

God Patiently Waits before Punishing Sin

God did not send his judgment on the nations neighboring Israel after a year or two or after they committed a sin or two. They had long lived in rebellion against the one true God, and he had allowed them to go their own way until the day of his judgment finally dawned. The rhetorical device Amos used to refer to the crimes of the nations expressed that their sin had overflowed God's limit: "For three crimes, even four." That numerical pattern expressed overflowing transgression—too many transgressions. It was like saying, "Your cup of committing crimes is full; no, it's overflowing—you've poured four gallons of sin into a three-gallon bucket! You've committed too many crimes. It's time for sin to stop and punishment to begin." From the first sin committed by humanity, sin has resulted in God's punishment. God's holiness and his righteous judgment of sin are built into the structure of the universe—sin leads to death. But God in his mercy often relents from punishing sin so we'll have opportunities to turn from sin and to him. He revokes the punishment our sin deserves (Exod 34:6-7; Acts 17:30-31; 2 Pet 3:9-11).

Sometimes parents see their child do something wrong, and they refrain from punishing the child. They give the child another chance; they let the child think about the wrongdoing. To use Amos's words, they relent. But imagine that the child does the same thing again, and again the parents mercifully relent from punishment. But then the child does it again, and then a fourth time, and the parents say, "Four crimes, and you deserved punishment every time. Every time we relented, but now we will *not* relent from punishing." That's what God was saying to the nations of Amos's day. They had committed barbaric acts of cruelty against their fellow man, and God had waited for their repentance. They did not repent, so God was sending his judgment.

God Uses His People to Call the Populations of All Nations to Himself

During the period of God's patient waiting, he sends his people with his word to warn sinners to turn to him. Before destroying Nineveh, God sent Jonah to preach there. God also used prophets like Elisha, Isaiah, Jeremiah, and Ezekiel to speak his word to the nations (2 Kgs 8; Isa 13–23; Jer 46–51; Ezek 25–32). To the extent that the nations heard such preaching, they had opportunities to believe God's word and repent. Furthermore, Israel was to be a witness pointing to the one true God and his pursuit of humanity (Gen 12:1-3). God's people were to live faithfully according to God's law with the result that the nations would learn of God, his greatness, his wisdom, and his nearness to Israel (Deut 4:5-7). Much of the Old Testament reveals that Israel largely failed to be faithful to God; it also reveals that the nations largely failed to repent based on the revelation God provided them.

God's Prophetic Word Comes to Pass

Through Amos, God announced that destruction was coming on Israel's neighbors as his judgment for their sin. Each of those nations was in fact destroyed. Soon after Amos preached, the Assyrians conquered Damascus and annexed Syria into the Assyrian Empire. Later, the Assyrians also conquered the other nations surrounding Israel and took the people into exile. If the remnant populations of those lands harbored any hopes of national restoration, such hopes were eliminated by subsequent conquests by the Babylonians and Persians. God's word came to pass.

What Does Jesus Do about the Crimes of the Nations?

To answer this question, we should first remember that everything we say about what God does is also true of Jesus, since Jesus is God. Still, the New Testament reveals further truth about the way Jesus relates to the nations. As we read Amos, we should bring this fuller revelation to bear on how we live.

Jesus Is Sinless

Amos cried out against the sins of the nations, but he did so as a fellow sinner. All the people in Judah and Israel were also sinners. Jesus is the only person who has lived without participating at all in the sins of humanity (Heb 4:15).

Jesus Spoke against Sin

Amos cried out against the crimes of the nations. Jesus did too. He came preaching repentance from sin (Mark 1:14-15; Luke 13:1-5) and God's wrath against sin (Luke 21:23; John 3:36). He calls his people to be separate from sin (Matt 5:48).

Jesus Died and Rose Again for Sinners

Jesus not only preached against sin. He loves sinners so much that he gave his life's blood to deliver them all from sin (Luke 19:10; Phil 2:5-11). He calls people to turn to him for the salvation and sanctification that only he can give. People do not have to face God's wrath that was expressed against the nations of Amos's time. They can turn to Jesus to be delivered from God's judgment. Through Jesus they are justified before God and freed from sin (Rom 3:23-26).

This section began with a reference to the barbaric modern crime of human trafficking. In 2010 six Christian teenage girls heard about that tragedy, specifically as it relates to Moldova, where trafficking is so common. One night during a sleepover they talked to one another about that evil and decided to take action. They planned fundraisers, mission trips to Moldova, and connections with existing ministries. They raised thousands of dollars for multiple ministries, all aimed at setting women and children free. The church I pastored at the time helped the girls' ministry by purchasing land in Moldova, erecting a building as a refuge for women, and carrying out evangelistic ministries that resulted in many women being delivered from the clutches of slavery and many people coming to salvation in Jesus. Today the ministry continues because six teenage girls decided to speak out against evil. (For more information, see Barney et al., *Save Our Sisters*.)

In every generation wickedness exists among the nations, and in every generation God calls his people to cry out against it and to call people to salvation in Jesus. He called Amos to do that, and he calls us. We cannot be silent while so many people are being harmed so badly. Robert Raines wrote a book of prayers; he titled one of the prayers, "What's Wrong with You, Lord?"

> The headlines hit me in the face again today. . . . There
> is so much sadness, so much that doesn't need to be . . .
> shouldn't be . . . it's unfair, it's horrible! How can you make
> a world in which people starve in Pakistan, nineteen-year-old
> boys kill each other, . . . fire destroys a whole family in that
> tenement house? . . . What's wrong with you, Lord? Can't you
> do something about it? You mean . . . you expect ME to do
> something about it? Oh . . . (Raines, *Lord*, 85)

Yes, God expects us to do something about it. Amos did something. He spoke out, and even though Amos was a courageous warrior against wrong, we dare not make him the hero of this passage of Scripture. God is the hero; he is the one who stood and stands forever opposed to injustice and violence. He called Amos and gave Amos his words to speak. One day, when three transgressions become four, God himself will act against wickedness. He will intervene and punish, expressing his righteous wrath against all sin. He will consummate this age of sin and introduce a new order—a new heaven and a new earth where wickedness will never again exist.

Reflect and Discuss

1. This section opens with an account of human trafficking. What additional crimes against humanity are being committed in the world today?

2. How are people in your community being affected by crime and violence?

3. In this section, the crimes of the nations are summarized into six types of sins. Can you think of an example of each type in the world today?

4. Where can we see evidence that God has given a sense of right and wrong to all people?

5. How does it encourage and/or convict you to think that God knows all our behavior and the behavior of all nations?
6. How is God's mercy expressed in his relationship with the nations and in the person and work of Jesus?
7. In what ways does God's future judgment of the nations motivate us to obey God's Word to us?
8. What are some ways we can be like Jesus in our relationship to a world full of sin?
9. If you had the opportunity to speak a message to the people of the world, what would that message be?
10. List specific actions you and your church can take to speak and work against the crimes of the nations and of your community.

Like the Gentiles

AMOS 2:4-16

Main Idea: God calls his people to live differently from those who don't know him.

I. **When We Sin like the World, God Will Punish Us like the World (2:4,6).**
II. **When We Have God's Word, God Expects Us to Obey It (2:4-8).**
    A. God has given us his Word (2:4).
    B. God requires that we receive and obey his Word (2:4).
    C. God punishes us when we disobey his Word (2:5-8).
III. **When We Rebel against God's Grace, God Punishes Us (2:9-16).**

In his Word, numerous times God calls his people to live differently from those who don't know him. For example,

> For this is God's will, your sanctification: that you keep away from
> sexual immorality, that each of you knows how to control his own body
> in holiness and honor, not with lustful passions, like the Gentiles, who
> don't know God. (1 Thess 4:3-5)

Sadly, sometimes people who profess to know and love God behave "like the Gentiles, who don't know God." Yet God communicates a way of thinking and living that will always contrast with the ways of the world, the flesh, and the devil. The Didache, a manual of discipleship in the church that originated in the early second century AD, describes the contrast between the two lifestyles in this way: "There are two ways, one of life and one of death; but a great difference between the two ways" (Roberts and Donaldson, *Ante-Nicene Fathers*, 377). Early church leaders used the Didache to disciple new believers because they wanted Christians to understand what the Bible says about the vast difference between the way of the world and the way of following Jesus.

God made plain to Israel that he wanted them to live differently, according to his law. For example, Leviticus 18:3-5 records that while Israel was still in the wilderness and before they entered Canaan, God said to them,

*"Do not follow the practices of the land of Egypt, where you used
to live, or follow the practices of the land of Canaan, where I am
bringing you. You must not follow their customs. You are to practice
my ordinances and you are to keep my statutes by following them; I am
the LORD your God. Keep my statutes and ordinances; a person will
live if he does them. I am the LORD."*

God promised continued life for his people when they walked in his way,
and he implied the end of life for those who walked in the ways of the
Egyptians or Canaanites. God later made that implication explicit. He
told Israel that living his way would lengthen life; living in disobedience
would invite his judgment and the end of life (Lev 26; Deut 27–28).
Through Amos, God announced that he was about to bring his promised judgment to pass.

When We Sin like the World, God Will Punish Us like the World
AMOS 2:4,6

In verse 4 God stated that his punishment was coming to Judah; in verse
6 God stated that his punishment was coming to Israel. God introduced
his judgment on both nations in the same way. It was the same way he
had introduced his judgment on the nations surrounding them. The
sins of Judah and Israel that Amos listed indicate that they were similar spiritually and morally to the Gentiles around them. We should not
assume the people of Judah and Israel were believers in the one true
God. On the contrary, when we read about the way they were living, it
seems that many or most of the people were not living by faith in him.
God chose Israel and Judah to be his people and live in a covenant relationship with him. Many of them were not doing so. Therefore, when we
speak of "Israel" and "Judah," we should be careful not to equate those
terms with the believing people of God. The historical books and the
preaching of the prophets make clear that Israel and Judah were political entities composed of believers and unbelievers.

   God was going to respond to Judah and Israel in the same way he
responds to all sin. The formula, "The LORD says: I will not relent from
punishing _____ for three crimes, even four, because . . ." was used
in the case of every nation, including Judah and Israel (1:3,6,9,11,13;
2:1,4,6). God was relating to Judahites and Israelites in the same way,

with the same words, as he was relating to the pagan nations around them. He was doing so because they were living in sin, as were the pagan nations around them.

Israel had weathered difficult relationships with all of those nations and had been at war with them at various moments in history. Only a generation before, Judah's King Amaziah had enticed Jeroboam's father, Jehoash, into war (2 Kgs 14:8-16; 2 Chron 25:17-24). Jeroboam also engaged in military action against his neighbors in extending the border of Israel during his reign (2 Kgs 14:25). In light of all their conflict with these nations, when the Israelites heard that God was going to punish them, they probably did not feel grief. But based on all that Amos wrote in his book about the Israelites, we can be confident they did not think they would suffer the same fate as other nations. God's announcement of judgment delivered by Amos was both unwelcome and surprising.

Most commentators make much of the geographical order of God's announcement of judgment against the nations (reviewed in chapter 2). It seems likely that such an order was intentional, a rhetorical strategy that crisscrossed Israel as Amos described the sins of neighboring people groups. As the Israelites who heard Amos agreed with God's punishment in each case, surely it would have become harder and harder for them to disagree with God's punishment of their own sin. Amos hemmed in the Israelites, geographically and morally, to impress on their conscience the truth that when we sin like the Gentiles, God will punish us like the Gentiles.

When We Have God's Word, God Expects Us to Obey It
AMOS 2:4-8

God Has Given Us His Word (2:4)

In verse 4 the Lord stated that Judah was guilty of rejecting his instruction and not obeying his statutes. Such sins may seem tame after reading about the violence of other nations in 1:3–2:3. Maybe that's what we think because we do not attach enough significance to the fact that the one true God of the universe has spoken to us in his Word. If the God who created us has spoken to humanity in Scripture, then no knowledge is as important as knowing what he has said. Nothing we can do is as important as doing what he tells us to do. May we never undervalue God's communication to us in his Word. As Francis Schaeffer put it,

> [M]an, beginning with himself, can define the philosophical problem of existence, but he cannot generate from himself the answer to the problem. The answer to the problem of existence is that the infinite-personal, triune God is there, and the infinite-personal, triune God is not silent. (*He Is There and He Is Not Silent*, 19)

We would not know how to define reality without God's Word; we would not know how to live successfully without God's Word.

Failing to treasure God's Word is heinous sin. When people do not respect what we say, they do not respect us. Showing a lack of respect for what God has said is showing a lack of respect for God, and that is blasphemy. When we treasure God, we will treasure his Word. When we love God, we will love his Word.

God Requires That We Receive and Obey His Word (2:4)

God's punishment was coming to Judah because the people were rejecting God's prophetic words to them (v. 4). Instead of rejecting God's Word, we are to receive it and order our lives according to its mandates. Years ago, for three summers I spent about a month each year participating in archaeological excavations in Israel. I loved being in that land, but being away from my family was hard. In those days, few people had email or cell phones. I was staying in a rustic area, and I had to walk all the way into town to use a pay phone. I did that once per week, but during the week it's an understatement to say that I looked forward to receiving letters from my wife. Every afternoon I rushed to the area where the mail was delivered to search for a letter from her. When I received a letter from her, I would take it back to my room, read it several times, laugh and cry as I read, cite parts of the letter to the professor who was my roommate, and quote portions of it to others over dinner.

I valued those letters highly because I love the person who wrote them. We value God's Word highly for the same reason. God sent us his Word because he loves us. If we love him, we'll love his Word. Since God loves us, he has given his book to us because he wants us to know the truth, and he wants us to know and love him. When we understand that, we'll understand what Jesus said: "Man must not live on bread alone but on every word that comes from the mouth of God" (Matt 4:4). When we love God, we must have his Word to live, and we'll live according to his Word. If the people of Judah knew God's Word, they were not obeying it.

God Punishes Us When We Disobey His Word (2:5-8)

Rejecting God's word and not obeying his law led to far-reaching consequences in Judah and Israel. In Judah's case, God said, "The lies that their ancestors followed / have led them astray" (v. 4). They chose to follow lies instead of God's truth. Specifically, "the lies that their ancestors followed" could refer to the worship of pagan gods practiced by Abraham's family of origin (Josh 24:2), or it could refer to something closer historically to Amos. Jesus said that the devil is "a liar and the father of lies" (John 8:44). His first temptation to sin involved an explicit denial of the truth of what God had said (Gen 3:1-5). Though we don't know the identity of the lies that led the Judahites astray, we know who was behind them—the same adversary who is behind all the lies we encounter today.

In the case of Israel, disobeying God's law led to a greedy, unjust, licentious disordering of society. Amos 2:6 says of Israel, "They sell a righteous person for silver." Evidently, they were selling righteous persons into slavery for a particular price in silver. Verse 6 also says they were selling "a needy person for a pair of sandals." Either (1) they were selling needy persons into slavery for the price of sandals, (2) they were selling needy persons into slavery because the needy people owed an amount that equaled the value of a pair of sandals, or (3) judges were accepting bribes as small as the value of sandals to convict poor people.

Verse 7 says, "They trample the heads of the poor / on the dust of the ground." The situation being described is unclear. Some translators see this as referring to trampling the heads of the poor into the dust (ESV, CSB). Others translate it as referring to panting for/coveting even the dust on the heads of the poor (NASB, KJV), desiring to destroy the poor whose heads are already in the dust, or desiring the land of the poor even though it further impoverishes them (Lev 25:23-34). What is clear is that Israelites were oppressing poor people.

Verse 7 also says, "A man and his father have sexual relations / with the same girl." Since Baalistic cult prostitution was practiced in Israel (1 Kgs 15:12; 22:46; 2 Kgs 23:7; Hos 4:14), this could refer to sexual promiscuity as part of a pagan fertility rite. It could also refer to some other decadent practice like incest or an orgy. One scholar proposes a nonsexual interpretation, suggesting that the woman was a hostess at a sacred banquet associated with Baalism (the banquet in 2:8 and 6:7); thus the sin was association with idolatry (Barstad, *Religious Polemics*, 33–36). Amos was not interested in describing the circumstances in lurid detail. He was simply stating their guilt for committing sexual sin. In doing so, God said they were "profaning my holy name." God's name is "holy" because God is holy; he is other than, separate, different. Thus, when Israelites behaved like the Gentiles, they were violating the otherness that was to characterize the people who belonged to the God who is holy. They were treating him as if he were not different from other gods, and they were living as if they were not different from other peoples.

In verse 8 Amos identified two more sins of the Israelites. First, "they stretch out beside every altar / on garments taken as collateral." According to Exodus 22:25, when Israelites took a garment as collateral from the poor, they were to return the garment the same day. That practice would ensure that the poor would be able to stay warm at night. Amos stated that Israelites were keeping such garments in disobedience to God's law. Archaeological excavation has unearthed a document that attests to the behavior Amos described. A day laborer in Israel complained to a local authority that the worker's supervisor had taken his cloak, presumably as collateral to make sure the laborer would finish his work quota. The worker wrote,

> Despite the fact that your servant had completed his assigned work, Hoshaiahu, son of Shobai, kept your servant's cloak. He has held my cloak for days. . . . All those who work in the heat of the day will surely certify that I am not guilty of any breach of contract. Please order my supervisor to return my cloak. (Matthews and Benjamin, *Old Testament Parallels*, 355–56)

The supervisor in question was an example of the behavior Amos was describing; he was not in compliance with Exodus 22:25 and was not showing compassion for his worker. Amos went on to describe Israelites "stretching out" on the garments near altars, either sleeping or eating on them. Also, "in the house of their God / they drink wine obtained through fines." That seems to indicate a banquet or party in a worship space that included drinking wine that had been used to pay a fine, or wine purchased with funds given to pay a fine. Either way, the banqueters were enjoying free wine, provided to them by the poor.

The Israelites were ordering their society according to greed, oppression, injustice, and carnal desire. In his law God commanded his people to care for the poor, but instead Israelites were oppressing the poor and using them to further their own material gain. God commanded his people to reserve sex for marriage, but instead Israelites were behaving "with lustful passions, like the Gentiles, who don't know God" (1 Thess 4:5).

When We Rebel against God's Grace, God Punishes Us
AMOS 2:9-16

The disobedience of the people of Israel was even more astonishing in light of the grace God had shown them in the past. In verses 9-11 God reviewed part of the history of his gracious dealings with Israel. First, God said, "I destroyed the Amorite as Israel advanced"—a reference to the conquest of Canaan. God also referred to the height and strength of the Amorites/Canaanites (v. 9), emphasizing that the conquest was his work of grace, since the Israelites could not have conquered Canaan without God's help. Second, God referred to his gracious deliverance of Israel from slavery in Egypt and his provision for them through the Sinai wilderness (v. 10). Third, God referred to his grace to Israel in sending persons to preach and live his word—prophets and Nazirites (v. 11).

God gave Israel his word. He rescued them from slavery in Egypt. He miraculously provided for them throughout forty years of wandering through the wilderness. He sent prophets to them to remind them of his law and call them to return to him. In light of all that God had done for Israel, surely they would recognize his goodness and grace to them and respond in grateful obedience. On the contrary, they rebelled against God in spite of all he had done for them. They enticed the Nazirites to break their Nazirite vows by drinking wine, and they commanded the prophets to stop preaching.

In verses 13-16 God spoke of the forms of his coming judgment against Israel. Some of the language is figurative, such as crushing them as a wagon is crushed under a full load of grain (v. 13). Some of the language, however, seems to be literal descriptions of military defeat—warriors and archers failing, people fleeing but not escaping, and the cavalry falling. Such events occurred only a few decades after

Amos preached. Under King Tiglath-Pileser III, the Assyrians began military incursions into Israel in the 730s BC. By 722 BC Israel's capital of Samaria fell to the Assyrians, and Israel ceased to exist as a political entity. The judgment of God had come in response to the sin of Israel (2 Kgs 17:5-18) and in fulfillment of his promise (Lev 26:14-33).

As Amos did, followers of Jesus should look back in history to recall all of God's gracious acts on our behalf. God has done even more for us than for Israel. For several chapters, the author of Hebrews developed the idea of the superiority of the new covenant over the old covenant, and then he asked,

> *How much worse punishment do you think one will deserve who has trampled on the Son of God, who has regarded as profane the blood of the covenant by which he was sanctified, and who has insulted the Spirit of grace?* (Heb 10:29)

Reviewing God's saving acts for us should compel us to gratitude, worship, and obedience. If we trample on God's grace by rebelling against him, we can expect his judgment.

Just as Amos could recall the exodus, the wilderness provision, the gift of the law, and the preaching of God's prophets, Christians today can recall God coming to us as a baby in Bethlehem, his sacrificial death for us on the cross, his resurrection, and his gifts of forgiveness, sanctification, the church, the Holy Spirit, and heaven. How can we rebel against God after all he has done for us? If we rebel, we will surely not escape God's condemnation for our sin (Rom 2:4-11). Thank God that followers of Jesus do not have to worry about eternal condemnation, since "there is now no condemnation for those in Christ Jesus" (Rom 8:1). God has given us eternal life as a gift when we put our faith in Christ (Rom 6:23). But because God is just, we will give an account for our works, and we do not want to lose our reward (1 Cor 3:11-13; 2 Cor 5:10).

Reflect and Discuss

1. This section includes a few passages of Scripture outside the book of Amos that call God's people to a holy life. Can you think of other passages with that theme?
2. Create a list of ways followers of Jesus will always be different from unbelievers, or "the Gentiles."

3. Identify behaviors in your life that are like unbelievers and do not reflect obedience to God's Word. Identify such behaviors in the church at large. What will it take for such behavior to change?
4. When Christians live like unbelievers, in what ways will God punish them?
5. How does it change your reading of the Old Testament to realize that not all Israelites and Judahites had put their faith in Israel's covenant God?
6. What are some ways we can assess the extent to which we treasure God's words to us in the Bible?
7. Read James 1:22. In what ways have you been a hearer but not a doer of God's Word? What have you learned from the Bible that you are not living?
8. What have you done to help the poor? What are you doing now? In what ways do contemporary societies oppress the poor?
9. Why was sexual sin a strong temptation for Israelites? Why is it a strong temptation today?
10. How has God shown grace in your life? List the ways. How should you respond to such acts of grace?

When God's People Stray

AMOS 3

Main Idea: Amos shows us how extreme backsliding can occur and how to avoid it.

I. God's People Stray When God Delivers but They Disobey (3:1-2).
II. God's People Stray When God Speaks but They Don't Fear (3:3-8).
III. God's People Stray When God Calls Them to a Mission but They Fail (3:9-10).
IV. When God's People Stray, God Will Punish, and None Will Escape (3:11-15).

In his book *Broken but Beautiful*, Joseph P. Conway tells of reading a newspaper article in his city's paper when he was about eleven years old. The article reported that a man had attempted to kidnap a woman in a local park and hold her for ransom. When the kidnapping did not go as planned, the man killed her. It was a horrible act, yet Conway writes that he was even more shaken when he read that the perpetrator was a deacon in a local church. Conway was a young Christian when he read those words. He knew deacons. He would never have thought they were capable of such an act. But it had happened. At age eleven, Conway writes, his innocence about the church was shattered (*Broken but Beautiful*, 8).

The innocence of many people has been shattered. Sadly, sin, even egregious sin, is in the church of Jesus Christ. Ten percent of Americans identify as Christians who once attended a church but don't anymore (Barna, "Meet Those Who Love Jesus"). Without doubt, one reason for such a statistic is the sin in the church. People have read about the abuses and scandalous cover-ups in the Catholic church. Among Protestants, people have seen one church leader after another exposed for sexual or financial impropriety. People by the thousands have concluded, "The church is broken. I've seen enough. Count me out."

When people read of the extent of sin in ancient Israel, a natural impulse is to be shocked and ask, "How could this have happened?" But when we take a hard look at God's people today, our shock diminishes as we realize God's people are still straying far from the holiness God intends for his people. In some cases, the people who stray are church members who have never been born again. That situation underscores the importance of a regenerate church membership. Sometimes those who stray are disciples of Jesus who lapse into the misery of sin. The third chapter of Amos helps us see how extreme backsliding can occur and how to avoid it.

God's People Stray When God Delivers but They Disobey
AMOS 3:1-2

In the first verse of chapter 3, God reminded the people of Israel that he had delivered them from slavery in Egypt. Israel was sinning against God's great grace (cf. 2:10). God's grace and kindness are meant to lead us to repentance (Rom 2:4), but the people of Israel were trampling on God's grace and rebelling against him.

In verse 2 God referred to his unique relationship with Israel: "I have known only you / out of all the clans of the earth." God was not denying his omniscience, as if he did not know other people groups. In Amos 1:3–2:3 and 9:7, God states that he knows other nations, he knows their deeds, and he has been involved in their histories. It's also true that God had a special relationship with Israel. He had established a unique covenant with Israel, he had given them his law, and the promised messianic seed of Abraham was to come from them. No other nation had received the benefit of such revelation and attention from God. As Israel was preparing to enter the promised land, Moses referred to the unique blessings God had showered on Israel, and Moses asked, "Has anything like this great event ever happened, or has anything like it been heard of?" (Deut 4:32). The answer is no. What God did for Israel was unique in human history. "I have known only you." And why did God act in that way toward Israel? Moses gave the reason: "Because he loved your ancestors, he chose their descendants after them and brought you out of Egypt by his presence and great power" (Deut 4:37). God chose Israel because he loved them.

The consequences of disobedience (Deut 4:3-5,21-22), Israel's responsibility to be an example to the nations (Deut 4:6-9), and the uniqueness of the relationship between God and Israel (Deut 4:31-38) should have been more than enough to motivate Israel to faithfulness to their covenant with God. Nevertheless, Israel was unfaithful to God, again and again. Chronologically, Amos stood on the other side of that long history of unfaithfulness. Through him, God reminded his people that they had been sinning against the powerful realities of his holiness, love, and grace—realities Moses had preached to their ancestors.

We might have expected God to say, "I have known only you out of all the clans of the earth, so because of that special relationship, I will exempt you from my judgment." But the fact that God had given them more revelation and more grace made them more accountable. Jesus said, "From everyone who has been given much, much will be required; and from the one who has been entrusted with much, even more will be expected" (Luke 12:48).

In Shakespeare's play *Henry IV*, as a young man Henry lives a wild, decadent life. But when his father, the king, dies, Henry changes. He realizes he has been given the crown through no achievement of his own, and he determines to live worthy of his status. At one point he says,

"The tide of blood in me
Hath proudly flowed in vanity till now:
Now doth it turn . . .
Where it shall . . .
flow henceforth in formal majesty." (*Complete Works*, vol. 11,
    266)

He realized the privilege and position granted to him called for greater responsibility and duty.

God gave Israel great privilege: the privilege of living in a covenant relationship with the God of the universe, the privilege of being a kingdom of priests. That privilege called for greater responsibility and duty. But after all God had done for them, they broke their covenant obligations and squandered their priestly position. So God said, "I have known only you / out of all the clans of the earth; / therefore, I will punish you for all your iniquities." It's a sobering word for us. How much truth has God revealed to us? We're responsible to obey and share that truth.

Just as God gave to Israel the gifts of deliverance, his word, and his grace, God has given gifts to us. In fact, everything we have is a gift from God. First Corinthians 4:7 asks us, "What do you have that you didn't receive?" Realizing that every gift we have, every breath we take, is a gift from God should motivate us to humility, gratitude, and obedience. God has given us our intellect, our voice, our time, our possessions, our athletic or musical abilities, our health, and so many other gifts.

Are we using those gifts for his glory or for our own pleasure? God also sacrificed himself on the cross for our sin (2 Cor 5:15-21), he forgave us and canceled the sin debt we owed (Col 2:13-14), he rescued us from spiritual death (Eph 2:4-5), he reconciled us to himself (Col 1:19-22), he adopted us into his family (Gal 4:4-5), and he gave us eternal life (John 3:16; Rom 6:23). Sinning against such lavish grace and love is showing a shameful level of ingratitude for what God has done for us.

When parents provide food, shelter, clothing, love, and guidance for a child year after year, how awful it is when a child chooses to rebel against such love and despise a parent. It's difficult to imagine such a level of ingratitude, but it happens all the time. Such parental love and grace, however, are finite and limited by the parents' sinful nature. God's love and grace are infinite and perfectly holy (Eph 3:18-19). He has provided for us not mere earthly gifts but a new nature and eternal life in heaven. To sin against such immeasurable grace is infinitely worse than committing sin against any fellow mortal. No wonder God's judgment was coming. No wonder God said, "I will punish you for all your iniquities" (Amos 3:2).

God's People Stray When God Speaks but They Don't Fear
AMOS 3:3-8

Beginning in verse 3, Amos presents a series of rhetorical questions that continues through the first part of verse 6. In verses 3–5, the six questions are identical in form, and the answer to each question is no. "Can two walk together / without agreeing to meet?" How unlikely is that? Two people walking side by side, matching stride for stride, merely by coincidence is a virtual statistical impossibility, and if we actually experienced it, we would feel awkward toward the stranger walking next to us. "Does a lion roar in the forest / when it has no prey?" That doesn't happen, and anyone who knows about the behavior of lions is aware of that. The same is true for young lions; they don't growl unless they have captured something. "Does a bird land in a trap on the ground / if there is no bait for it? / Does a trap spring from the ground /when it has caught nothing?" Those things don't happen either.

Verse 6 has two more rhetorical questions, but the questions appear in a different form from the first six. The Christian Standard Bible reflects the difference by translating them as questions that expect a positive answer, not negative as the previous six questions. The change in form serves as a grammatical signal that the content is about to change. "If a ram's horn is blown in a city, / aren't people afraid?" Yes, one purpose of blowing such a horn was to warn the residents of a city that danger was approaching, so people were naturally afraid when they heard that sound. And that question brings Amos to the finale to which all his rhetorical questions have been building.

All of Amos's rhetorical questions have something in common: the answer is absolutely certain. Amos was using those questions to prepare his hearers to understand that what he was about to say next was also absolutely certain. Specifically, three powerful truths are certain. First, God rules his world in such a way that he superintends all events, good and bad. As Amos expresses it, "If a disaster occurs in a city, / hasn't the Lord done it?" (v. 6). Yes, the Lord has done it. Second, God is not mute regarding his plans; he reveals his work in redemptive history. "Indeed, the Lord God does nothing / without revealing his counsel / to his servants the prophets" (v. 7). The Israelites should have known that, after God had used Moses to give his law and used the prophets to preach his truth (Amos 2:11-12). Third, when God speaks, people should respond with worship and obedience. Amos says, "A lion has roared; / who will not fear? / The Lord God has spoken; / who will not prophesy?" (v. 8). The lion here is God. When God speaks his word to a prophet, the prophet prophesies that word to the people. When God roars his word to the people, those people fear. Such responses to the revealed word of God should be as certain as the answers to all Amos's rhetorical questions.

Why should we respond with fear to God's word? In the case of the Israelites during Amos's lifetime, fear was especially appropriate because God's word through Amos was an announcement of coming judgment. But fear is always a proper response to hearing God's word. God says, "I will look favorably on this kind of person: one who is humble, submissive in spirit, and trembles at my word" (Isa 66:2).

In the Bible, the words *fear not* and *do not be afraid* occur hundreds of times. God has clearly communicated the message that his people are not to be afraid of the things other people fear. On the other hand, the Bible repeatedly states that we are to fear God. Proverbs 9:10 says, "The fear of the Lord is the beginning of wisdom." We don't *begin* to live wisely until we fear God. A lot of people fear people more than they fear God. Proverbs 29:25 says, "The fear of mankind is a snare, / but the one who trusts in the Lord is protected." The snare of the fear of mankind is the trap of thinking about what people think instead of what God thinks. *What do they think about the way I look or the way I talk? What's their opinion of me?* And we think that way to the neglect of thinking about what really matters, which is what God thinks of us. Are our hearts right before God? Who knows? We're preoccupied with wondering what people think about us—we're ensnared.

When we fear God instead of man, we do what God wants, even if it means going against the grain. Shiphrah and Puah were the two Hebrew midwives Pharaoh commanded to kill the Hebrew male babies in Egypt. In a courageous act of civil disobedience, they disobeyed the man who had the power to put them to death. Why? Exodus 1:17 says, "The midwives . . . feared God." They did *not* fear the most powerful man in the world; they feared God. If they disobeyed Pharaoh, they knew they would have to answer to him. But they also knew that if they disobeyed God, they would have to answer to him. Jesus said, "Don't fear those who kill the body, and after that can do nothing more. But I will show you the one to fear: Fear him who has authority to throw people into hell after death" (Luke 12:4-5). Jesus said we should not fear people; we should fear God, who can send us to eternal judgment in hell.

Even after we become Christians, we continue to fear God. Philippians 2:12-13 is addressed to Christians: "Work out your own salvation with fear and trembling. For it is God who is working in you both to will and to work according to his good purpose." In other words, the one who is working in you is God, so live out your salvation with a healthy fear of him. Some people hear about fearing God and they say, "I thought we were supposed to love God and feel close to God." Yes! Jesus said the greatest commandment is to love God, but he also said to fear God. As we emphasize loving God, we cannot exclude fearing God; we cannot forget the holiness, power, and judgment of the God we are to love.

God's People Stray When God Calls Them to a Mission but They Fail
AMOS 3:9-10

When God made a covenant with his people at Mount Sinai, he told them, "If you will carefully listen to me and keep my covenant . . . , you will be my kingdom of priests and my holy nation" (Exod 19:5-6). The role of a priest is to represent God to people and to intercede for the people to God. God's covenant intention from the beginning was for the entire nation of Israel to be a "kingdom of priests." All Israel was to represent the one true God to the world and intercede for the world to God. As Moses was calling the next generation to obey God's covenant stipulations, Moses said,

> *Carefully follow them, for this will show your wisdom and understanding in the eyes of the peoples. When they hear about all these statutes, they will say, "This great nation is indeed a wise and understanding people."* (Deut 4:6)

God's covenant with Israel had a missional purpose. God intended for other people groups to look at Israel's obedience to his commands and conclude that he is the one true God and living in a faithful relationship with him is leading a successful life.

The Old Testament indicates that Israel never fulfilled God's missional purpose for them. When they arrived in Canaan, instead of living according to God's law, they began to adopt the religious practices and immoral lifestyle of the Canaanites. Idolatry was ubiquitous throughout the history of Israel. By the time of Amos's generation, Israelites had been mixing the worship of God with the worship of Baal and other deities for more than six hundred years, and Israel was rife with sin.

Verses 9-10 underscore how far Israel had strayed from God's missional calling. Instead of Israel displaying to the world the wisdom of following God's word, God invited neighboring nations to witness how awful Israel had become. He invited them to "assemble on the mountains of Samaria, / and see" all the turmoil and oppression in the capital city. Israel's sin had advanced so far that even pagan nations would be able to identify Israel as wicked. Such a scenario is the opposite of what God had planned for his people. God had called Israel to be a witness to the world, but now God was inviting the world to witness Israel's sin.

God has also called today's church to a global mission. We are to live differently from the people who do not know and follow the one true God. Those people will see the wise way we live and be drawn to the God who tells us to live that way. Jesus called us to be "the light of the world," and he said, "Let your light shine before others, so that they may see your good works and give glory to your Father in heaven" (Matt 5:14-16). We live so that people see our good works, and the result is that they glorify God, because he is the one who told us to live this way. Jesus also said we are witnesses to the world (Acts 1:8) through telling the gospel story, and he commanded his followers to make disciples of all nations (Matt 28:19-20).

Sin compromises the church's ability to fulfill God's mission. Sin can become so common that the church may actually become a negative witness. When sin becomes deeply imbedded in the life of the church, a community or nation can look at the church as an example of the way *not* to live. God's people should pray that no church will ever reach that point. We should pray that when the world looks at any church they will think of our Savior, not our sin. What can happen to the witness of a church can also happen to the witness of an individual Christian. Christians can become so involved in sin that they are living more like the sinful culture than like our sinless Savior. Such sin spoils their witness for Christ. When people look at such Christians, they think of the power of sin, not the power of our Savior to set us free from sin. We do not want the world to be invited to watch churches or Christians in order to see how awful they have become.

When God's People Stray, God Will Punish, and None Will Escape
AMOS 3:11-15

"Therefore" in verse 11 introduces the consequence of Israel's sins mentioned in verses 9-10, and the consequence is God's judgment. The theme of the final five verses of chapter 3 is God's coming judgment, and God delivers a fourfold message regarding that judgment. First, his judgment would be **military**. In verse 11 God states, "An enemy will surround the land; / he will destroy your strongholds / and plunder your citadels." It seems best to interpret that statement as literal, not figurative, especially in light of the fact that exactly what the verse describes occurred about forty or fifty years after Amos prophesied (724–722 BC). The Assyrian army surrounded Samaria and besieged the city for three years. In 722 BC, Assyrian soldiers breached the city, and Samaria fell. That event marks the end of the northern kingdom of Israel. Through Amos and others, God announced that Israel's fall was God's judgment against the sinful kingdom. The Assyrian army was the immediate cause, but God was bringing it about because of the extent of Israel's wickedness.

Second, God's judgment would be **violent**. In verse 12 God symbolized his judgment as a lion dismembering a sheep. Only a piece of an ear and a few legs remain after the lion is finished with its attack. Some commentators point to the custom of a hired shepherd providing pieces of a sheep to the owner to prove the shepherd did not steal or lose the sheep (Gen 31:39; Garrett, *Amos*, 97–98; Andersen and Freedman, *Amos*, 408). Such a custom may have been familiar to Amos's hearers, but the point of this verse is not the responsibility of the shepherd but the total destruction of the sheep. The point is also not that part of Israel would be spared but that the sheep is dead. This is sarcasm; God was mocking those who were saying that he would deliver Israel. "Yes," Amos replies, "Israel will be spared, in the same way a piece of a sheep's ear is spared after a lion's attack." Of all the buildings in all the cities in Israel, "only the corner of a bed / or the cushion of a couch" will be spared. If someone were to say, "At least something is saved," it would be a tragic joke. "No! Everybody is gone and everything is destroyed."

Third, God's judgment would be **aimed at the centers of false worship**. When God said, "Listen and testify against the house of Jacob" (v. 13), he was continuing to address Ashdod and Egypt (v. 9), calling those pagan nations to listen to the evidence against Israel and to testify that Israel was guilty. Israel was guilty of corrupt worship, so God would target religious centers in his judgment against them. He mentions "the altars of Bethel"—surely a synecdoche for the entire shrine at Bethel, and perhaps also its personnel. "The horns of the altar will be cut off" indicates total destruction. The worship site at Bethel was illicit, built when the kingdom split as a competitor to the legitimate temple in Jerusalem. At that time its eventual destruction was prophesied (1 Kgs 12:27–13:3). Here Amos also prophesied its destruction, and it was indeed destroyed by Josiah over a century after Amos prophesied (2 Kgs 23:15).

Fourth, God's judgment would be **aimed at signs of opulence**. The "winter house" and "the summer house" may refer to the two royal palaces built in a former generation by King Ahab, one in Jezreel and the other in Samaria (1 Kgs 21:1,18). An Aramean king named Barrakab, roughly a contemporary of Amos, also recorded references to his winter house and his summer house (King, *Amos, Hosea, Micah*, 64–65). Other wealthy people may have had similar arrangements, as wealthy people today own multiple homes. "The houses inlaid with ivory" also would have been owned by wealthy people; ivory was rare and had to be imported from Africa. The book of Amos shows that wealthy Israelites were oppressing the poor and likely growing wealthier by taking advantage of the poor. God said, "I will demolish" the multiple houses of the wealthy; their richly decorated houses "will be destroyed, / and the great houses will come to an end."

How do contemporary Christians apply this stern word of judgment? First, we give heed to ourselves. God will judge us according to our works. Perhaps we should hold Romans 8:1 and Ephesians 2:8 in one hand and 2 Corinthians 5:10 and Hebrews 2:3 in the other hand. Romans 8:1 affirms, "There is now no condemnation for those in Christ Jesus." Christians will not be condemned by God's judgment; he gave us the gift of eternal life when we put our faith in Jesus (John 3:16; Rom 6:23). We are "saved by grace through faith," not works (Eph 2:8). Jesus bore the judgment for our sin on the cross; he took God's righteous wrath for our sin on himself so he could offer us free forgiveness (2 Cor 5:21). Praise his name! Thus, our eternal salvation is not contingent on our good works.

In the other hand we hold the fact that God will judge us in the end somehow according to our works. Second Corinthians 5:10 is addressed to Christians; it says, "We must all appear before the judgment seat of Christ, so that each may be repaid for what he has done in the body, whether good or evil." We will answer to God for what we do. Hebrews 2 also warns of an accounting for the way we live out our salvation in Christ. After referring to God's judgment of sin in the times before Christ, the writer asks concerning salvation in Christ, "How will we escape if we neglect such a great salvation?" (v. 3). If God punished Israel for their sin against his grace, how will we escape judgment if we sin against God's greater grace in Christ? Again, Christians need not worry about eternal judgment; all the promises of God regarding our eternal home in heaven are true, and we will experience their glorious fulfillment. But the Bible affirms that in some way God will hold us accountable for our deeds. That sobering truth motivates us to shun sin and seek holiness.

Second, in applying God's strong word of judgment through Amos, we should remember that one day God will condemn sin finally and completely. God's judgment of Israel, and of every other nation in the past, was penultimate. One day God will eradicate all evil, injustice, wrong, immorality, hatred, and prejudice. God will cause right to prevail, and his people will enjoy being in his presence without sin forever. Sin will not be in heaven, but God will be there, and so will those whose names are written in the Lamb's Book of Life (Rev 21:1-8,22-27). Praise his name!

Before God's final judgment, God is calling people to himself from every tribe and every nation so that every person will avoid eternal judgment and live in his eternal presence. His church is extending his invitation to the nations and calling all people to come to faith in Jesus before it's too late. "God is making his appeal through us" (2 Cor 5:20). We have put our faith in Jesus, and he has saved us. Now we are part of God's plan to tell all people about the salvation he offers. "A lion has roared; / who will not fear? / The Lord God has spoken; / who will not prophesy?" (Amos 3:8).

Reflect and Discuss

1. This section begins with a story about sin in the church. Do you know such stories? Recall them silently and pray that such events will not be repeated and that God will strengthen you, protect the vulnerable, and heal his church.
2. Reflect on God's great gifts of love and grace to us. What should be our response to God's grace?
3. How is it infinitely worse to sin against God's immeasurable grace than to commit sin against any fellow mortal?
4. Recall what this section states about fearing God. Do you have a biblical fear of God? How do you know?
5. Should God's Word cause us to fear? Why or why not?
6. Why do you think people fear people more than they fear God?
7. How is God's mission for the church similar to and different from God's mission for Israel? Are you fulfilling God's mission for his church?
8. How does the church's purity relate to the church's mission?
9. Consider what this section states about God judging Christians according to our works. What difference might that truth make in our lives and in the church?
10. How can believers in Christ today be assured of their eternal salvation and presence in heaven?

Let Them Eat Cake

AMOS 4:1-5

Main Idea: Amos condemned rich people who were oblivious to the plight of the poor and needy.

I.   Let's Serve the Poor, Not Mistreat Them (4:1).
II. God Punishes People Who Mistreat the Poor (4:2-3).
III. Religious Rituals Won't Make Things Better (4:4-5).

Marie Antoinette was born and raised in Austria in the middle of the eighteenth century. When she was a teenager, she was betrothed to Louis XVI of France, who was the crown prince. In 1774, Louis XVI ascended the throne, and Marie Antoinette was the queen of France before she was twenty years old. She had been born into a wealthy family in Austria, and she became even more wealthy as queen. During the days of her reign, a poor crop harvest and other factors led to an increase in poverty. She continued to live an opulent lifestyle, spending much of her time in the palace in Versailles, separated from the common people in the streets of Paris. Such disparity between the wealthy and poor classes caused increasing turmoil in France. In the midst of the crisis of poverty, reputedly Marie Antoinette heard someone comment that the poor had no bread to eat, and she replied, "Let them eat cake."

Today, people question whether Marie Antoinette actually said those words, since documentation is sparse and late (Cunningham, "Did Marie-Antoinette?"; Nadeau, "The Real Story"). But no one doubts the existence of the sentiment expressed by that statement—callousness toward the poor on the part of the rich. One doesn't need to search far to find stories of aristocrats who are oblivious to the plight of common people. And lack of sympathy is certainly not limited to women; wealthy men have also demonstrated insensitivity to people of meager means. Of course, many people of great wealth are among the most kind, generous, and compassionate people on the planet, but Amos was addressing people who seem to have been none of that.

184

Let's Serve the Poor, Not Mistreat Them
AMOS 4:1

Amos 4 begins with an imperative: "Listen to this message." Those same words begin chapters 3 and 5, and in every case the verb is in the imperative form. What follows the imperative that heads those three chapters are oracles that highlight four big ideas: God's gracious work in the history of Israel, Israel's current rebellion against God, the judgment of God that was about to fall on Israel, and the offer (at least implied) to return to a faithful relationship with God. The three chapters and their oracles differ in their details, but they toll essentially the same warning.

The oracle in chapter 4 begins by specifically addressing "cows of Bashan." Bashan was a geographical region east of the Sea of Galilee, a large area stretching from well south of the sea into the hills north of the sea. Bashan was agriculturally rich; the references to Bashan in the Old Testament indicate that the name was proverbial for fertile crops and well-fed livestock. Amos was using "cows of Bashan" as a figurative reference to people, and these "cows of Bashan" were on "the hill of Samaria." Samaria was the capital of the northern kingdom of Israel, and it was located on a hill. No cows grazed on the acropolis of Samaria; people lived and worked there, including the royal family and their courtiers. Amos, then, was referring to those people, at least some of them, as cows. Calling someone a cow in the time of Amos was surely no more complimentary than calling someone a cow today. And since "cows of *Bashan*" were well-fed cows, Amos was also referring to the wealth of these people, their size, or both. When Amos addressed his audience in that way, he surely had their attention, though probably not their affection. These opening words indicate that Amos was not preaching this message to win friends but to deliver a stern warning from God.

The fact that Amos was figuratively referring to people, not literal cows, is made more clear by the sins these "cows" were committing. They were oppressing the poor and crushing the needy (v. 1). This is the second time Amos referred to oppression on the hill of Samaria (3:9). "Oppress the poor and crush the needy" are synonymous phrases. Amos was using different words to state the same information twice, hammering down the fact that the wealthy cows on the acropolis were mistreating the poor.

Also, women were saying to their husbands, "Bring us something to drink." "Bring" is an imperative, so they were ordering their husbands (literally "lords") to fetch something so they could imbibe. Amos was portraying drunkenness, laziness, or both. In that culture, women typically served the food, but these women were reversing that cultural convention and telling someone else to serve them. They were eating more than they needed, like cows in Bashan, and ordering others to serve their drinks (Stuart, *Hosea–Jonah*, 1987, 332). So, while they were oppressing people who were struggling to meet their basic needs, they were also demanding that others work to fulfill their selfish desires. These aristocrats were living in opposition to the way God had told his people to live, and Amos flatly declared their sin.

Mistreating the poor violated laws God had given to Israel. For example, God told them they were not to charge interest to the poor, they were not to pervert justice for the poor in a lawsuit, they were to leave some of their harvest in the field for the poor to glean, under some circumstances they were to open their homes for the poor to live with them, and they were to be generous and give to the poor (Exod 22:25; 23:6; Lev 19:10; 23:22; 25:35; Deut 15:7-11). Using the same word translated "oppress" in Amos 4:1, Deuteronomy 24:14 says, "Do not oppress a hired worker who is poor and needy, whether one of your Israelite brothers or one of the resident aliens." Thus, in oppressing the poor and crushing the needy, the cows of Bashan were disobeying a list of commands God had given Israel. In fact, it's possible they had lived unfaithfully for so long they were no longer even aware of the contents of God's law (Hos 4:6; Amos 3:10).

In the age of the new covenant in Christ, God still expects his people to act with compassion for the hurting and marginalized. We follow a Lord who lived that way. Jesus stopped to help blind Bartimaeus when everyone else was telling Bartimaeus to be quiet and stay out of the way (Mark 10:46-52). Jesus helped a man in the region of the Gerasenes who was tormented by demons; everyone else had been avoiding him (Luke 8:26-39). Jesus engaged a woman in conversation at a well in Sychar, and she was the kind of woman that "respectable" men would have avoided (John 4:1-27). Such ministry is a countercultural way to live. It puts others first instead of self. The way of our culture is to love ourselves. The way of our sinful, fallen flesh is also to love ourselves. It's not the way of Jesus, who gave himself away as a sacrifice for others. We follow the one who said that he "did not come to be served, but to serve, and to give his life as a ransom for many" (Mark 10:45).

If we limited ourselves solely to the message of the previous paragraphs, we could arrive at something like "the social gospel." The social gospel can be defined as confining the message of the New Testament to ethical imperatives like "Work for justice!" and "Care for the poor!" If doing good in society is the sum of our message, we are not preaching the gospel of Jesus Christ. The gospel is that God came to us in the man Jesus, who was and is God the Son. Jesus lived a sinless life, died on the cross as the atoning sacrifice for the sins of humanity, rose from the dead on the third day, is alive today, and gives new and eternal life to all who put their faith in him as Savior, forgiving their sin and giving them a new nature. That is the gospel, and the new nature we have in Christ includes rejecting sinful behaviors and practicing righteousness. Jesus, through his presence in us, empowers us to live as he lived, to live as God directs us to live in his Word. Part of that kind of life is caring for the poor and refraining from any mistreatment of the poor. Corporately, every local church will maintain a ministry that shows care for the poor, compassion to the marginalized.

The gospel is not merely a social message; it is a spiritual message with a social mission. We put our faith in Jesus, and he abides in us and changes us into new people. As a result, we live differently, witnessing to the life-changing gospel of Jesus and serving others in the name of Jesus (see Rom 6:1-23; Gal 5:22-25; Eph 2:8-10; Phil 2:12-13). Second Corinthians 5:15 says that Jesus "died for all so that those who live should no longer live for themselves, but for the one who died for them and was raised." The people who have life in Jesus have an entirely new purpose for living; we no longer live for ourselves; we live for Jesus. This is the message we share with the world: all people need to be reconciled to God, and Jesus died as the sacrifice for their sins and rose again so that if they put their faith in him, he'll reconcile them to God, forgive their sin, and give them abundant life. As a result, they'll stop living for themselves, which leads only to misery, and they'll begin living for Jesus, which leads to joy.

God Punishes People Who Mistreat the Poor
AMOS 4:2-3

After briefly describing the sinful lifestyle of the indolent elites in Samaria, Amos turned to the consequences of such behavior. Amos

knew this word of judgment would be fulfilled because "the Lord GOD
has sworn by his holiness" (v. 2). In the Bible, the word *holy* means "to be
other than, different, set apart." To refer to a person or thing as "holy"
is to refer to that person or thing as different, not common. To refer to
God as holy is to refer to him as other than us; he is God, not human.
It's not merely that he is good to a higher degree than we are—we are
loving, he is more loving; we have strength, he has more strength, etc.
God is completely other than us. He is loving in a way we will never be
loving; he has power that is incomparable to anything human. In fact,
it's a sin to treat God in the same way we treat people. In Psalm 50, God
lists many of the sins of Israel, and one of them was, "You thought I was
just like you" (Ps 50:21). We should understand all God's attributes in
light of his holiness. His love is holy love, his power is "his holy arm"
(Isa 52:10), and his law is his holy law (Rom 7:12).

When God swears by his holiness, he is swearing by that which
makes him God—his otherness. As God, he cannot and will not make
an oath that he will not keep. "God is not a man, that he might lie, or
a son of man, that he might change his mind. Does he speak and not
act, or promise and not fulfill?" (Num 23:19). In Psalm 89:33-37 God
emphasizes the certainty of the permanence of his covenant with David
by saying, "I have sworn an oath by my holiness" (Ps 89:35).

In God's announcement of coming judgment in Amos 4:2-3, in
the original text a few of the pronouns are masculine. Amos specifies
females several times in verses 1-3, but he may have added the masculine
gender to indicate that men as well as women were guilty and should
expect to face God's judgment. As for the form of God's judgment, the
reference to the people being taken away "with hooks" and "with fish-
hooks" (v. 2) alludes to exile. Assyrians and other peoples in the ancient
Near East often led their captives into exile with ropes through the nose
or lip. Tiglath Pileser III was the first Assyrian king to invade Israel only a
few decades after Amos preached, and he left records indicating that he
followed that practice (Niehaus, "Amos," 393). The reference to going
"through breaches in the wall, / each woman straight ahead" (v. 3) is
also a reference to the military conquest of Samaria. When invading
soldiers laid siege to a city, eventually they would use a battering ram to
break through the city walls (King, *Amos, Hosea, Micah*, 72–73, 86–87).
Amos prophesied such a future for Samaria, and when it happened,
the women he had been addressing would exit the city through the
holes in the walls made by their enemies. Such a fate would be a tragic

reversal of the Israelite conquest of Jericho, when the Israelites entered the city "each man straight ahead" (Josh 6:20). The Assyrians did indeed lay siege to Samaria in 724 BC, and by 722 BC the city fell. Amos also announced that the residents of Samaria would be "driven along toward Harmon." The location of Harmon is unknown, but it was likely located north of Syria since the Assyrians would be returning in that direction.

Practices like leading people into exile by stabbing hooks into their bodies and stringing them on ropes seem barbaric to modern people, but in their public art the Assyrians displayed such cruelty. Their art also shows that they impaled people on poles and flayed their skin. They were advertising their cruelty in order to intimidate potential enemies and keep their vassals submissive. In Amos's case, however, the Assyrians were not advertising brutal exile; God was announcing it through his prophet.

Religious Rituals Won't Make Things Better
AMOS 4:4-5

Amos invited his hearers to attend worship at Gilgal and Bethel. Gilgal was the first place Israel camped after entering the promised land, and it seems that it became an important meeting point (Josh 4:20-24; 5:9). Since Gilgal is not mentioned in any city lists in the Old Testament, it's possible that it never became a town that was permanently populated; it was more of an ongoing religious center, an area devoted to worship (Andersen and Freedman, *Amos*, 430–32). It was a worship site when Amos preached, as was Bethel. Bethel was probably the primary place of worship; Amaziah the priest called Bethel "the king's sanctuary and a royal temple" (Amos 7:13). Bethel had been a place of worship since Jeroboam I built an altar there to compete with the temple in Jerusalem (1 Kgs 12:26-30).

We typically think of inviting people to worship as a good thing to do, and we think that when people accept our invitation and they attend worship, they'll be doing something good. But what if a time of worship becomes so twisted that it leads people further away from faithfulness to God instead of closer to faithfulness to God? The preaching of the eighth-century prophets (Amos, Hosea, Micah, and Isaiah) indicates that worship in Israel and Judah had become corrupt. The lifestyle of worship leaders and worship participants was morally compromised. Such intransigent immorality meant their worship was mere ritual that did not alter their path of sin. Ritualism divorced from righteousness was not the kind of worship God had commanded Israel to observe. Therefore, Amos's invitation to "come to Bethel and rebel; / rebel even more at Gilgal" was dripping with irony. The place where the people should have been doing something righteous was, in fact, a location where they were committing rebellion against God.

Amos continued his mockery of their wrongheaded religion by encouraging them to "bring your sacrifices every morning, / your tenths every three days. / Offer leavened bread as a thanksgiving sacrifice, / and loudly proclaim your freewill offerings" (vv. 4-5). God had not commanded his people to offer sacrifices every day, and he had commanded them to bring the tithe every three years (Deut 14:28-29). Amos sarcastically encouraged them to sacrifice something every day and bring a tithe every three days, as if to say, "Since the *quality* of your worship is no good, maybe *quantity* will help."

At the conclusion of worship, a priest would be expected to announce God's acceptance of the sacrifice and his pleasure in the worshipers. Instead, in Amos's satire of worship, the people themselves "loudly proclaim" or boast about their offerings. And instead of God's pleasure, Amos said only the Israelites were pleased: "That is what you Israelites love to do" (v. 5). What good are excessive observances of religion when the religious people are practicing sin? Amos's words communicate that no amount of religion, or religious ritual, can compensate for hearts that remain separated from God and deeds that remain steeped in sin. "Israel loved religious activities. That is not the same thing as loving God" (Billy Smith, *Amos, Obadiah, Jonah*, 88). As we read these verses, we should feel the incongruity between right religion and oppressing the poor. Religion that is pleasing to God makes us compassionate and generous to the poor (Amos 5:21-24; Micah 6:6-8; Jas 1:27).

Jesus delivered stern words to the scribes and Pharisees of his day because their many rituals did not result in righteousness. Since they sat "in the chair of Moses" and were supposed to know and teach God's law, Jesus told people, "Do whatever they tell you, and observe it." But then he said, "Don't do what they do, because they don't practice what they teach" (Matt 23:2-3). God's Word is good; we follow it. Hypocritical religious leaders are not good; we don't follow them. Like Amos, Jesus went on to tell the scribes and Pharisees that their rituals were not acceptable because they were neglecting "the more important matters of the law—justice, mercy, and faithfulness" (v. 23). The result was the same for the religious leaders in Amos's day and in Jesus's day: as Jesus put it, "On the outside you seem righteous to people, but inside you are full of hypocrisy and lawlessness" (v. 28).

Authentic faith in the one true God is not merely a matter of ritual. When we exercise saving faith, God changes us on the inside (Ezek 11:19; 36:26; John 3:3-7; 2 Cor 5:17). As a result, our behavior is also changed (Jas 2:14-26). The church of Jesus Christ has always practiced rituals—gathering for worship, sharing the Lord's Supper, baptizing, attending business meetings that are such terrific fun, etc. But these are all expressions of a heartfelt and life-altering love relationship with God. If they are something other than that, they are worse than worthless because God is not pleased, and we risk giving people the impression that empty ritual will suffice. With God, it never will suffice; he has told us that in his Word. He has told us that a relationship with him will result in serving the poor, not mistreating them, because he punishes people who mistreat the poor, and religious rituals won't make things better.

Reflect and Discuss

1. Amos addressed the wealthy elites as "cows of Bashan." How do you think the elites reacted to that? How would people react today if addressed in that way?

2. Amos criticized the "cows of Bashan" for drunkenness and/or laziness. Can you think of analogous persons or groups in any contemporary society?

3. Reread the laws regarding the poor that are referenced in this chapter. If all those laws were implemented in a society, what would that society look like?

4. Define the "social gospel." How is that gospel different from and similar to the gospel of Jesus?

5. Why should followers of Jesus be involved in caring for the poor?

6. Can you say honestly that you are living for Jesus, not for yourself?

7. Define God's holiness. How should God's holiness affect the way we live?

8. Why was the worship of the Israelites corrupt? How do people corrupt worship today?
9. Describe the way ritual and righteousness were related in the corrupt worship of Israel, and describe the way ritual and righteousness are related in worship that pleases God.
10. Why do people today think religious ritual can compensate for sin?

When God Spoke through Suffering

AMOS 4:6-13

Main Idea: God made life bitter for Israel to help them discover the insufficiency of their lives without him and to show them the wretchedness waiting for them in the end if they did not come to know God.

I. **Heed God's Call to Repentance (4:6-11).**
II. **Prepare to Enter God's Presence (4:12).**
   A. God is in control.
   B. God's ways are inscrutable.
   C. God is a participant in our suffering.
   D. All creation is marred by sin.
   E. God offers salvation from sin and its consequences.
   F. Disasters provide a foretaste of God's consummation of this age.
   G. A time of suffering is a time to turn to God.
III. **Praise God because of His Greatness (4:13).**

A seminary student met with me and told me that God was calling him to help people who are struggling with the kinds of problems he faced before he came to faith in Christ. That led him to share with me his salvation testimony. Before his salvation, his life story consisted of one tragedy after another. Each instance of suffering, he said, was sent by God to get his attention and call him to repentance.

Suffering is not our preferred mode of communication from God, but it is not our prerogative to determine how God will speak to us. C. S. Lewis wrote, "God whispers to us in our pleasures, speaks in our conscience, but shouts in our pains: it is His megaphone to rouse a deaf world" (*The Problem of Pain*, 81). As for my student friend, when he was in his twenties, he had experimented with drugs and had quickly become addicted. That addiction began to control his life, and he was miserable. Then one day he crashed his car into another car. The crash resulted in only minor injuries, and at some point after the crash, he sat down on the street curb next to his car. The other driver, whom he had just rammed with his car, sat next to him and began to share the gospel with him. He knew his life was spinning out of control, and he was powerless to stop it. So the truth that God loves him and has a wonderful plan for his life came as extraordinarily good news. He put his faith in Jesus. God saved him spiritually, and he healed him physically. Miraculously, his desire for drugs was no longer present. He told me he thought that car crash was the final disaster in a series of disasters in his life, all of which God had been using to arrest his attention so he would turn to him. Again and again he had refused to turn to God, until finally God used the car crash and a Christian witness.

To return to C. S. Lewis, Lewis argues that God allows pain in our lives to warn us of eternal pain that's in store for us if we don't turn from our sin and to convince us that life really is not sufficient without God. Pain, then, makes us less satisfied with life as it is right now.

> Try to believe . . . that God, who made . . . people, may really be right when He thinks that their modest prosperity and the happiness of their children are not enough to make them blessed: that all this must fall from them in the end, and that if they have not learned to know Him they will be wretched. And therefore He troubles them, warning them in advance of an insufficiency that one day they will have to discover. . . . He makes that life less sweet to them. (*The Problem of Pain*, 85)

God made life "less sweet" for Israel to help them discover the insufficiency of their lives without him and to show them the wretchedness waiting for them in the end if they did not come to know God.

Heed God's Call to Repentance
AMOS 4:6-11

In Haggai 2:17, God said to Judah, "I struck you—all the work of your hands—with blight, mildew, and hail, but you didn't turn to me—this is the LORD's declaration." Jeremiah also referred to God's using suffering, or discipline, to call people to repentance:

> "LORD, don't your eyes look for faithfulness?
> You have struck them, but they felt no pain.
> You finished them off,
> but they refused to accept discipline
> . . . , and they refused to return." (Jer 5:3)

In the lifetime of the prophet Joel, an army of locusts invaded and devastated the land. Joel affirmed that God sent the disaster of the locust plague to call people to repentance, referring to the locust swarm as "his army" and "his camp," and in that calamity God called, "Turn to me with all your heart" (Joel 2:11-12). So, when we hear a testimony like my student's, we can believe it's credible that God was using suffering to reach him, since God says in his Word that he has used suffering to call people to himself.

The Bible teaches that sin leads to suffering. Personal sin leads to personal suffering; universal sin leads to universal suffering. But can we look at a particular example of suffering and conclude that it is the result of a particular sin? Sometimes that's not difficult to do. A man drinks alcohol for decades and gets sclerosis of the liver. A woman smokes for decades and contracts lung cancer. Not a lot of mystery there. But we are not divinely inspired prophets; the Holy Spirit is not inspiring us to write authoritative interpretations of instances of human suffering. Drawing a line from some suffering back to a sin is usually impossible, so it's foolish to speculate and pronounce, "This is God's message in this suffering!" Job's friends tried and failed to connect Job's suffering with some sin he had committed, and we should learn from their failure.

On the other hand, we believe the Scriptures, including prophetic books like Amos, are divinely inspired and authoritative. When the prophets record God saying that a particular circumstance of suffering is the result of someone's sin, we know sin is the reason for that suffering. Amos was one such prophet, and God sent him to announce to the people of Israel that he had been calling them repeatedly to repent of sin, and his calls had been in the form of disasters he had sent them. He named five such disasters. First, God sent famine. He said, "I gave you absolutely nothing to eat in all your cities, / a shortage of food in all your communities" (v. 6). "Absolutely nothing to eat" is literally "cleanness of teeth," a figurative reference to the fact that the people did not have the opportunity to use their teeth to eat because they had no food. Such famines were not uncommon in the ancient Near East. "All your cities" and "all your communities" indicate that this famine was widespread. It was also sent by God; he takes credit for it. God concludes this oracle by saying, "Yet you did not return to me." God's goal in sending the famine was for the people to return to him. God makes that statement here five times: "Yet you did not return to me." God's purpose in disciplining them was redemptive, but they refused God's overtures and suffered to no good end.

Second, God sent drought. God says, "I also withheld the rain from you / while there were still three months until harvest" (v. 7). The timing of the drought was during the rainy season. At the time they needed the rain to water the crops, it did not come. Unlike the famine, though, some communities had water: "I sent rain on one city / but no rain on another." So the cities without water staggered to a city with water. Still they "were not satisfied" (v. 8).

Third, God sent two additional calamities that prevented food production. "Blight and mildew" were plant diseases, and "the locust" was an insect that could devastate crops (v. 9). Even after this third disaster, the people did not return to God.

Fourth, God sent both "plagues" and "the sword" (v. 10). We don't know why God mentioned those two together except that they occur together in God's law where he promised to send both as his judgment for the unfaithfulness of his people (Lev 26:25; Deut 28:49-61). God specified "plagues like those of Egypt" (v. 10). Israel was opposing God's will as Egypt had done, so God was punishing them as he had punished Egypt.

Fifth, God "overthrew" some of the people. God uses the same word *overthrew* that he used to refer to his judgment of Sodom and Gomorrah ("demolished" in Gen 19:25; see also Jer 20:16). God does not specify the method of this overthrowing. It was sufficient to state the fact of it. God's statement that they had been "like a burning stick / snatched from a fire," gives the impression that many of them may have barely escaped. Still they did not return to God. Five rounds of disasters, and all of them were meant to cause the Israelites to turn to God. God ends this review of the tragedies he sent to Israel with a final use of the refrain: "Yet you did not return to me— / This is the LORD's declaration" (v. 11).

By Act 4 of Shakespeare's *Hamlet*, Ophelia's father has been murdered, Gertrude's son has been taken away, Claudius thinks Ophelia has lost her sanity, and people are spreading the false rumor that Claudius killed Ophelia's father. In the midst of all that tragedy, Claudius says, "When sorrows come, they come not single spies, but in battalions" (*The Tragedy of Hamlet*, 209). God sent battalions of sorrows to Israel, one after another. Unlike my student friend, however, tragedy did not cause the people to turn to God in faith. When God gave his law to Israel through Moses, he promised this kind of suffering if they strayed from him (Lev 26:14-33; Deut 28:15-44). They should have recognized all these calamities as God's promises coming to pass because of their sin. The disasters were his calls to repentance; they should have heeded the calls.

Prepare to Enter God's Presence
AMOS 4:12

In the first two lines of verse 12, God refers to what he has been describing in the previous six verses. He repeats that he will act in judgment against sin: "That is what I will do to you." Throughout this passage, God emphasizes that the suffering Israel experienced came from him. God uses the first-person form of verbs eleven times. Twice he adds a first-person pronoun for emphasis. God sent this suffering. The idea that God is the source of any suffering poses a problem for some people. Yet the Bible affirms here that God sent this suffering to Israel for the purpose of leading them to repentance. It is helpful to put this passage in the context of other biblical truths regarding God's relationship to suffering. Here we present seven such truths. The Bible teaches more about suffering than these seven truths, but perhaps these will help us as we contemplate Amos 4.

God Is in Control

God created everything that exists by speaking it into existence. One day he will bring everything in the universe to a holy and just consummation, and in the meantime, "by him all things hold together" (Col 1:17). Amos 4 is a reminder that God controls things like famine, drought, plagues, and even war. Humans make choices that lead to suffering, but somehow in God's sovereign providence, he is ultimately in control. The world is not out of control; it is under God's control. First Samuel 2:6-7 says, "The LORD brings death and gives life; / . . . The LORD brings poverty and gives wealth." God is also in control of the destinies of nations. Acts 17:26 says he has made every nation, and he determines the allotted times and boundaries for their existence. God is in control.

God's Ways Are Inscrutable

Isaiah 40:28 says,

> *Do you not know?*

Have you not heard?
The LORD is the everlasting God,
the Creator of the whole earth.
He never becomes faint or weary;
there is no limit to his understanding.

The last statement can be translated literally, "There is no searching of his understanding." In other words, God's understanding is so great that we cannot search for it and find it. "Inscrutable" means "not easily understood." *God* is not easily understood; his ways are mysterious to us. We cannot fully comprehend all God does because he is God and we are mortals. If we could fully understand all he does, then he would be no greater than we are. In times of suffering, when we say to our friends and neighbors that God is in control, they ask, "Then why doesn't he fix this problem?" or "Why does he allow that to happen?" So we say, *God* is in control; I'm not in control. He's the one who understands; we don't understand all his ways, and we *cannot* understand because he's God and we're not. That's the reason we worship and obey him: he is God. Why did God send famine, drought, and other forms of suffering to Israel at that particular moment in Amos's lifetime? God determines the form and timing of his judgments, we do not, and it's likely that the number of factors he considered is virtually infinite so that we could not even grasp his reasons. Why not? Because his understanding is beyond our searching.

God Is a Participant in Our Suffering

He is the almighty God of the universe who created and controls all that is, and he is holy beyond our comprehension. But he loves us, cares about us, and has compassion for us. Jesus looked at a crowd of people and "he felt compassion for them, because they were distressed and dejected, like sheep without a shepherd" (Matt 9:36). God has compassion for us when we suffer; when we hurt, he feels with us. Did God feel compassion for Israel in Amos's lifetime, even in their sinful state? In the same century, when God continued to speak of his coming judgment on Israel, he said through Hosea, "How can I give you up, Ephraim? / How can I surrender you, Israel? / . . . my compassion is stirred!" (Hos 11:8). God is affected by our sin and suffering; he suffers with us. He has suffered finally and redemptively on the cross when he invited suffering on himself to become the sacrifice for our sin so we could be forgiven and reconciled to him.

All Creation Is Marred by Sin

Romans 8:22 says, "The whole creation has been groaning together with labor pains until now." All the created order is suffering the consequences of sin. Famines, droughts, plagues, and war were not part of God's original creation. Suffering and death entered the world as the consequences of human sin. Now the created order groans under the weight of sin and death. When we see people suffering and remember that it's the consequence of the presence of sin in the world, it should cause us to hate sin, and thereby the world's suffering can have a sanctifying effect in our lives.

God Offers Salvation from Sin and Its Consequences

During times of suffering and disaster, we tell people that God offers salvation from the sin that besets every person and causes suffering. God is the Judge, and he will pass judgment against sin. But he also offers the remedy for sin and deliverance from judgment if we will put our faith in Jesus the Savior, who can deliver us from sin and its eternal consequences. God calls all people to himself to give them eternal salvation.

Disasters Provide a Foretaste of God's Consummation of This Age

Jesus said, "There will be famines and earthquakes in various places. All these events are the beginning of labor pains" (Matt 24:7-8). The famines, droughts, plagues, and pandemics of this present age are birth pangs. Disasters are contractions that tell us something greater is about to happen. A new age is in the future. In the present age we suffer, but that suffering is the birth pain that will lead to the perfect age God has in store for his people. One day the curse of sin will be reversed, and the entire cosmos will reflect the glory of God. That day has not yet come, so in the meantime we see a creation that is marred by human sin.

A Time of Suffering Is a Time to Turn to God

The Bible affirms this truth repeatedly. In the book of Psalms, for example, every circumstance of life was an occasion for psalmists to turn to God. When they experienced grief, they prayed. When they felt depressed, they prayed. When they faced an uncertain future, they prayed. When they suffered, they turned to God. Amos, too, urged Israel to turn to God. In verse 12 Amos wrote, "Israel, prepare to meet your God!" They had refused to return to God in the past, but it was not too late to turn to him.

Today's world is reeling in pain—disease, death, war, injustice, abuse, corruption. Is this not a time to turn to God and call out to him for help? Who would be willing to say, "God, we've got things under control. We'll call you if we need you, but we're all good here." Instead of turning to God, a lot of people turn to other people: "We'll get through this as long as we pull together. We've got one another!" Followers of Jesus want to help people, too; that's what Jesus did, and it's what he told us to do. But we also know human beings have needs that only God can meet. So, especially in times of difficulty, we turn to God. And one day we *will* meet him. When we die, we will stand in his presence. Are we prepared for that moment?

Praise God because of His Greatness
AMOS 4:13

At first glance, the final verse of Amos 4 may seem out of place. The shift in theme from the preceding verses is obvious. However, the verse is a perfect conclusion to the chapter both in form and theme. Anyone reading the final verse of Amos 4 in the original language would notice parallels with the first verse of the chapter. The first verse introduces the "cows of Bashan," the wealthy women of Samaria who were oppressing the poor while selfishly demanding the fulfillment of their own desires. The original text of verse 1 has three participles describing them: "oppressing," "crushing," and "saying." The final verse of the chapter describes God, who is opposite from the oppressive upper class because he cares for the poor and is perfectly righteous. The original text returns to the use of participles to describe him: "forming," "creating," "revealing," "making," and "striding." Thus, the ending of the chapter causes us to recall the beginning of the chapter and invites us to contemplate the contrast between Israel's sin and God's greatness.

What does Amos proclaim about God's greatness in verse 13? First, God created all. He "forms the mountains" and "creates the wind." Both those verbs appear in the first two chapters of Genesis to refer to God's creative activity. The word translated "creates" is the word that appears in Genesis 1:1; it is unique in that only God is the subject of that verb in all the Old Testament. God also "reveals his thoughts to man." The thoughts, or musings, here are most likely humans' thoughts, since that is the way this word is used elsewhere in the Old Testament (Niehaus, "Amos," 407). God knows what we are thinking (Ps 139:1-4; Heb 4:12).

God is also "the one who makes the dawn out of darkness." Literally, this line reads, "the one making dawn darkness." It may refer to God making the dawn and the darkness or to God making the dawn into darkness. The point is that God has power over light and the heavenly bodies. He also "strides on the heights of the earth." Amos provides an anthropomorphic picture of God walking on the mountains. Humans must make the arduous climb to arrive at the heights; God steps down and treads on them as his path. God is indeed great. The known universe consists of trillions of stars spread out over billions of light-years. God measures it all with his hand (Isa 40:12). He knows all things visible and invisible, and he has the power to alter anything in the universe at any time according to his will.

Amos's expression of praise serves as a fitting conclusion to this chapter. Why should people repent of sin and turn to God? Amos 4:6-13 gives three emphatic answers. First, unfaithfulness leads to suffering God's judgment (vv. 6-11). Second, all are going to stand before God to give an account (v. 12). Third, God is infinitely great and therefore infinitely worthy of our worship and obedience (v. 13).

We began this section with words from C. S. Lewis about pain as God's megaphone. Lewis also wrote this:

> Until the evil man finds evil unmistakably present in his existence, in the form of pain, he is enclosed in illusion. . . . No doubt Pain as God's megaphone is a terrible instrument; it may lead to final and unrepented rebellion. But it gives the only opportunity the bad man can have for amendment. It removes the veil; it plants the flag of truth within the fortress of a rebel soul. (*The Problem of Pain*, 83)

Pain shouts at us the truths that sin leads to suffering, God calls us from sin to himself and to the new life that only he can give, and we need God's help and salvation. Whatever our present circumstances may be, we need him, so let's turn to him.

Reflect and Discuss

1. What have been your greatest moments of suffering? What helped you endure those times?
2. Describe some biblical examples of God speaking through suffering.
3. In Amos's time, God used disasters to call people to return to him. How is God calling people to turn to him today?
4. In difficult times, how are we helped by knowing God is in control of the world?
5. How can we make suffering an opportunity to share the gospel?
6. What do we say to people who ask how God can send disasters if he loves us?
7. Suffering in the world is the result of sin. How does knowing that fact help us?
8. When we turn to God in times of pain, what do we pray?
9. What lessons has God taught you through suffering? How has suffering helped you grow?
10. Why should we repent of sin and turn to God? What are the answers to that question given in Amos 4:6-13?

What It Takes to Turn from Sin

AMOS 5:1-13

Main Idea: When we mourn the presence of sin, seek God, and contemplate God's greatness, with God's help we can turn from sin.

I. Mourn the Presence of Sin (5:1-3).
II. Seek God, Not Just Religion (5:4-7).
III. Contemplate the Greatness of God (5:8-9).
IV. Consider the Consequences of Sin (5:10-13).

The book of Lamentations is one of the most poignant collections of grief poetry ever written. Jerusalem had fallen to the brutal Babylonian army (586 BC). The Babylonians had ransacked the holy temple and burned the city to the ground (2 Kgs 25:1-15). Jerusalem was the place where God had caused his name to dwell. Many of the people believed Jerusalem could not fall because God would not allow it to fall (Jer 7:1-8). But it did fall. More than a hundred years earlier (701 BC), the Assyrians had besieged Jerusalem, and God had miraculously spared the city (2 Kgs 18:13–19:37). Not this time. The mourning of the Jews over the death of their holy city is understandable, as is a book of mourning like Lamentations.

The grief expressed in Lamentations demonstrates how ancient people felt when their capital city fell. In the northern kingdom of Israel, the capital was Samaria. When it fell (722 BC), surely the people mourned. God allowed Amos to see the fall of the northern kingdom before it happened. It's understandable, then, that Amos would lament the death of Israel before it happened. He knew that in the near future it *would* happen because God allowed him to see it. Thus, Amos's fifth chapter opens with a lament over fallen Israel.

The Old Testament has a range of words that refer to lamenting or mourning. To open this chapter, Amos used a word that refers to a poem of bereavement, a lamentation, or a dirge. It was chanted, or sung, during mourning rites and funerals (Coppes, "*qînâ*," *TWOT*, 2:798). When Saul and Jonathan died, David "sang the following lament" (2 Sam 1:17). When Josiah died, Jeremiah "chanted a dirge"

(2 Chron 35:25). In those laments, Amos's word appears, as it does in prophetic passages that anticipate the death of a nation (Judah in Jer 9:20; Tyre in Ezek 26:15-17; Egypt in Ezek 32:2).

Mourn the Presence of Sin
AMOS 5:1-3

Amos's lament was for the "house of Israel" because "she has fallen; / Virgin Israel will never rise again." By this fifth chapter of Amos, Amos's hearers or readers should be aware of the reason Amos is anticipating Israel's fall. Israel's sin, her unfaithfulness to God's covenant with her, had long invited the fulfillment of God's promises of judgment. Amos announced in multiple ways that God's judgment was about to fall; now he does so in the form of a dirge, lamenting the certain reality of Israel's demise. Israel is dead and the funeral is beginning.

In light of the circumstances, calling Israel "virgin" cannot be a statement about moral purity (Garrett, *Amos*, 137). Possibly "virgin" should be taken politically, since at the moment of Amos's ministry Israel was free, unconquered, independent of other countries (Harper, *Amos and Hosea*, 107). Also, Israel in Amos's time, like a virgin, was "ready to enter the most exciting and fulfilling time of her life . . . but tragedy strikes and wastes her potential; her untimely death . . . brings to an end . . . God's wonderful plans for her" (Gary Smith, *Hosea, Amos, Micah*, 312). Amos portrayed that end graphically in verse 3 as a crushing military defeat. Such a defeat would occur when the Assyrians invaded Israel.

The lament form was another means of convincing the people of their true spiritual and moral condition. In the book of Amos, the prophet delivers stern condemnations of sin and declarations of judgment. Perhaps the mood of his delivery changed as he recited this lament. Did he do so in plaintive tones, perhaps even weeping (Gary Smith, *Hosea, Amos, Micah*, 311)?

We don't know the way Amos originally delivered these words, but we know the Bible calls us to mourn the presence of sin. Joel called people to mourn the results of a locust plague—bare farmland and famine (Joel 1:5-20). Then he called them to mourn the cause of the suffering—their sin (2:12-17). The apostle Paul expressed gladness that Christians in Corinth had grieved their own sin and had repented, and he distinguished between godly grief that leads to repentance and worldly grief that leads to death (2 Cor 7:6-11; 1 Cor 5:1-2). Paul also wrote that he would grieve if he discovered that some believers had not repented (2 Cor 12:21). James exhorted people to weep over the reckoning that awaited them because of their sin (Jas 5:1-6).

When sin is present, we mourn. Do we mourn over the fact that rape and murder are common occurrences? Do we lament racial bigotry or inequity? Do we grieve over sin in the church? Do we weep when people are deceived into thinking homosexuality is just another kind of lifestyle or that killing a baby in his mother's womb is just a choice? Amos's dirge was a fitting literary form in his circumstances. Israelite society was rife with egregious sin and headed for death, and that was cause for grief.

Seek God, Not Just Religion
AMOS 5:4-7

We need God's help to turn from sin. God saves us from sin, leads us away from temptation (Matt 6:13), and gives us the power to live without sin. Through Amos, God told the people of Israel to seek him. Amos preached that death was coming to Israel as a whole, but he held out hope of survival for at least some of the people. Maybe through Amos God was even offering hope to all Israel in the exhortation, "Seek me and live!" (v. 4). That imperative is repeated in verse 6, "Seek the LORD and live." The survival of Israelites was dependent on whether they sought the Lord. If they knew God's law, that would not be surprising, since the law often portrays obedience as a matter of life or death (Lev 10:6-9; 15:31; Deut 6:1-2; 17:18-20; 28:58-66; 32:45-47).

Amos also wrote, "Do not seek Bethel / or go to Gilgal / or journey to Beer-sheba" (v. 5). Amos mentioned Bethel and Gilgal as worship sites elsewhere in his prophecy (3:14; 4:4-5; 7:10-13). He never refers to them in a positive way. A worship site was also located at Beer-sheba (2 Kgs 23:8). Beer-sheba was located in the far south of the southern kingdom. Israelites would have crossed the border into Judah to make a pilgrimage there. That explains Amos's use of the verb translated "journey." Beer-sheba was a sacred site perhaps because both Abraham and Jacob worshiped at Beer-sheba, and Abraham lived there (Gen 21:33; 22:19; 46:1). Some Israelites were substituting the pursuit of religion for the pursuit of God. Amos told them to stop doing that. He also gave them a good reason to stop seeking those places: they were going to suffer God's judgment. He wrote, "Gilgal will certainly go into exile, / and Bethel will come to nothing" (v. 5).

The progressive poetic structure of these lines is difficult to miss (Garrett, *Amos*, 139). The Holy Spirit inspired it and Amos recorded it, surely aware that the form amplifies the emphasis on seeking God and the futility of seeking religion.

> *Seek me and live!*
> > *Do not seek Bethel*
> > > *or go to Gilgal*
> > > > *or journey to Beer-sheba,*
> > > *for Gilgal will certainly go into exile,*
> > *and Bethel will come to nothing.*
> *Seek the LORD and live.* (Amos 5:4-6)

Seeking God is essential for all people at all times. Our desire should be the same as the psalmist when he wrote, "God, you are my God; I eagerly seek you. / I thirst for you; / my body faints for you / in a land that is dry, desolate, and without water" (Ps 63:1). Do we seek God as a thirsty man seeks water in a dry, desolate land? Another psalm expressed it this way: "My heart says this about you: / 'Seek his face.' / LORD, I will seek your face" (Ps 27:8). Most local churches produce some sort of pictorial directory of their church family, either digitally or in print. By using such a directory, church members can get to know other members. To accomplish that, churches place pictures of their members in the directory. What do they photograph to help people get to know one another? Their feet? Their hands? No, they take pictures of the members' faces. We know one another by our faces. God wants us to seek his face (2 Chron 7:14). He wants us to know him in a personal way.

Some people are eager to seek the hand of God—his blessings of comfort, guidance, and provision. Seeking God's hand is not wrong; he's the one to whom we look for comfort, guidance, and provision. But it's possible for the benefits and blessings God gives to become subtle substitutes for God himself. The gifts can become objects of greater attention and affection than the one who gives the gifts. When we seek God, what matters most is hearing from God himself, knowing God. Some believers want to seek God, but in reality it doesn't happen because of busyness, wandering thoughts, or distractions. Sin can also prevent us from seeking God. We can be satisfied to appear to seek God instead of actually seeking him. We can idolize tradition, so that we're willing to seek God only if meeting with him fits the patterns to which we have grown accustomed. Even in times of personal or corporate worship, it's easy to be distracted by trappings, forms, or personalities with the result that we expend more energy thinking about those things than seeking God. Intimate fellowship with God—seeking him and knowing him—is the magnificent obsession of followers of Jesus. Right now,

> Turn your eyes upon Jesus,
> Look full in His wonderful face,
> And the things of earth will grow strangely dim
> In the light of His glory and grace. (Helen H. Lemmel)

Contemplate the Greatness of God
AMOS 5:8-9

The psalmist wrote, "The heavens declare the glory of God, / and the expanse proclaims the work of his hands" (Ps 19:1; see also Ps 8). Gazing at the night sky reminds us of the beauty, enormity, and complexity of the created order. Our next thought is of the greater beauty, enormity, and complexity of the one who created it all. Amos also considered the night sky, and he expressed praise to the God who made it.

Amos 5:8-9 constitutes the second of three brief passages of praise in Amos (also 4:13 and 9:5-6). Commentators often refer to these passages as hymns, or hymn fragments. To modern believers, such a designation implies they were used, or even sung, in worship. Lacking any evidence of such use, we probably do well to consider them hymns in only the broader sense of praise poetry. The praise passage in Amos 5:8-9 mentions two constellations: "Pleiades and Orion." "Pleiades" translates a Hebrew word that probably means "flock" or "group" (Brown et al., "*kwm*," *BDB*, 465), and Pleiades is a group of stars that represented a group of sisters in Greek mythology. "Orion" appears with "Pleiades" in Job 9:9 and 38:31. It is typically translated "Orion" possibly because of the relatedness of Orion to Pleiades. Since God made all the stars in the universe, why did Amos praise God as "the one who made" only two constellations? Amos was writing poetry, not a paragraph in a textbook about systematic theology or astronomy. These words were chosen probably because of the sound of the words or the images or feelings evoked by them.

The point of this praise poetry is to extol God's greatness. Constellations are far beyond our reach; we can only gaze at them in wonder. God made them. We can only observe "darkness" and "dawn," "day" and "night"; but God can turn one into the other whenever he chooses. "The water of the sea" overpowers us; it sinks our ships, it floods our towns, and we're vulnerable to its slightest undertow. God "summons the water of the sea," and it comes to him like a trained pet; he "pours it out over the surface of the earth" like he is emptying a glass of water. To further express that God is greater than humans, next Amos states, "He brings destruction on the strong" (v. 9). The original text repeats "destruction" in the next line, which states that God brings destruction "on the fortress" also. The strongest humans and their strongest buildings are no match for God.

The Bible contains many poems of praise for God's greatness. When we read such descriptions, one proper response is to contemplate his greatness in contrast with our smallness. Such meditation naturally leads us to offer God heartfelt praise. Have you ever known someone who was in the custom of worshiping, but when he faced an enormous problem, he didn't feel like going to church, so he skipped? He didn't feel like continuing with his personal or family times of worship, so he skipped that too. When people make such decisions, they underestimate the power of praise. May we never lose sight of God's greatness; may we never cease to offer him praise. Even in the midst of writing about Israel's sin and empty religion, Amos stopped to give God praise. Remembering and reciting who God is can sustain us through every circumstance.

Consider the Consequences of Sin
AMOS 5:10-13

Jesus said, "Everyone who commits sin is a slave of sin" (John 8:34). Romans 6:23 says, "The wages of sin is death." The Bible also affirms that sin alienates us from God (Eph 4:17-19; Col 1:19-21). Sin leads to consequences—slavery to sin, alienation from God, and death. In fact, God announced that sin leads to death before humanity committed the first sin. God told Adam and Eve that if they disobeyed him and ate the forbidden fruit, they would die. They disobeyed, and they died. Sin has been resulting in death ever since (Gen 3:1-19). The consequences of sin should motivate all people to repent of sin, turn to God in faith, and follow his way. Amos repeatedly reminded Israelites of the consequences of sin.

Verses 10-13 provide another catalog of Israel's sins. Amos mentions hating "the one who convicts the guilty / . . . , and they despise the one who speaks with integrity" (v. 10). So they hated the application of justice and the statement of truth. They also trampled the poor and impoverished them even further (vv. 11-12), which Amos had pointed out earlier (2:6-8). As a result, Amos told them they were going to suffer. They had been building "houses of cut stone" and planting "lush vineyards" (v. 11). God said through Amos that they would not live in those houses and they would not reap the benefits of their vineyards (v. 11). The consequences for their sins would come. In the near future, they would lose material blessings. In the more distant future, their nation would be conquered, and the people would be exiled.

In the face of widespread evil and certain judgment, Amos counseled silence: "Therefore, those who have insight will keep silent / at such a time, / for the days are evil" (v. 13). God had called Amos to speak against sin, announce God's coming judgment, and call people to repentance. Beyond that, what could be said? Bartering with God is fruitless. Claiming that sin is not that bad contradicts God. Better to "keep silent."

Once we know the consequences of sin, it seems like we would never commit another sin. But it doesn't work that way. People continue to feel the power of temptation and to give in to it. Near the end of the movie *Indiana Jones and the Last Crusade*, the Holy Grail is found. It's the object for which many people have searched for twenty centuries. To the people who have been looking for it, it's the ultimate archaeological find. A woman is holding the Grail when suddenly the ground beneath her splits apart. She falls into a deep chasm, and the Grail falls from her hand and lands on a nearby ledge. Indiana Jones grasps one of her hands and saves her from falling to her death. He is holding her with one hand and tells her his grip is slipping. To survive, she must grasp his other hand with her free hand. But she can only look at the Holy Grail, and she says, "I can reach it." It's so obvious that if she reaches for the Grail she'll fall to her death. But her desire for the Grail overcomes her, and instead of contemplating the consequences of her action, she reaches out for the prize and she falls. Then, only seconds later, Indiana Jones is in the same situation. He's dangling over the abyss, and the Grail is just out of reach. This time it's his father holding one of his hands to save him while Indiana reaches for the Grail with his other hand. His father tells him, "I can't hold you." But Indiana just looks at the Grail and says, "I can reach it," even though just seconds before he had pleaded with the woman to take *his* hand. But his father calls to him once more, and just in time he comes to his senses and gives his father his other hand instead of reaching for the Holy Grail.

All people know what it's like to be drawn like a magnet to some Holy Grail, to be lured from what we know is right, to feel we must have the object of our desire. Sometimes we're tempted so much that we find it difficult to remember that the consequence of sin is falling into the abyss. That's the reason we need to hear our Father's call to contemplate the consequences of sin. We cited the first part of Romans 6:23: "The wages of sin is death." The next words in the same verse are, "But the gift of God is eternal life in Christ Jesus our Lord." Let us mourn the presence of sin in the world and in our lives. Let us seek God, not just religion. He's the only one who can save us and empower us. Let us contemplate God's greatness and consider the consequences of sin. When we do all of that, with God's help we can turn from sin.

Reflect and Discuss

1. Recall a time when you experienced grief. What caused you to mourn?
2. Would the death of your nation, or any nation, cause you to mourn? Why?
3. Why was a lament an appropriate form of speech for Amos to use?
4. What is the difference between godly grief and worldly grief?
5. How can awareness of our emotional response to sin and its effects help us measure our spiritual health?
6. What does it mean to seek God's face? How are you seeking God?
7. List some realities that have hindered you from seeking God in the past. How have you overcome those challenges?
8. What can we learn about God from observing the sky or other parts of creation?
9. How does the regular practice of praising God affect the way we live?
10. In what ways should we remind ourselves of the consequences of sin?

When God's People Live in a Wicked Culture

AMOS 5:14-27

Main Idea: God called his people to walk the opposite direction from the culture around them.

I.   We Walk in the Opposite Direction (5:14-15).
II. We Keep the End in View (5:16-20).
III. We Renounce Compromised Religion (5:21-27).

Not all of the Israelites in Amos's day had exercised faith in the one true God. Their deeds revealed the condition of their hearts. In every area of life—religion, commerce, family life, treatment of the poor, and entertainment—they were demonstrating rebellion against God and his law. Such rebellion does not arise from a heart that is trusting in God. James wrote, "What good is it, my brothers and sisters, if someone claims to have faith but does not have works? Can such faith save him?" and "Faith without works is dead" (Jas 2:14,26). When we know God in a saving relationship, the way we live will be different because we are different people (2 Cor 5:17; Eph 2:8-10). Furthermore, through Amos God was at the point of condemning Israel, and God does not condemn his people (Rom 8:1).

When Amos called people to repent, he was calling people to turn, and the nature of their turning would depend on their spiritual condition. For the Israelites who had never put their faith in God, their turning would consist of putting their trust in him as their God for the first time. Some Israelites had put their faith in God. Their turning would consist of changing their lifestyles to align with God's word instead of resembling the lifestyles of unredeemed Israelites and their pagan neighbors.

When contemporary preachers call people to repent, we are doing something similar to Amos's preaching. We are calling unsaved people to put their faith in Jesus the Savior, and we are calling followers of Jesus to live in a way that is consistent with their faith. As the apostle Paul wrote to Christians, "Walk worthy of the calling you have received"

(Eph 4:1), and "You were once darkness, but now you are light in the Lord. Walk as children of light" (Eph 5:8). Amos's words can help contemporary believers walk worthy of our calling in Christ. When we live in a culture where we're surrounded by people who are not walking with God and living in sin, what do we do?

We Walk in the Opposite Direction
AMOS 5:14-15

Years ago, an episode of the television show *Seinfeld* had to do with opposites. The character named George Costanza decides that every decision he has ever made has been wrong and his life is the opposite of what it should be. George says that to Jerry Seinfeld, who then says to George, "If every instinct you have is wrong, then the opposite would have to be right." That makes sense to George, so he resolves to start doing the opposite of what he would do normally. He introduces himself to a woman and says the opposite of what he would usually say. He says, "My name is George. I'm unemployed and I live with my parents." She's impressed and agrees to date him. On the date, George does the opposite and doesn't shave, and she loves it. He gets an interview for a job with the New York Yankees, where he also does the opposite of his instincts and criticizes the owner to his face for the way he runs the team, and George gets the job.

The show is just comedy, but the writers of the episode actually articulated an important biblical truth. Our nature is so affected by the fall, by our own sinful inclinations, and by a corrupt culture that if we rely on our instincts, we will live in unfaithfulness to God and in sin. The unredeemed people of Israel who lived during the lifetime of Amos were living that way. Would the people who knew and loved God live in the same way? Amos called them to do the opposite of what the culture around them was doing.

Amos told them, "Pursue good and not evil" (v. 14). "Hate evil and love good" (v. 15). Twice Amos used the word *evil*. Anyone who had heard Amos preach would have been well aware that Israelite society was evil. Amos preached against specific sins Israelites were committing. He called God's people to be different, to go in the opposite direction. The apostle Paul wrote to Christians in Rome about the unregenerate people of his day,

They do what is not right. They are filled with all unrighteousness,
evil, greed, and wickedness. They are full of envy, murder, quarrels,
deceit, and malice. They are gossips, slanderers, God-haters, arrogant,
proud, boastful, inventors of evil, disobedient to parents, senseless,
untrustworthy, unloving, and unmerciful. Although they know God's
just sentence—that those who practice such things deserve to die—
they not only do them, but even applaud others who practice them.
(Rom 1:28-32)

Like Paul, Amos named specific sins in his preaching ministry.

Yet Amos held out hope for some Israelites if they would turn from
evil and "establish justice at the city gate" (v. 15). He said, "Perhaps the
LORD, the God of Armies, will be gracious / to the remnant of Joseph."
God was ready to be gracious because that is his nature. "The LORD is
a compassionate and gracious God, slow to anger and abounding in
faithful love and truth" (Exod 34:6). However, God does not bless sin.
He would be gracious to "the remnant," to those of "Joseph," or Israel,
who turned from sin. Sadly, under the new covenant it is also true that
not everyone will be saved, only those who want to be saved. Hell has
been called God's great compliment to human free will. God will allow
people to be separate from him if that is what they choose. When people
around us are walking away from God, God's people walk in the opposite direction—toward him.

We Keep the End in View
AMOS 5:16-20

The beginning of verse 16 seems to assume that many people would not
turn from sin and only a remnant would be saved, since God announces
that people would be wailing, crying out in anguish, and mourning in
the streets. Whatever will happen exactly, it will involve the death of people, since God mentions "professional mourners." God says that the reason for this future death and wailing is, "I will pass among you" (v. 17).

When God shows up to a group of sinners, the result is his judgment
against them. Thus, Amos introduced his comments about the coming
"day of the LORD." Evidently, some of Amos's contemporaries spoke
positively about the day of the Lord since Amos referred to those "who
long for the day of the LORD" (v. 18). Perhaps these people thought
the Lord would save Israel unconditionally, no matter how the people

related to him or to others. Amos makes clear that his generation was rife with rebellion against God, but amazingly some people expected God to exalt them when he passed among them on the day of the Lord.

Amos replied to their benighted view of God's visitation by saying, "Woe to you who long for the day of the LORD!" (v. 18). "Woe" to them—how sad for them to expect something from God that would not come to pass. The day of the Lord would bring the opposite of what they expected: "darkness and not light" (vv. 18,20). Amos parodied the awfulness of the day of the Lord by portraying someone trying unsuccessfully to escape it:

> *like a man who flees from a lion*
> *only to have a bear confront him.*
> *He goes home and rests his hand against the wall*
> *only to have a snake bite him.* (v. 19)

Poor guy. He had a super-rough day, but at least he winds up in the safety of his own home. Not so fast. While he was running for his life from a lion and then a bear, a snake slithered into his house. Amos was saying, "You can run but you can't hide. On the day of the Lord, he's going to visit you with his judgment, and he knows where you live." Because of God's delay, some people may say, "I escaped God's judgment!" They escaped it the way that guy escaped the lion and then the bear. But they haven't escaped utterly. God's judgment against sin is coming.

The prophet Malachi wrote that God was coming to his temple, and he asked, "Who can endure the day of his coming? And who will be able to stand when he appears?" (Mal 3:2). When God shows up to judge, who will be left standing? Both Amos and Malachi knew the people in their times wanted God to show up. They both affirmed that God was coming, but they both also said that his coming would not be as pleasant as the corrupt nation was thinking.

Followers of Jesus are often discouraged by the fact that wickedness is so prominent and goes unchecked and unpunished. It will not always be so. One day Jesus is going to return. The New Testament also refers to a "day of the Lord" that is still future for our generation (Phil 1:6; 1 Thess 5:1-3). One day God will eliminate all evil and reward all righteousness. The first time Jesus came, he was condemned by wicked people. But when he comes again, he will condemn all wickedness. When Jesus returns, the kings of the earth will war against him but to no avail. He will triumph over all (Rev 19). When people today think of Jesus, they think they can take him or leave him. But when he returns, every person will be either with him or against him. There will be no middle ground, only battleground. Relativism will be no more; one side will be good and the other side will be evil, and good will win. Pluralism will be no more because in the end only one religion will matter—the religion that exalts Jesus. Humanism will no longer exist. Nobody will be saying, "We can figure this out. The governments of humanity, or our educational systems, will improve this." In the end only Jesus wins and those who are with him.

These days, people talk about being "on the right side of history." In other words, as our culture moves in the direction of embracing more and more sin, celebrating such sin puts us on the cutting edge of progress, on the right side of history. The people who use that sort of language don't know where history is headed. Our culture is not progressing; it's degenerating into more perversion and greater deception. Only God determines where history is heading, and he has decreed that history is heading toward the consummation of this age when he will express his holy wrath against sin and will reward his people eternally. Jesus will be enthroned, the earth will be restored to its lost glory, and heaven will rejoice. In this age, the devil hates us and oppresses us, but in the end he loses, and it's not even close. God loves us and has given himself to save us. In the end he wins and he wins forever. Hallelujah! In the midst of our struggles and doubts during the wicked age in which we live, this is the end God's people keep in view.

We Renounce Compromised Religion
AMOS 5:21-27

Evidently the people of Israel loved to practice religion, but it was *their* religion. God spoke to Israel about "*your* sacrifices . . . *your* tenths . . . *your* freewill offerings . . . that is what *you Israelites* love to do" (Amos 4:4-5; emphases added). Their religion wasn't about what God had *told* them to do; it was about what they *wanted* to do. So they loved it. But in chapter 5 Amos wrote what God thought about their worship (vv. 21-24).

Their religion was unrelated to righteousness. Attendance at their so-called worship was not causing them to seek justice and care for the poor. It wasn't even drawing them closer to God. The forms of worship had become formality. Amos mentioned nothing in their religion about loving God and nothing about loving people—the hallmarks of right religion. Their religion was doing what they wanted to do to make them feel better. God said he hated their worship.

When I was in my twenties, I produced an interpretive paraphrase of the book of Amos, with some built-in application based on what the text says. Here's the way I paraphrased Amos 5:21-24. I was pastoring a rural church at the time.

> *I hate all day singing and dinner on the grounds. You are in a festive mood at your fellowships; when I see them I am nauseated. The size of your tithe does not matter to Me, and I don't even care how much you give above the tithe. Go ahead and sacrifice all you want; someone will pat you on the back, but I won't. And turn down the sound system when you sing—I'd rather not hear it. While you have been burning your . . . rock and roll music, I have been burning your . . . Christian music. It used to be beautiful, but you have replaced caring for the poor with concerts, showing love to the unlovely with Christian shows. Now I want you to show Me something else—love your neighbor; feed the hungry; help the sick; lift up the down-trodden. That is how I want you to show your love for Me.*

It's a sobering thought that God could hate our worship. About three hundred years before Amos, God went on record as preferring obedience to worship forms. He said through Samuel, "To obey is better than sacrifice" (1 Sam 15:22). No amount of worship participation can compensate for a disobedient life.

When contemporary Christians gather for corporate worship, we typically sing strong words about our worship of God, our love for him, and our commitment to serve him. It's important that we make sure the words we sing are heartfelt and the worship we offer is sincere, lest we make worship a sham, something God hates. We ought to think about what we're committing to do. Before we *sing* it, we should be sure we're ready to *do* it. God hates empty, phony worship. Amos 4:4 says that kind of worship is just a multiplication of rebellion.

Through Amos, God stated what he does not want: worship that's unrelated to righteous living. God also stated what he wants: "Let justice flow like water, / and righteousness, like an unfailing stream" (v. 24). God wants justice and righteousness from his people. The book of Amos shows that Israelites were practicing plenty of injustice and unrighteousness. God looked for the opposite from his faithful people—justice and righteousness.

In America, we should be grateful for the justice system in our country, and in our pledge of allegiance to our flag we say that we're a nation with "justice for all." But we also see evidence that equal justice does not exist for all. Throughout history the courts of virtually every civilization have been weighted in favor of the wealthy. God's Word leaves no doubt that God is on the side of justice. Deuteronomy 32:4 says of God, "All his ways are just." Psalm 140:12 says, "The LORD upholds / the just cause of the poor, / justice for the needy."

God commands his people to promote and pursue justice. Isaiah 1:17 says, "Learn to do what is good. / Pursue justice. / Correct the oppressor. / Defend the rights of the fatherless. / Plead the widow's cause." In other words, God's people are to treat all people fairly and compassionately. When people are mistreated, we are to "correct the oppressor." Also, we are to make a special effort to help the weak—the fatherless and the widows. Fairness and compassion are not presented in the Bible merely as ideals but as behaviors that will characterize the lives of God's people individually and corporately. Through Amos, God called for justice and righteousness to flow like a stream in Israel.

God continued to address Israel's wicked worship in the final verses of chapter 5. First, he asked Israel a rhetorical question: "Was it sacrifices and grain offerings that you presented to me during the forty years in the wilderness?" (v. 25). God's point is either that Israel did not offer sacrifices regularly to God at all during the forty years in the wilderness or that they offered sacrifices, but God's focus had never been mere ritual. All along, God had looked at the condition of the worshipers' hearts and the righteousness of their lives. Passages like Exodus 24; 40:29; Leviticus 8–10; and Numbers 7–8 indicate the observance of worship in the wilderness, but all those passages describe events that occurred at the beginning of the wilderness sojourn. In light of the context, it is most likely that the point here is "to emphasize that sacrifices and grain offerings alone are not of primary importance to the Lord" (Niehaus, "Amos," 433; see also Jer 7:21-23).

Many Israelites loved their religion and valued it over obedience, but they were getting religion wrong. They were taking up images they had made named "Sakkuth" and "Kaiwan" (v. 26). Those were idols, false gods, and probably both of them were astral deities (Andersen and Freedman, *Amos*, 533–34). Idolatry was ubiquitous throughout the history of Israel, and Amos's lifetime in the eighth century BC was not an exception. The difference in this case was that God's punishment for their centuries of idolatry was growing close. Here God says, "I will send you into exile beyond Damascus" (v. 27). God fulfilled that promise when the Assyrians conquered Israel a few decades after Amos preached.

Through Amos, God called his people to walk the opposite direction from the culture around them. God calls his people today to do the same. Second Corinthians 6:17 exhorts Christians, "Come out from among them / and be separate, says the Lord; / do not touch any unclean thing." How do we live differently from people around us who don't know God in Christ? Do we decide to do better and then do it through sheer determination? No, we are far too influenced by our sinful flesh to obey God on our own. Jesus said, "You can do nothing without me" (John 15:5). If we want to change, we need Jesus. And Jesus does change us. Second Corinthians 3:18 says that as we are in the presence of Jesus and behold his image, we "are being transformed into the same image from glory to glory; this is from the Lord."

So, if we want to conform our lives to the truth of God's Word, we need Jesus. Praise his name, Jesus offers his salvation to every person by his grace to make them into new creations! And to his church Jesus offers his sanctification to transform us from one degree of glory to another.

Reflect and Discuss

1. This chapter begins with the truth that saving faith results in good works. What kinds of good works demonstrate our salvation? (See 1 John.)
2. What will cause greater numbers of people in the world to repent of sin and turn to faith in Jesus?
3. What kind of repentance is needed in the lives of followers of Jesus? In what ways should you repent now?
4. What consequences might Christians have to face if they walk in the opposite direction from the culture around them?
5. How did Amos describe the coming day of the Lord? If the day of the Lord occurred and God appeared in your community or in your church, what might be the results?

6. Why do people who are living in sin expect an encounter with God to go well for them?
7. How are Christians helped by thinking about the end of history?
8. How can our practice of religion become something we enjoy but that is contrary to God's Word?
9. What causes God to hate our worship? Does God ever hate the way you worship?
10. What should the church of Jesus be doing to promote justice? What should you be doing?

Pride before Israel's Fall

AMOS 6

Main Idea: Amos gives a picture of the way pride was playing out in Israel and its coming consequences.

I. **What Does Pride Look Like (6:1-6)?**
   A. Puffed up and clueless (6:1-3)
   B. Pampered and carefree (6:4-6)
II. **How Does God Respond to Pride (6:7-14)?**
   A. God declares his hatred of pride and announces his judgment (6:7-8).
   B. God will bring down human accomplishments (6:9-11).
   C. God reveals the absurdity of sinful reasoning (6:12).
   D. God manifests his greatness (6:13-14).
III. **What Will We Do with Pride?**

Proverbs 16:18 says, "Pride comes before destruction, / and an arrogant spirit before a fall." That proverb has often been shortened to the well-known saying, "Pride goes before a fall." In an article in *Scientific American*, Steve Mirsky referred to a study done by researchers in Great Britain that explored the accuracy of that adage. The study was purely tongue-in-cheek and published first as a bit of humor in the Christmas issue of the *British Medical Journal*. The researchers asked a test group of British citizens, "During the past 30 days, to what degree did you feel proud?" Then the researchers asked the study participants if they had fallen down recently. After all the answers were submitted, the researchers crunched the numbers and as it turns out, the odds of having had a fall "was 19% lower for people with high levels of pride." Mirsky cited the researchers as concluding, "Contrary to the proverb, our findings suggest that pride may actually be protective against falls rather than being a contributing factor" ("Staggering Discovery," 74).

Of course, the authors of the study were surely aware that the biblical proverb has nothing to do with falling down physically. The point is that pride leads to another kind of fall—dishonor and distress. People think pride will result in exaltation, but it leads ultimately to humiliation.

The sixth chapter of Amos begins with the second of three woe oracles (5:18; 6:4). "Woe" is used primarily in two ways in the Old Testament: mourning for the dead and announcing imminent suffering as the judgment of God (Eidevall, *Amos*, 164). In Amos 5:18 "woe" follows a description of impending death and mourning. Chapter 6 continues the theme of coming disaster. The primary reason for the arrival of God's judgment is Israel's pride. The central message of the chapter is in the middle, where God says, "I loathe Jacob's pride."

What Does Pride Look Like?
AMOS 6:1-6

Amos's confrontational words to the leaders of Israel indicate that they were pursuing a course of self-delusional pride that would lead to their downfall. Amos gives a picture of the way pride was playing out in Israel and its coming consequences. In Amos's picture, we can see the way pride often looks in our lives too.

Puffed Up and Clueless (6:1-3)

In verse 1 Amos addressed "the notable people" in Samaria and Zion, or Jerusalem. Evidently to some extent he was issuing a warning to both nations, though the remainder of the chapter refers to Israel only (vv. 1,8,14). The leaders to whom Amos preached thought their nation was "first." It's doubtful that Israel at this point in history was first in anything and even more doubtful that Amos thought so. The prophet was being sarcastic, but it's also likely that "first" was an accurate description of the leaders' opinions of themselves and their leadership of the country. They thought they were the best; they thought they were winners. They were deluded. Amos preached that the only way they would be "first" was being the first to be captured and carried into exile (v. 7).

These people were also "at ease," a phrase that translates a word used positively a few times in the Old Testament, as when Isaiah referred to Jerusalem as "a peaceful pasture" (Isa 33:20). However, the word is also used negatively to refer to a sort of casual arrogance (Cohen, "*sha'nan*," *TWOT*, 2:893–94). God used this word to refer to Sennacherib's "arrogance" (2 Kgs 19:28). They were also "secure on the hill of Samaria." "Secure" translates a word that often refers to trusting in God (2 Kgs 18:5; Ps 9:11; Isa 26:3-4). But these people were not trusting in God; they were trusting in the hill of Samaria. Samaria was built on a hill, rising about three hundred feet above the valley, and "beautifully constructed casemate walls" surrounded the acropolis on the top of the hill (King, *Amos, Hosea, Micah,* 36). So besieging and conquering Samaria would not have been easy, and the people thought they were justified to trust in it. But Amos pronounced "woe" over them because God had called Israel to trust only in him. Plus, the prophet knew Samaria was doomed.

In verse 2 Amos urged the people to go to three different locations to confirm that Israel and Samaria were not better. Calneh and Hamath were cities in Syria, and Gath was in Philistine territory. As long as the Israelites compared themselves with themselves, they looked like the first and the best. Amos told them that if they would check out a few other places, their "greatness" would seem ordinary. Furthermore, Amos reminded them that an "evil day" was coming, hastened by their sin, and their leadership was only a "reign of violence" (v. 3). They were clueless; they were saying they were great, but to God they were anything but great. Their boasting about themselves and their nation was empty political propaganda arising from pride, not reality. Whoever bought into the arrogant lie, woe to them.

Pampered and Carefree (6:4-6)

Amos described a scene of luxury and laziness. The people were not working; they were lying on ivory beds, "sprawled out on their couches," and eating two kinds of meat, a sure sign of wealth (v. 4). On the other hand, they expended a significant amount of energy in throwing parties. They were following the example of King David but in the wrong way. David had worked to make music to express praise to God; they worked to produce music for their parties (v. 5). And the typical cups or flasks were not big enough for the wine at their parties; they drank "wine by the bowlful" (v. 6).

While these Israelites were occupied so zealously with partying and inebriation, they were showing no care for the sorry spiritual state of the nation and were oblivious to the fact that they were ripe for God's judgment. Amos told them it was not the time to party; it was the time to "grieve over the ruin of Joseph," a reference to the sin of Israel and its looming downfall (v. 6). Ecclesiastes 3:4 says there is "a time to weep and a time to laugh; / a time to mourn and a time to dance." The time during which Amos preached was a time to weep and mourn, but the people were laughing and dancing. They were "doing what the Gentiles choose to do: carrying on in unrestrained behavior, evil desires, drunkenness, orgies, carousing, and lawless idolatry" (1 Pet 4:3).

Doesn't the church today have as much reason to grieve as Amos had? Western culture is rife with the practice of sin, approval of sin, and mockery of those who preach against sin. Meanwhile, many people in the church go about their lives as if nothing were wrong and pursue the same kind of entertainment the world pursues. Their time is occupied with the same music, the same movies, and the same Internet sites as the people who do not know Christ. Where is our grief over "the ruin of Joseph," over the moral degeneration and spiritual emptiness of people all around us? Churches are filled with Christians who spend more time looking at the television and social media than reading God's Word and listening to Bible teaching. They talk on their phones and text more than they talk to God.

What would Amos say if he were preaching today? He would likely preach in the same way he preached in his day; he would name sins and condemn them. Billy Sunday was a popular evangelist at the turn of the twentieth century. He was known for his straight-talking condemnation of sin. He once said,

> I'm against sin. I'll kick it as long as I have a foot. I'll fight it
> as long as I have a fist. . . . I'll bite it as long as I've got a tooth.
> And when I'm old and fistless and footless and toothless,
> I'll gum it till [sic] I go home to glory and it goes home to
> perdition. (Galli and Olsen, *131 Christians,* 75)

Billy Sunday and Amos told it like it was. They were not familiar with that bush around which many preachers beat. Amos named the sins of the people of Israel. He said they thought they were the best, but they were the worst.

How Does God Respond to Pride?
AMOS 6:7-14

Amos introduced verses 7-14 with "therefore." In the book of Amos, that word typically stands between a description of Israel's sin and an announcement of God's judgment. Chapter 6 follows that pattern; verses 1-6 depict Israel's sin, and verses 7-14 describe God's coming judgment.

God Declares His Hatred of Pride and Announces His Judgment (6:7-8)

Amos agreed with the people in Israel who thought they were the first (v. 1). But the first of what? In a play on the word *first*, Amos said they would be "the first of the captives" to go into exile. He also said their feasting would "come to an end" (v. 7). In the next verse, God introduces his word to Israel in the strongest possible way. He uses his name twice and states that he is swearing by himself, and nothing higher exists to ensure the strength of an oath. His oath is, "I loathe Jacob's pride / and hate his citadels." God hates both their pride and the object of their trust—the strength of their city, their "citadels." Instead of saying, "A mighty fortress is our God," they were saying, "Our city's mighty fortress is our god." They were trusting in themselves and in what they had built. Therefore, God declares that he "will hand over the city and everything in it" (v. 8). Only three or four decades after Amos preached this oracle, exactly that happened: lofty Samaria fell ingloriously to the Assyrians.

Some people are surprised to hear that God hates anything, but God hates pride. Amos 6:8 states that. So does Proverbs 6:16, which says, "The LORD hates six things; / in fact, seven are detestable to him," and in the list that follows, "arrogant eyes" is at the top (v. 17). God hates pride.

Pride started early. In the garden of Eden, to tempt Eve to eat the forbidden fruit, the serpent said, "You will be like God" (Gen 3:5). At the heart of the first sin was the desire for self-exaltation—to be as great as God. In the archetypal sin, the object of worship shifted from God to self. Whenever that first sin is repeated, "other-centeredness and humility are replaced by self-centeredness and pride" (Liederbach, *Chasing Infinity*, 86). Pride is a sinful root in our hearts that bears all kinds of poisonous fruit. How many divorces have been caused by pride because spouses insisted on their own way? How many church splits have been caused by pride because church members did not humble themselves? How many jobs have been lost because employees would not submit to others? Contemplate the devastating consequences of pride, consider that pride is a universal problem, and we can begin to understand why God hates pride.

God Will Bring Down Human Accomplishments (6:9-11)

The scene in verses 9-11 seems to be the aftermath of a city's destruction. Ten men are "left in one house." Typical family dwellings did not have space for that many men. Perhaps they were jammed into a small space to hide from invaders, or perhaps this was a larger building like the palace. The presence of a "burner" indicates extraordinary circumstances, since usually Israelites burned only animals (Gary Smith, *Hosea, Amos, Micah*, 341). This seems to indicate that many people died suddenly, as in the result of a terrible military defeat. Amos also describes what seems to be a search for survivors. Someone calls into a house, "Any more with you?" to determine whether any more survivors are present. Sadly, the answer from within the house is, "None." Then come the words, "Silence, because the LORD's name must not be invoked." Maybe the survivor in the house thought mentioning the Lord's name would summon him to come, and then he realized that the Lord's coming in judgment had caused the devastation of the city. He did not want the Lord to come again; don't even mention his name. Verse 11 summarizes God's announcement of complete destruction from the greatest to the least.

The destruction Amos described was coming to people who thought all was well. They were living as if they could continue in sinful pride with no consequences, but Amos declared that consequences were on the way. In the United States, every year, a day or two before Thanksgiving Day, virtually every local TV station sends a reporter out to a turkey farm and films a pen of turkeys. The farmers have been fattening them for Thanksgiving Day, and the reporter will say something like, "Well, Jim, it doesn't look like they've seen the menu for Thanksgiving dinner. I don't think they have any idea what's going to happen to them." Amos told the "first," proud Israelites that they had everything a turkey could ever want. As they pecked around their little barnyard, they were getting fatter and fatter. But slaughter day was coming. Amos was preaching about people who had everything in this world but nothing in the world to come except judgment. So many people are in that condition today. What a great tragedy! Will the church stand like Amos and warn people to turn from pride to the one true God?

God Reveals the Absurdity of Sinful Reasoning (6:12)

A friend of mine once said, "Sin makes people stupid." He was right. Sinful desires like lust and covetousness short-circuit rational thinking; people don't think about the consequences. Years ago, a young couple sat in my office for help with troubles in their marriage. They mentioned two major issues—the husband was going to strip clubs and spending hundreds of dollars, and they were facing financial challenges. Amazingly, he had not made the connection between those two problems. Sin had made him stupid.

Through Amos, God confronted Israel with the absurdity of their thinking. "Do horses gallop on the cliffs?" he asked. No, they do not. "Does anyone plow there with oxen?" Again, no; it's not possible, and it doesn't make sense to try. If they tried to have a horse race on a cliff or tried to plow there, the animals would refuse. Israel did not have horse sense; they were dumber than an ox. They were doing something that seems impossible to a clear-thinking person. God said, "You have turned justice into poison / and the fruit of righteousness into wormwood" (v. 12). Amos was using wordplay. The word translated "poison" is a homonym of the word already used twice in this chapter about pride: "first" (vv. 1,7). It's as if Amos was saying they thought they were the first, but they were doing the worst.

God Manifests His Greatness (6:13-14)

In verse 13 God quotes the people as exalting their greatness again. They were boasting over capturing two cities, Lo-debar and Karnaim. "Lo-debar" is a named town elsewhere in the Old Testament (2 Sam 9:4-5; 17:27). It means something like "not a thing," or "nothing." So it's also possible that Amos was continuing his wordplay with a sarcastic respelling of "Debir," another city in the Transjordan. Either way, capturing a place called "Not Much" is hardly a cause for boasting. Also, "Karnaim" means "two horns," and horns were symbols for strength. Hence, it was likely also a pun when Israelites said that they had captured "Karnaim / for ourselves by our own strength."

Again, Israel was boasting in themselves. If they had conquered those two cities, it was because God allowed them to do it. But they gave God no credit; they said they did it "by our own strength." First Corinthians 4:7 asks questions that are appropriate for the Israelites of Amos's day: "Who makes you so superior? What do you have that you didn't receive? If, in fact, you did receive it, why do you boast as if you hadn't received it?" God had given Israel everything they had. But they continued to be proud.

In contrast with the people of Israel who were boasting over insignificant accomplishments, God was truly great, and he was about to manifest his greatness. He told Israel, "I am raising up a nation / against you, house of Israel." Far from capturing small towns, God was raising up an entire nation against Israel. Furthermore, the people of that invading nation were going to oppress Israel "from the entrance of Hamath / to the Brook of the Arabah." Those geographical locations were at the northernmost and southernmost limits of Israel and Judah. Israel was boasting about capturing a town called "Not Much," but God was going to alter the length and breadth of the promised land. God opposed the pride of Israel in Amos's day, and God still opposes pride.

What Will We Do with Pride?

Pride convinces us that we're better than other people and that we don't need anyone else; we don't even need God. James 4:6 says, "God resists the proud but gives grace to the humble." Surely no one wants God to resist them, but God resists the proud. On the other hand, God says, "I will look favorably on this kind of person: / one who is humble, submissive in spirit, / and trembles at my word" (Isa 66:2). God hates pride and resists the proud; God gives grace to the humble and looks favorably on them.

A proper response to reading Amos 6 is to join God in hating the pride in our hearts, to confess it as sin, and to renounce it. Instead of allowing pride into our hearts, we follow biblical directions for our lives like Paul's words in Romans 12:3, "I tell everyone among you not to think of himself more highly than he should think," and Peter's words in 1 Peter 5:6, "Humble yourselves, therefore, under the mighty hand of God, so that he may exalt you at the proper time."

Pride was one of the sins that caused Jesus to be crucified as our sacrifice, and that alone should cause us to hate pride. The Puritan pastor Lewis Bayly, in one of his prayers, reflects on pride as one of our sins for which Jesus died, though he had no pride in himself:

> What had you done, my Savior, . . . to be falsely accused and unjustly condemned? What was your offense? Whom did

you ever wrong, to be scourged with whips, crowned with
thorns, reviled, buffeted, and beaten? . . . To be lifted upon
the cursed tree, to be crucified among thieves? To endure
such a sea of God's wrath? . . . I can find no offense in you.
The centurion who executed you confessed you to be the very
Son of God. The thief that hung with you said you had done
nothing wrong. So what caused this cruel disgrace, suffering,
and death? Lord, I caused your sorrows. My sin brought about
your shame, my failings your injuries. . . . I was proud; you
are humble. I was disobedient; you became obedient. I ate
the forbidden fruit; you hung on the cursed tree. O Lord, let
me never forget your infinite love. Amen. ("I Am the One
to Blame")

When we meditate on the fact that our pride caused Jesus's suffering
and death, surely we feel the opposite of pride—shame. Yet we do not
have to remain in disgrace; Jesus died and rose again so the sin of pride
would be forgiven and we could be free from pride and submissive to
our Lord Jesus forever. Praise his name!

Reflect and Discuss

1. Why do pride and ignorance of our sin often go together?
2. Israelites were trusting in the strength of Samaria instead of trusting
   in God. What do people put their trust in today?
3. Why does measuring ourselves by other people, or by ourselves,
   often lead to pride?
4. How can followers of Jesus grieve over sin yet remain joyful?
5. How do Christians speak against sin, as Amos did, yet act in a
   kind and gracious way to people?
6. God hated Israel's pride. What sins do you hate in your life?
7. What problems or conflicts can you think of that have been
   caused by pride?
8. Why is it difficult to tell unredeemed people that God's eternal
   judgment is coming?
9. How does sin make people stupid?
10. What are some ways for believers to eliminate pride?

Standing in the Gap

AMOS 7:1-9

Main Idea: When God showed Amos visions of punishment, Amos asked God to stay his hand, but when Israel did not repent, God's judgment was inevitable.

I. God Speaks to His People.
II. God Is in Control of the Destiny of Persons and Nations.
III. When God Is Going to Send His Judgment, He Warns in Advance.
IV. God's People Should Pray for God's Mercy.
V. God Hears and Responds to Prayer.
VI. God Is Gracious to Undeserving People.
VII. The Time Will Come When Opportunities for Repentance Have Passed.

In past years, many churches included a children's sermon in their time of worship. Typically, the person who led that teaching time would gather the children at the front of the church and ask them to look at something the leader had brought to show them. Then the leader would talk about how that object illustrated a scriptural truth. That brief talk was often referred to as an object lesson.

The Bible contains numerous object lessons because God often spoke to his people through symbolic objects or actions. The introduction to Amos's prophecy describes the contents of his book as "what he saw." Most of Amos's book consists of words that God showed Amos. Chapter 7 records visions God showed Amos—a swarm of locusts, a great fire, and a plumb line next to a vertical wall (see 8:1-3 and 9:1-4 for two additional visions).

The word translated "swarm of locusts" occurs only here and in Nahum 3:17, where it is parallel to a more common word for locusts, so it seems the meaning "swarm of locusts" here is reliable. Locust swarms were not uncommon in the ancient Near East, and they still occur. Locust plagues have decimated vegetation in areas as large as entire countries. For example, in 1915 locusts swarmed the region where the nation of Israel is located. According to an eyewitness, locusts flew overhead for five days, darkening the sky. Such a description explains why plagues of locusts have been so feared. In areas where subsistence farming is common, an infestation of locusts can annihilate the food supply (Firmage, "Zoology," 1150). In the vision God showed Amos, the locusts began their devastation "after the cutting of the king's hay" (v. 1) and before the general population could reap their harvest.

The second vision God showed Amos was "a judgment by fire." In Amos's opening messages announcing God's judgment on the nations, he referred to fire coming on all the nations except for Israel (1:4,7,10,12,14; 2:2,5). Those announcements of judgment seem to refer to literal fires as a result of military incursions. Amos mentions fire in relation to Israel in 5:6, but there the meaning seems to be figurative, referring to God himself spreading "like fire" among his people. The fire here in Amos's vision doesn't seem to be a natural phenomenon since "it consumed the great deep and devoured the land" (v. 4). In the past, God had sent literal fire to pass judgment on Sodom and Gomorrah for great wickedness (Gen 19:24), to manifest his power on Mount Carmel (1 Kgs 18:20-39), and to express his judgment on messengers from King Ahaziah (2 Kgs 1:1-12). But the fire Amos saw seems visionary, not literal, whether "the great deep" refers to the Mediterranean Sea or to subterranean waters (Eidevall, *Amos*, 196). God was showing Amos that great devastation was coming to Israel (see also Deut 32:22 and Isa 66:15-16).

The third vision God showed Amos was the Lord himself standing next to a wall "with a plumb line in his hand" (v. 7). Builders used plumb lines in the same way carpenters use levels today—to make sure vertical walls are straight. God said, "I am setting a plumb line among my people Israel." God was checking Israel with a plumb line to determine if they were straight. Both God and Amos knew Israel was not straight spiritually or morally, so God said, "I will no longer spare them" (v. 8).

God Speaks to His People

In these visions, God was speaking to Amos, and God still speaks to his people. Acts 13:2 says this about the church in Antioch: "As they were worshiping the Lord and fasting, the Holy Spirit said, 'Set apart for me Barnabas and Saul for the work to which I have called them.'" While they were worshiping, God spoke to them. During Paul's second missionary journey, he and his companions were trying to decide where to travel next, and more than once the Holy Spirit gave them specific direction, once through a vision in the night (Acts 16:7-9).

When the Holy Spirit spoke to the church in Antioch, how did that happen? Did the people hear an audible voice? Was there a majority vote about God's will? We don't know. And we don't know how the Holy Spirit made his will known regarding the direction of missionaries' travels. God speaks to us in different ways at different times. What we know is that God speaks to his people. It's up to us to listen, and we listen by reading God's Word, asking God for direction in prayer, gathering with God's people for worship, listening to the counsel of mature believers, and remaining sensitive to the Spirit's leadership. If we remain submissive, in his time God will make his way known.

God Is in Control of the Destiny of Persons and Nations

God sees the future because he is in control of the future. He reveals some of the future to us, as he did to Amos, but he knows all of the future—every possibility, every future reality. He knew his judgment was on its way to Israel. God's response to Amos's prayer in these verses seems to indicate that the timing and the means of God's judgment remained contingent at this point. However, all the details were fixed in the mind of God, and he revealed the fact of his coming judgment to his prophet Amos and through Amos to Israel.

God could reveal the future of Israel because he was in control of the future of Israel, as he is in control of the future of every nation. When God spoke to Jeremiah at the potter's house, he stated the same fact (Jer 18:7-11). He said that if a nation turns to him, he will bless it. If a nation does evil in his sight, he will uproot it.

It's possible that it was difficult for Israelites to accept the message of the doom of their nation since things were looking up during the days of the ministry of Amos (Andersen and Freedman, *Amos*, 588–91, 600). Jeroboam II was leading Israel to extend its borders, and God was behind those events (2 Kgs 14:25-27). But God knew the spiritual apostasy and moral depravity in Israel would eventuate in his judgment. God would cause Israel to fall under the weight of her own sin, and he was beginning to reveal those plans to his prophet. As the book of Amos demonstrates, God's plans were perfectly just since Israel's future doom would be the consequence of Israel's wickedness. Ultimately, Jeroboam II was not in charge of Israel's future; God was. He rules every nation, and in his Word he states the principles by which he rules: if a nation seeks him and obeys him, he will bless it; if a nation turns from him and disobeys him, that nation will face ruin.

God is still in control of the destiny of persons and nations. He has not resigned his position as the sovereign Ruler of the universe. The decisions of people in Washington, Beijing, Moscow, Tokyo, and Tehran are important, but where man rules, God has the power and prerogative to *overrule*. In a hundred years, all current human rulers will be dead, as will many nations. God will still be on the throne. Therefore, God's people ponder the destiny of nations by reading both the news and the Bible because the one who wrote the Bible is the one who controls the nations.

When God Is Going to Send His Judgment, He Warns in Advance

The entire book of Amos could be regarded as God's warning to Israel that his judgment was coming. As Amos 3:7 says, "The Lord GOD does nothing / without revealing his counsel / to his servants the prophets," and in these visions God was revealing his counsel to Amos. Throughout Scripture God warned of his coming judgment. He revealed to Abraham his plan to visit Sodom and Gomorrah with judgment (Gen 18:17-33). As early as the lifetime of Moses, God told Israel they would be cursed if they were unfaithful to his covenant with them (Lev 26:14-45; Deut 28:15-68). God used the prophet Nahum to announce that Nineveh was facing imminent destruction because of the extent of their rebellion against him, but approximately 150 years earlier God had sent Jonah to warn the people of Nineveh to turn from their sin lest his judgment fall on them (Jonah 1:1-2; 3:1-10).

God has also warned our generation that his judgment is coming. Romans 2:5 refers to "the day of wrath, when God's righteous judgment is revealed." And people who are unrepentant are "storing up wrath" for themselves. Second Peter also refers to "the day of judgment and destruction of the ungodly" (3:7). The book of Revelation communicates repeatedly the message that God will reward the saved and pass judgment on the wicked (e.g., Rev 19–20). People should believe God's warning about future judgment against evil. In the past, when God has announced his judgment, his judgment has always come.

God's People Should Pray for God's Mercy

Praying in times of crisis is common—so common that such prayers even have a name: "foxhole prayers." Even people who pray rarely or never are willing to pray when they are facing the possibility of disaster. Sargon II, king of Assyria from 722 to 705 BC, prayed to the goddess Nanaya for deliverance from locust plagues:

> The evil locust which destroys the crop/grain,
> the wicked dwarf-locust which dries up the orchards,
> which cuts off the regular offerings of the gods and
>   goddesses—
> (Verily) Ellil listens to you, and Tutu is before you—
> May by your command it be turned into nothing. (Hurowitz,
>   "Joel's Locust Plague," 598)

In that moment of crisis, Sargon II prayed a useless prayer to a lifeless god for help.

When God showed Amos the vision of destruction by locusts, Amos also prayed. The difference is that Amos spoke to the living God. He said, "Lord GOD, please forgive!" Amos based his request for mercy on Israel's lack of size, asking God, "How will Jacob survive since he is so small?" (v. 2). When God showed Amos the vision of destruction by fire, Amos prayed again, this time praying, "Lord GOD, please stop! How will Jacob survive since he is so small?" (v. 5). This is the only time in the Old Testament that intercession for Israel was based on Israel's smallness, but it is not the only time a man of God interceded for Israel and prayed for God's mercy.

In the wilderness, when the Hebrews complained about their misfortunes, God sent fire that consumed some of the people. Moses "prayed to the LORD, and the fire died down" (Num 11:1-2). On another occasion in the wilderness, Israel believed the negative report of the ten spies to Canaan and did not go forward to take the promised land. God was ready to send his judgment, but Moses interceded, praying, "Please pardon the iniquity of this people" (Num 14:13-19). In response, God allowed Israel to survive, but the generation that had rebelled perished in the wilderness.

In Ezekiel 22 God furnished Ezekiel a long list of Judah's sins. As a result of Judah's unrepentant sin, God was announcing his judgment. Then in a remarkable statement, God told Ezekiel,

> *I searched for a man among them who would repair the wall and*
> *stand in the gap before me on behalf of the land so that I might not*
> *destroy it, but I found no one. So I have poured out my indignation on*
> *them.* (Ezek 22:30-31)

God said he had looked for an intercessor, but he "found no one"
to stand in the gap, so his judgment was not abated. If someone had
prayed, God would have at least delayed his judgment. Sin had made a
"gap" through which God's judgment was going to enter. It is possible
to stand in such a gap and repair it by prayer, and it would be repaired
fully by repentance and reformation. In the case of Ezekiel's Judah, no
intercessor appeared, so God was pouring out his wrath.

Amos stood in the gap. Though Israel's sins were many and God's
coming judgment was just, Amos asked God, "Please forgive!" and
"Please stop!" Such prayers give a glimpse into the prophet's heart.
Amos did not want Israel to fall under God's judgment. Amos preached
against Israel's sin, but evidently he felt no animosity for the people. He
asked God to stay his hand of judgment. God's people today should contemplate Amos's prayers and their results. Has the judgment of God on
nations in the West been delayed because of the prayers of God's people?
Are we faithful in praying for our sinful culture? What might be the positive results if all of God's people were willing to "stand in the gap"?

God Hears and Responds to Prayer

When Amos saw the visions of God's coming judgment, he asked God
to forgive (v. 2) and to stop (v. 5). In answer to each prayer, "The LORD
relented concerning this" (vv. 3,6). Though Israel's sin was great, God
heard Amos's prayers and responded in mercy.

Did God change his mind? Did Amos's prayers convince God that
his planned judgment against Israel was a wrong course of action? The
answer to both those questions is no. The word translated "relent"
should be distinguished from the word translated "repent." The latter
word refers to turning from wrongdoing or to simply "turning." It is
used to refer to God only in the latter sense and only twice (Mal 3:7,
"Return to me, and I will return to you;" and Hos 14:4, "My anger will
have turned from him"). The word translated "relent," used in Amos 7
and elsewhere to refer to God, can refer either to emotion or volition.
Judges 2:18 carries the emotional sense: "The LORD was moved to pity
whenever they groaned because of those who were oppressing and

afflicting them," where "moved to pity" is the word in Amos 7:3 and 6 (see also Gen 6:6; Judg 21:6,15; 1 Sam 15:10,35). Comparing 1 Samuel 15:11 and 15:29 demonstrates both the duality of this term and God's changelessness. In verse 11 God says, "I regret that I made Saul king" (the emotional sense). Verse 29 says, "The Eternal One of Israel does not lie or change his mind, for he is not man who changes his mind," where "change(s) his mind" translates the same word that is "regret" in verse 11. These two statements would constitute a contradiction if it were not for the complexity of meaning in this word.

Knowing the meaning of the term translated "relented" in verses 3 and 6 does not fully explain God's actions. In response to Amos's prayers, God decided not to bring to pass the visions of the locusts and the fire. God also spoke of destroying Israel in the wilderness, but Moses interceded and God "relented" (Exod 32:14). God told Samuel that he regretted, or relented from making Saul king. Samuel "cried out to the LORD all night" (1 Sam 15:11). Was Samuel interceding, asking God to change his course and allow Saul to continue as God's choice? If so, it did not work because the next day Samuel announced to Saul that God had rejected him as king (vv. 23,26). During Jeremiah's lifetime, the sin of Judah became so extensive that God told Jeremiah not to pray for the people; intercession was pointless because God's judgment was fixed (Jer 7:16; 11:14; 14:11). The same was true with the latter visions God showed Amos (7:7-9; 8:1-3; 9:1-4). God announced the outcomes of the visions and gave Amos no opportunity to intercede. The time comes when no amount of intercession can reverse the effects of a lack of repentance.

God determines that the outcome of some circumstances is fixed, established in the mind of God, and therefore unalterable. However, God determines that the outcome of other circumstances is only potential, and the outcome will be to some degree contingent on human decisions, specifically the decision about whether to obey God. In such cases, "there is an implied 'if' in all God's words" (Maclaren, "Ezekiel, Daniel," 195). Such an "if" in God's dealings with persons and nations doesn't undermine his omniscience; it underscores his patience, his responsiveness to people, and his desire to redeem. God does not overlook sin; he condemns it. He does not ignore repentance; he forgives. God's posture toward humanity does not change; he responds to people as they change (Moseley, "When God Repents," 65–67). He also responds to prayer.

The Bible presents God's foreknowledge on the one hand and his response to human action on the other hand as compatible. Our best response to the Bible's presentation is to rejoice and give God praise for his mercy. In his great love he does not want any to perish, and in his long-suffering mercy he has ordained at times that a delay in his judgment is no contradiction in answer to prayer.

God Is Gracious to Undeserving People

When Amos interceded for Israel, God relented of the locust plague and the fire. As far as we know, no repentance occurred to move God to relent. The people did not deserve God's delay in punishment; the delay was based solely on God's decision to be gracious in answer to prayer. God showed grace to undeserving people. God's grace at that moment should cause us to rejoice and give praise to God; he relates to sinful people like us with grace! Thank God that he is "a compassionate and gracious God, slow to anger and abounding in faithful love and truth" (Exod 34:6). And thank God for the ultimate and most perfect expression of his grace: his coming to us in Jesus. He not only came to us; he took our sins on himself on the cross and died as our sacrifice so we can be reconciled to God. As Titus 3:5-7 says, "He saved us—not by works of righteousness that we had done, but according to his mercy— . . . so that, having been justified by his grace, we may become heirs."

The Time Will Come When Opportunities for Repentance Have Passed

Amos preached that God's judgment was coming. When God showed him visions of his judgment, Amos asked God to stay his hand of punishment. When God relented, waiting for repentance, surely Amos continued to preach and warn Israel of God's judgment, perhaps even more urgently.

> The people must then follow by responding in genuine repentance. . . . Failure to act in this period of grace . . . would, however, ensure a reinstatement of the judgment . . . , intensified by the added guilt of rejecting the pardon. (Andersen and Freedman, *Amos*, 640)

Indeed, Israel failed to repent, and God reinstated his judgment.

When God showed Amos the next visions, he gave Amos no opportunity to intercede, and God showed no willingness to relent. The time allowed for repentance had passed, and the time of punishment for rebellion had come. This was the same kind of moment expressed in Amos 1:3–2:3, when God stated repeatedly, "I will not relent." God had shown Israel kindness in waiting, and "God's kindness is intended to lead you to repentance" (Rom 2:4). Israel did not repent, so God's judgment was on its way.

The time will come for every person when the opportunity for repentance is past. Perhaps that time will come when Jesus returns. Perhaps that time will come at death, for "it is appointed for people to die once—and after this, judgment" (Heb 9:27). All people can be ready for that day, persevere through God's judgment, and receive the reward of eternal life. "If you confess with your mouth, 'Jesus is Lord,' and believe in your heart that God raised him from the dead, you will be saved" (Rom 10:9). And, "There is now no condemnation for those in Christ Jesus" (Rom 8:1).

Reflect and Discuss

1. God used object lessons to speak to Amos. Can you think of other object lessons in the Bible?
2. How does God speak to his people today?
3. How can a church know what God is leading them to do together?
4. In what ways does it help God's people to know that God is in control of the destinies of persons and nations?
5. What should be the response of government leaders to the fact that God is in control of history?
6. How do God's people warn this generation that God's judgment against sin is coming?
7. Can you recall instances when you asked God to show mercy to undeserving people? How should you pray in that way in the future?
8. What should be our response to the truth that God sometimes relents of judgment in answer to prayer?
9. How was God's grace demonstrated in his relationship with Israel in the time of Amos?
10. How should followers of Jesus communicate the fact that one day the time of God's gracious patience will be over?

False Versus True Religion

AMOS 7:10-17

Main Idea: In the clash between Amaziah and Amos, we can see contrasts between false and true religion.

I. **False Religion Prioritizes Human Authority;**
   True Religion Is Based on God's Authority (7:10-13).
II. **False Religion Views Ministry as a Profession;**
   True Religion Views Ministry as a Divine Calling (7:14-15).
III. **False Religion Works to Preserve the Status Quo;**
   True Religion Responds to the Spirit of God (7:16).
IV. **False Religion Is Destined for God's Judgment;**
   True Religion Is Destined to Inspire People to Know God (7:17).

When I was about twenty years old, I attended a worship service in a traditional Baptist church. The church had invited a man to speak who was popular but didn't really fit the profile of a Baptist minister. The sanctuary was packed to hear him. During his sermon, a man in the congregation stood up and loudly said, "Hey! I don't like what you're saying!" The speaker stopped his sermon, and the large auditorium was completely silent. The man remained standing, and after a brief pause, he said again, "I don't like your stories; I don't like what you're saying!" As soon as this awkward scene began, some men stood up and moved toward the man. After a few moments, which seemed like a long time, they reached him and ushered him out of the room.

I was shocked that a heckler had interrupted the sermon, but I was also surprised by what the speaker did next. As soon as the heckler was out of the room, he said, "Let's pray," and he began his prayer by asking God to help us all to listen carefully to people like that heckler who had shocked us with words that seemed inappropriate and unsettling. He then asked God to help us remember that during the ministry of Jesus a lot of people looked at him as little more than a heckler—a misfit who disrupted the religious status quo. To this day I remain impressed that the speaker that night not only refrained from criticizing the man who heckled him but even had the clarity of thought and humility to consider out loud that perhaps our respected religious gathering could benefit by being interrupted by a nonconformist. Typically, the religious establishment is not so open to criticism. Amos's ministry is exhibit A; he was an outsider to the religious establishment in Israel. He was not a native of Israel; he hailed from the southern kingdom of Judah. He was not a prophet or a priest; he was a herdsman and dresser of sycamore figs (v. 14). Amos was of the wrong vocation and from the wrong location. But God gave Amos a message to preach to Israel, and part of that message was a denunciation of the religious status quo. Amos pronounced God's displeasure with Israelite religion because for all its rituals it did not result in righteousness. In light of Amos's negative message about Israel's religion, we're not surprised that eventually one of Israel's religious leaders wanted to have a chat with Amos. Amaziah was that religious leader; he was the priest at Bethel. In the clash between Amaziah and Amos, we can see contrasts between false and true religion.

False Religion Prioritizes Human Authority; True Religion Is Based on God's Authority
AMOS 7:10-13

When readers of the book of Amos are introduced to Amaziah, he's reporting to King Jeroboam about Amos's preaching. That was the act of someone who saw himself as an employee of the king and responsible to keep him informed. Such a situation was common in the ancient Near East. Prophets and priests were often in the employ of the royal class, and their job was to secure the blessing of the gods on the royal house and on the nation (Nissinen, *Prophets and Prophecy*, 16–17). Amaziah's connection to Jeroboam is also demonstrated by the fact that he referred to the worship site at Bethel as "the king's sanctuary and a royal temple" (v. 13). "Bethel" means "house of God." Its former name was Luz; the patriarch Jacob renamed it Bethel after God met with him there (Gen 28:10-19). The irony is that Amaziah called the "house of *God*" the "sanctuary of the *king*," and he doubled the irony by adding that it was "a *royal* temple." So Amaziah referred to the area in two ways, both of them excluding the name of God that was actually part of the site's name, and both of them including references to the king and kingdom. Amos was preaching the word of God as a prophet called by

God, but Amaziah had his ear tuned to the nation's government and the nation's populace.

In Amaziah's report to Jeroboam, he represented Amos in the most unlikable way possible, and it seems that he even stretched the truth. First, he stated, "Amos has conspired against you," implying treason against the king. Amos had certainly preached against the sins of the nation and her leadership, but there is no indication that he was part of a conspiracy against the king. Amaziah's statement, "The land cannot endure all his words," is a testimony to the powerful effects of Amos's preaching, but it was also a pejorative exaggeration. The land would do well to hear and heed "all his words." And it seems clear that Amaziah was attempting to elicit Jeroboam's opposition to Amos when he reported, "Amos has said this: 'Jeroboam will die by the sword'" (v. 11). Amos had not said exactly that. In 7:9 Amos preached that God said, "I will rise up against the house of Jeroboam / with a sword." However, "the house of Jeroboam" refers to the dynasty of Jeroboam, and it did indeed come to an end when Jeroboam's son and successor Zechariah was assassinated (2 Kgs 15:8-10). Some people may have interpreted Amos's words as a prediction of Jeroboam's violent death, but that's not exactly what Amos said (Billy Smith, *Amos, Obadiah, Jonah*, 134). Amaziah was creatively paraphrasing Amos to enhance the negative impression he was giving Jeroboam.

Amaziah's allegiances were clear. He stood with Israel's morally compromised king and against God's prophet. Amos's allegiances were also clear. More than forty times Amos used phrases like, "The Lord says," "the Lord has spoken," and "the Lord God has sworn." Amos stood with God and his word. We could say that Amaziah lived an early version of "political correctness." To answer the question, "What should I believe and teach?," politically correct people consider what political leaders and the culture think. Amos was concerned with theological correctness. To answer the same question, he listened to God's word. All people must answer that question: What should I believe and teach? As we form our belief system and opinions, to whom will we look for help? Will we look to human authority—the latest social media post from a hero, a political leader, a loved one—or will we look to God and his unchanging Word?

Amos's commitment to base his life and message on God's authority set him apart from, and against, some powerful people like Amaziah. Amos was not the first to endure opposition from powerful people because of faithfulness to God, and he wasn't the last. King Ahab had

Micaiah the prophet thrown into prison (1 Kgs 22:24-27). Isaiah's opponents mocked him (Isa 28:9-10). The men of Anathoth told Jeremiah they would kill him if he didn't stop preaching, and King Zedekiah put Jeremiah in prison (Jer 11:21; 37:18). John the Baptist told Herod that he should not live with his brother's wife, so Herod had him arrested and later beheaded (Mark 6:16-18). Jesus always spoke God's word because he is God, and the religious authorities of his day opposed him and killed him. When God's people base their lives and message solely on God and his Word, it's likely that people who are invested in a corrupt culture, or even a corrupt religion, will oppose them.

False Religion Views Ministry as a Profession; True Religion Views Ministry as a Divine Calling
AMOS 7:14-15

Both Amaziah's words and Amos's response to Amaziah indicate that Amaziah viewed prophecy as a professional guild, and Amos was not part of the guild. When Amaziah told Amos to leave Israel and return to Judah, Amaziah said, "Earn your living and give your prophecies there" (v. 12). "Earn your living" is literally "eat bread." Amaziah's point was that "Amos should earn his living by performing his services as a professional prophet in Judah" (Garrett, *Amos*, 221). The leader of the religious establishment told Amos to get out of town. Amaziah's words are laced with financial implications. He was telling Amos that he wasn't going to make a living in Israel preaching against Israel's sin.

Amos's response indicates that he understood what Amaziah was saying. He told Amaziah what he did to earn a living, and it wasn't preaching. He said, "I was not a prophet or the son of a prophet; rather, I was a herdsman, and I took care of sycamore figs" (v. 14). "The son of a prophet" does not necessarily refer to being blood related to a prophet; that phrase appears elsewhere in the Old Testament to refer to bands of prophets, probably prophetic apprentices (1 Kgs 20:35; 2 Kgs 2:3-15; 4:1,38; 5:22; 6:1; 9:1). One translator renders Amos's statement, "I was not a prophet's disciple" (Niehaus, "Amos," 459). Amos was telling Amaziah that he was making what logicians call a category error. Amaziah was incorrectly placing Amos in the category of "professional prophet," but Amos did not belong in that category because he made his living by other means.

If Amos was not a professional prophet, why was he preaching? Amos said, "The LORD took me from following the flock and said to me, 'Go, prophesy to my people Israel'" (v. 15). Amos was literally minding his own business of caring for flocks and caring for an orchard, but God took him. God had a job for Amos to do, a message for Amos to deliver. Amos wasn't preaching in Israel because Amaziah had invited him, and he wasn't going to leave because Amaziah told him to go. And Amos wasn't preaching because he needed a job; he was preaching because of an inner conviction that God recruited him and told him to preach. God took Amos in the same way God said to Isaiah, "Go!" (Isa 6:9), in the same way he said to Jeremiah, "I chose you // . . . speak whatever I tell you" (Jer 1:5-7), and in the same way he said to Ezekiel, "I am sending you" (Ezek 2:3). Amos, Isaiah, Jeremiah, and Ezekiel—they all spoke God's word because God sent them. Their work was not a job; it was a divine calling.

God has a calling and a message for his people today. Jesus said in Matthew 28:19-20, "Go, therefore, and make disciples of all nations, baptizing them in the name of the Father and of the Son and of the Holy Spirit, teaching them to observe everything I have commanded you." That's our call, our commission. God is sending his church to this broken world to carry the message of Jesus's salvation and healing. We don't have to be professionals; we need to obey God's call.

As for the church's leaders—those called by God to teach and lead—the church looks to them to give evidence of a spiritual call from God, not just a desire for a career in religion. When they give themselves to lead the church, the church should pay them (1 Cor 9:3-14; 1 Tim 5:17-18), but that's not their motivation for serving. And the nature of their work is radically different from any other profession in its origin, its methods, and its aims.

> The mentality of the professional is not the mentality of the prophet. It is not the mentality of the slave of Christ. . . .
> Our business is to weep over our sins (James 4:9). Is there professional weeping? . . . The aims of our ministry are eternal and spiritual. They are not shared by any of the professions. . . . The professionalization of the ministry is a constant threat to the offense of the gospel. It is a threat to the profoundly spiritual nature of our work. . . . The love of professionalism . . . kills a man's belief that he is sent by God

to save people from hell and to make them Christ-exalting, spiritual aliens in the world. The world sets the agenda of the professional man; God sets the agenda of the spiritual man. (Piper, *Brothers*, 1–3)

Amos, who was faithful to God's covenant with his people, viewed his ministry as a divine calling to preach God's word. False religion, embodied in the priest Amaziah, did not even recognize God's word when he heard it.

False Religion Works to Preserve the Status Quo; True Religion Responds to the Spirit of God
AMOS 7:16

Amaziah made his living at the sanctuary in Bethel. According to Amaziah's own words, it was the king's sanctuary. Amaziah's job was to preserve that institution for the king, his employer. Amos posed a threat to the status quo at that religious center. He had preached that God was saying, "I will punish the altars of Bethel / on the day I punish Israel for its crimes; / the horns of the altar will be cut off / and fall to the ground" (3:14). He had sarcastically told the Israelites, "Come to Bethel and rebel" (4:4), and he told them, "Do not seek Bethel" (5:5). Amaziah was a worship leader at Bethel, maybe the chief leader, and Amos had said that God hated their worship (5:21-24). The messages Amos had been preaching threatened the existence of the worship center at Bethel. Amaziah derived his identity from that institution, and Amos had preached against it. Amaziah was the establishment, and as the popular saying about the establishment goes, "Come weal or woe, the only status they know is quo." Amos had heard God say that the status quo was rife with sin, and Amos was interested in covenant faithfulness to God, not preserving sin or institutions that protected sin.

Amos had no respect for Bethel's worship and worship leaders because he was captivated exclusively by what God was saying, and God was saying that what was happening at Bethel was wrong. True religion is not bound to a human institution, especially a sinful human institution. True religion listens to and follows the leadership of the Holy Spirit.

In a traditional setting, we're tempted to value preserving the institution and its traditions instead of listening to and following the leadership of God's Spirit. It can happen so easily. When we're members of a religious institution that has stability, security, and tradition, we're surrounded by the signs of religious success—a beautiful building, preaching that is amplified, beautiful music from trained musicians, attractive Bible study materials, and people who dress the way we expect religious people to dress. The whole experience has an air of respectability, so much so that it's easy to look at some little storefront church with a feeling of superiority, as if we're the tried and true, the established, the acceptable, but they're the novices, the faddish. So we don't listen to their message. If we're ever tempted to think that way, we should remember that Amos was the equivalent of a street preacher—one who was unpopular at that. In the eyes of the religious establishment, he was an undesirable, a pariah, but he spoke the word of God. The church should be more like Amos than Amaziah: we follow the leadership of the Spirit of God; we don't just work to preserve the status quo.

False Religion Is Destined for God's Judgment; True Religion Is Destined to Inspire People to Know God
AMOS 7:17

Amos also said to Amaziah, "You say: / Do not prophesy against Israel; / do not preach against the house of Isaac" (v. 16). Amaziah was one of the people about whom Amos had preached earlier, who "commanded the prophets, / 'Do not prophesy'" (2:12). Then, ironically, Amos proceeded to preach to Amaziah.

Amos introduced his prophecy with the words, "This is what the Lord says" (v. 17), again calling Amaziah's attention to the fact that his words were not his own but God's. And God's words concerning Amaziah's future were ominous:

> "Your wife will be a prostitute in the city,
> your sons and daughters will fall by the sword,
> and your land will be divided up
> with a measuring line.
> You yourself will die on pagan soil." (v. 17)

All those outcomes would not have been unprecedented in a conquered land. Many people would be killed, like Amaziah's children; many people would be exiled to "pagan soil," like Amaziah himself; the land would be parceled up among the conquerors; and some women who remained would resort to prostitution to survive, like Amaziah's wife. Amos was saying what he had said before: Israel was going to be conquered. Amaziah had misquoted Amos in his report to Jeroboam, but one statement he made was accurate. Verse 11 says that Amaziah reported, "Amos has said . . . , 'Israel will certainly go into exile from its homeland.'" In verse 17 Amos said exactly those words in the same form: "Israel will certainly go into exile / from its homeland." Amos confirmed that Amaziah was accurate about that prophecy, and Amos also stated that the heartrending effects of military defeat would be felt in Amaziah's own family. Within a few decades the Assyrian army would begin its subjugation of Israel, and neither Amaziah's prestigious religious position nor his relationship with King Jeroboam would protect him from the onslaught that was to come.

Let's consider two final words of application from this historic encounter between a prophet of God and a compromised priest. First, it took courage for Amos to say such strong words to the priest who had the ear of the king. Today we hear the call to "speak truth to power." Amos did that, not because of a slogan but because God called him and he obeyed. When we please God, sometimes powerful people will be displeased. But Amos feared God more than people. If we're going to be used by God, we'll have to do the same. Living like Jesus often is possible only when we fear God and no one else. When we fear God, what matters is *God's* assessment of our lives, not what people think of us. When we fear God, we'll do what God wants, even if it means going against the grain. Amos did that, even though the king could have executed him for speaking God's truth. To do what Amos did, we need to fear God more than people. We also need a call from God, and we have that in his Great Commission to his church.

A second final application arises from remembering that Israel, including Amaziah, faced a tragic future that could have been avoided by turning in faith to the one true God. All people also face a tragic future for all eternity unless they put their faith in Jesus as Savior. Romans 6:23 states it simply: "The wages of sin is death, but the gift of God is eternal life in Christ Jesus our Lord." Jesus makes the difference in this life and in the life to come. Ultimately, the difference between false and true religion is Jesus. True religion exercises faith in him, follows him, and worships him.

False religion exists in this world, but it will not exist in the next world. In that eternal world, every knee will bow to Jesus, and every tongue will confess that he is Lord to the glory of God the Father (Phil 2:8-11). In that eternal world, the kingdoms of this world will become the kingdom of the Lord Jesus, and he will reign forever (Rev 11:15). Followers of Jesus should take heart. Though we may have to face an Amaziah in this world occasionally, we are preparing to live forever in our eternal home, where only true religion exists.

Reflect and Discuss

1. This section begins with a story about a heckler. Was Amos a heckler? Why or why not? Was Jesus a heckler?
2. Why is traditional religion typically not open to criticism?
3. In today's false religion, what human authorities are important?
4. What are some differences between "political correctness" and true religion?
5. When contemporary believers follow Jesus and speak God's truth in love, from where might they expect opposition?
6. What are some differences between professionalism and a divine calling?
7. How can the contemporary church guard against fostering a spirit of professionalism among pastors?
8. What callings does every follower of Jesus have from God?
9. How can a traditional church prioritize the leadership of the Holy Spirit over the preservation of the status quo?
10. How do followers of Jesus develop the courage to fear God instead of people, even when people oppose them?

Three Facts that Change Everything

AMOS 8

Main Idea: The impending approach of the end should lead us to compassion for others and a determination to worship only God.

I. **The End Is Coming, and It Includes God's Judgment (8:1-3).**
    A. For Israel, the "end" meant the nation's final fall (8:3).
    B. For many people, the end will mean eternal punishment.
II. **Knowing God Leads to Showing Compassion (8:4-6).**
III. **Only the One True God Is Worthy of Our Worship (8:7-14).**
    A. We worship God because he is holy (8:7).
    B. We worship God because he is the ruler of the universe (8:8-10).
    C. We worship God because only he has spoken to us (8:11-13).
    D. We worship only God (8:14).

A few times in years past, I have read statements that were prefaced by words like, "This changed my life." I remember those statements. For example, one man wrote that when he was a young man, his big brother asked him, "Charles, when are you going to get serious about God?" That question changed his life. Another man wrote that he had struggled with prioritizing all the people in his life—work people, church people, friends, family, etc. A friend gave him a suggestion: start with the people who are going to be standing around your grave after you die; put them first. That statement changed his life. God's Word is filled with truths that will change our lives. We encounter three such truths in the eighth chapter of the book of Amos.

The End Is Coming, and It Includes God's Judgment
AMOS 8:1-3

For decades, newspapers and magazines have published variations of the iconic cartoon that depicts a guy walking on a sidewalk wearing a sandwich board that says, "The End Is Near." Actually, he's right. We don't know how near the end may be, but it's coming, and it's probably nearer than we think.

What would we think if we received that message "The End Is Near" not from a guy wearing a sandwich board but from God himself? Would it change our lives? It should. Amos received that message in the form of a vision God showed him. The first three visions God showed Amos are in chapter 7, and in chapter 8 Amos recorded that God showed him "a basket of summer fruit" (v. 1). God then asked, "What do you see, Amos?" (v. 2), like a parent would ask a preschooler who is learning his words: "What do we call this?" Amos needed to say the words to get the point. The Hebrew word translated "summer fruit" sounds much like the Hebrew word for "end," and that was the point of the vision. When Amos said the word for "summer fruit," God said, "The end has come for my people Israel" (v. 2). Not only did the word for "summer fruit" sound like "end," but the summer fruit was also the end of the harvest season (Andersen and Freedman, *Amos*, 796). This symbol was doubly symbolic. Israel was ripe for judgment, and the end was near.

For Israel, the "End" Meant the Nation's Final Fall (8:3)

"Temple songs will become wailing." Why? People were going to be mourning and singing laments over all the people who died during the conquest of Israel. Verse 3 is rated TV-MA: "Many dead bodies, thrown everywhere!" What a terrible sight! Gary Smith depicts the horror of the scene:

> There soon will be dead bodies lying everywhere. The military defeat will be complete, and the dead bodies will remain in a disgraceful unburied state, available for vultures and wild animals to eat. All one can do is gasp in horror at the enormity of the slaughter, turn one's eyes away from the mutilated carnage and bloated bodies, and flee from the unbearable stench of death and rotting flesh. (*Hosea, Amos, Micah*, 382)

That horrible sight would become a reality a few decades after Amos's ministry. The Assyrian army would invade, and the nation of Israel would meet its end. Anyone who thinks "many dead bodies, thrown everywhere" is an exaggeration is not familiar with the power and cruelty of the Assyrian Empire during this time. An enormous depiction of the Assyrian conquest of Lachish shows Assyrian soldiers impaling people on poles, decapitating others, and carrying others away as captives (Hoerth, *Archaeology*, 351). God knew the barbaric military practices of Assyria, and he knew they would bring those practices to Israel.

Israel rebelled against God over and over. God called them to repentance again and again, but they kept turning from God instead of turning to him. Therefore, God was going to punish them for their sin in accord with his promise in the covenant (Lev 26:14-45; Deut 28:15-68). The end of Israel was Israel's fault. The end of Israel was also God's work—an expression of his holy wrath against sin. The end of Israel was also Assyria's work. God used the Assyrians to accomplish his will. That did not exonerate Assyria from guilt; it was an expression of God's inscrutable sovereignty over historical events. On the day of Pentecost, the apostle Peter preached this about Jesus: "Though he was delivered up according to God's determined plan and foreknowledge, you used lawless people to nail him to a cross and kill him" (Acts 2:23). Peter placed both facts side by side: Jesus's crucifixion was according to God's "plan and foreknowledge," and Jesus's crucifixion was performed by "lawless people" employed by conspirators, all of whom were guilty of sin. The same would be true of the end of Israel. Israel's end was according to God's plan and foreknowledge because of Israel's unrepentant sin; it was his judgment. Israel's end would also be the sinful deed of the Assyrian army, and they would be guilty of sin. Those two facts are perfectly compatible in the infinite mind of God.

For Many People, the End Will Mean Eternal Punishment

Amos preached God's message that God's judgment was coming to Israel, and it did come. God's Word also says that God's judgment against sin is coming to every person individually and to the world universally. "Many dead bodies, thrown everywhere" is terrible, but God's final judgment will also be terrible. Many people in postmodern, pluralistic Western cultures give all kinds of reasons for not believing in God's coming judgment against sin, but such reasons will not stop God's judgment from coming. Many people in Amos's Israel also did not believe God's judgment was coming, but their unbelief did not alter God's holiness or impede his righteous judgment against sin. People today dismiss the idea of eternal punishment in hell, and they mock preachers who speak about it. They say, "He's only trying to scare people into putting their faith in Jesus." Actually, people *should* be scared of hell. Jesus said of those who are not his, "These will go away into eternal punishment, but the righteous into eternal life" (Matt 25:46 ESV).

Justice has long been a popular topic in the news and on television. Television shows like *CSI* and *Law and Order* have been some of the most popular shows in television history. Evidently people enjoy watching the collection of evidence and the prosecution of the guilty. The assumption of such shows is that people who are guilty should be brought to justice and punished. People think the same about real-life crimes; we're distressed when someone who commits a crime does not get justice. A young man who is poor is caught with drugs and gets three years in prison; a senator's son is guilty of the same offense, and he gets his hand slapped. Where's the justice in that? It's ironic that people in our culture expect good judges to punish wrongdoing, and when a guilty person is not punished, they say, "That's not right," but when Christians say that God *does* punish guilty sinners, people say, "God should not do that; he should let them go."

The truth of the justice of God, his wrath against sin, has fallen on hard times. But God's wrath is not the invention of angry preachers. God refers to his wrath throughout his Word. Second Thessalonians 1:8-9 says when Jesus returns, he will inflict "vengeance with flaming fire on those who don't know God and on those who don't obey the gospel of our Lord Jesus. They will pay the penalty of eternal destruction from the Lord's presence." God's wrath is real. In Revelation 20:15, the apostle John saw what will happen at the end of the age, and he wrote, "Anyone whose name was not found written in the book of life was thrown into the lake of fire." God's wrath will be expressed against ungodliness. For many people the end will mean eternal punishment. That fact changes everything, so it should change everyone's life. An old fable describes a student asking his rabbi, "Rabbi, when should people repent?" The old rabbi answered, "People should repent just before they face God's judgment." "But," the student said, "they don't know when they will face God's judgment." "Exactly," said the rabbi, "So they should repent now, while they have an opportunity before God's judgment comes."

Knowing God Leads to Showing Compassion
AMOS 8:4-6

Earlier in the book of Amos, God denounced Israel for mistreating the poor and needy (2:6-8; 4:1; 5:11-12). In chapter 8, God repeated that denunciation in verses that are in the middle of God's announcement that his judgment was coming on Israel. The location of this condemnation reminds readers that mistreatment of the poor was a reason God's judgment was coming.

How did Israelites "trample on the needy / and do away with the poor of the land" (v. 4)? According to these verses, they did so in three ways. First, they said, "We can reduce the measure / while increasing the price / and cheat with dishonest scales." Literally this says, "Make the ephah small and the shekel large." An ephah was something like a bushel basket. When these dishonest merchants sold customers "an ephah" of produce, they were actually selling less than an ephah because their basket was smaller than the standard. And if people paid in silver, they weighed the silver on scales, and the merchant provided a counterweight on the other side of the balance. When the merchant made "the shekel large," his counterweight was heavier than a shekel, so customers had to place more than a shekel of silver on the scale to pay for the product.

Second, verse 6 cites Israelites as saying, "We can buy the poor with silver / and the needy for a pair of sandals." The law God gave his people allowed for a poor person to "sell" himself as a hired worker to someone in order to pay debts and live, but the poor were not to be regarded as slaves, and they were to be released after a period of time (Lev 25:39-43). This legal provision was for extreme cases, used only as a necessity and at the initiation of the poor person. Amos 8:5-6 describes a different situation: purchasing the poor was a goal for materialistic merchants. Their aim was not to help the poor survive but to build their own portfolio. And the amount they paid was low: "a pair of sandals" was not worth much.

A third greedy practice was to "sell the chaff!" (v. 6). The chaff was the dry, fine casing of the grain. Typically it is used as fodder for animals or as mulch for the soil. Since chaff is not grain, it should not be sold as grain, but the merchants these verses describe were adding it to the grain they sold and thus increasing the bulk of their produce with worthless filler. That practice no doubt contributed to impoverishing the poor even further by charging them for something they could not eat. And these merchants did not practice their unethical business dealings reluctantly. Verse 5 says they were eager for religious observances like the new moon and the Sabbath to end so their customers would return to the market and selling could resume. Religious holidays were just nuisances that interrupted their dishonest merchandising.

The Israelites to whom Amos referred here were committing the sins of lying, greed, stealing, and mistreatment of the poor. Such sins were leading to the judgment of God. God's law requires not only honesty in business but also compassionate care for the poor. Israelites were to allow poor people to glean in their fields so they would have something to eat (Exod 23:10-11; Lev 19:9-11; 23:22). The poor could sell their land and their labor to pay debts and survive, and God provided multiple means for the redemption of their land so the land could stay in their family and the poor could continue to be free (Lev 25:23-41; Deut 15:12-18). God also told his people to give to the poor to help them (Deut 15:7-11). Furthermore, God himself cares for the poor. Psalm 69:33 says, "The LORD listens to the needy." And Isaiah 25:4 says God is "a stronghold for the poor person, / a stronghold for the needy in his distress."

In the old covenant period, faithfulness to God included showing compassion to the poor, and the same is true in the new covenant period. Jesus quoted Isaiah 61 to say that part of his mission was "to preach good news to the poor . . . / to proclaim release to the captives / and recovery of sight to the blind, / to set free the oppressed" (Luke 4:18). During his earthly ministry, Jesus fed the hungry, healed the sick, and set the demon possessed free. He spent time with marginalized people, so much so that his enemies called him "a friend of . . . sinners" (Matt 11:19). And Jesus was poor, living the life of an itinerant teacher.

Following Jesus's example of caring for the poor and hurting, the early church made it a priority to "remember the poor." The apostle Paul wrote that he had "made every effort" to do that (Gal 2:10). Paul also worked to collect a generous offering for the poor church in Jerusalem (1 Cor 16:1-3; 2 Cor 8-9). James warned against showing favoritism to the wealthy and dishonoring the poor (Jas 2:1-9). The apostle John wrote,

> If anyone has this world's goods and sees a fellow believer in need but withholds compassion from him—how does God's love reside in him? Little children, let us not love in word or speech, but in action and in truth. (1 John 3:17-18)

Followers of Jesus are not to withhold compassion. If God's love resides in us, we will show compassion to the poor. We will express love, not in theory or rhetoric but in action.

Members of the church of Jesus Christ are to be the opposite of the
Israelites Amos described in Amos 8. We use our income to help the
poor; we don't make dishonest income *from* the poor. I have seen followers of Jesus who are close to me find ways to help the poor. A Christian
young couple I know found an apartment complex with a high concentration of refugees from about thirty different countries. They moved
into that complex so they could live among the refugees, offer help of all
kinds, and share the gospel. A Christian physician was practicing medicine in a successful practice where he was part owner. He wanted to help
more poor people, so he and his family moved to another state to work
in an inner-city clinic that provides health care to the underserved—
refugees, the homeless, and the poor. A Christian couple with four
children looked for ways they could help the poor. Instead of joining a
church with a large children's program, they joined an inner-city church
that participates in ministries to the poor. Such stories could be multiplied many times over. Christians have built hospitals, benevolence ministries, and disaster relief organizations all over the world to help hurting
people. Knowing God leads to showing compassion.

Only the One True God Is Worthy of Our Worship
AMOS 8:7-14

Who, or what, we choose to worship is an expression of our deepest
commitment, our highest priority. Therefore, making a statement like,
"Only the one true God is worthy of our worship," inevitably changes
the trajectory of our lives. Worship is not an activity we participate in
once per week; it is a daily decision about who or what will guide our
lives, who or what will be of primary importance to us. "Worship is . . .
an attitude of heart that finds expression in the daily living of life. In
reality, worship is a lifestyle" (Owens, *Return to Worship*, 38). Our feelings and decisions regarding family, finances, schedule, relationships,
career, and hobbies (everything!) will be governed by whom we worship.
Amos 8:7-14 resumes the subject of future judgment. The details of the
coming judgment in these verses express enough about the nature and
greatness of God to demonstrate why everyone should worship only him
and why the Israelites should have been worshiping only him all along.

We Worship God because He Is Holy (8:7)

Why was God bringing his judgment on sinful Israel? He is holy. Therefore, he is perfectly just. Israel was rebelling against God and committing egregious, unrepentant sin against him. To allow such sin to continue without judgment would not be just.

When contemporary Christians read accounts of God's judgment against sin, we should remember that God is holy. That means he is different from us; he is God and not man. His righteousness, justice, mercy, love, goodness, patience, and grace are not just better than ours. He is in a different category, a category that consists of only one because only he is God. He is incomparable. Nothing and no one in the universe can rival him; therefore, we should allow nothing and no one to compete with him for our worship. People tolerate sin, excuse sin, ignore sin, and commit sin. God does not because he is perfectly holy. Only he, therefore, is worthy of our worship.

We Worship God because He Is the Ruler of the Universe (8:8-10)

Verses 8 and 9 describe planetary and even cosmic upheavals: the land quaking up and down like the rising and falling of the Nile River and the sun going down at noon so the sky is dark at midday. It's possible to interpret these images as figurative descriptions of some literal cataclysmic event, like the Assyrian conquest of Israel. It's also possible to interpret the images as literal descriptions of events in space and time: the sky will literally darken in the middle of the day. Some interpreters think the reference to the land shaking may be a prophecy of a coming earthquake, perhaps even the earthquake mentioned in Amos 1:1 (Andersen and Freedman, *Amos*, 193). Other prophets also referred to such cosmic events, always caused by God's power (Isa 24:1-4; Jer 4:28; Joel 2:10,30-31). The intense grief God describes in verse 10 is certainly literal.

We worship only the one true God because only he has the power to control the entire planet. Indeed, every molecule moves according to his will. Only he sets the stars and planets on their courses, and only he can stop them in place by speaking the word. The verses in Amos that describe God's power over all nature serve as incentives to worship and obey God as the sovereign Ruler of the universe and the rightful Ruler of our lives.

We Worship God because Only He Has Spoken to Us (8:11-13)

Verses 11 through 13 describe another form of God's judgment: "a famine . . . / of hearing the words of the LORD." This punishment seems suited to Israel's crime. Since they had not wanted God's word, they would not have it. Even when people attempted to find God's word, they would not be able to find it (v. 12). The situation described in these verses could have likely occurred after the fall of Israel and during the exile. Israelites would be scattered throughout the Near East, only limited copies of God's law would have existed, and many people would not have access to one.

People who reject God and people who have strayed from God don't value God's word and don't want it. But what would life be like if God took his word away completely? Wickedness and lawlessness would increase even more, and even some of the godless would long for the days when God's word was known by some and restrained some evil.

All people should value the fact that the one true God of the universe has spoken (2 Tim 3:16-17; 2 Pet 1:20-21). Since the eternal God has spoken, is it not obvious that we, his creation, should value and submit to what he has said? The Bible is God's Word, and the fact that it is God's Word necessarily means his people will treasure it, read it, learn it, and live by it. In the late fourth century AD, the church father John Chrysostom commented on this verse and referred to the tragedy that some Christians impose on themselves a famine of God's Word:

> While one famine can torture the body, the other famine affects the soul, this very thing that the Lord threatened to inflict on them by way of punishment we now of our own volition secure for ourselves despite God's show of care for us and his provision. (*Homilies on Genesis*, 94)

Thank God for his Word! Other gods have not spoken. The prophet Jeremiah described the false gods: "Like scarecrows in a cucumber patch, / their idols cannot speak. / They must be carried because they cannot walk. / Do not fear them for they can do no harm— / and they cannot do any good" (Jer 10:5). The writer of Psalm 115 also contrasted the one true God with useless gods: "They have mouths but cannot speak, / eyes, but cannot see. / They have ears but cannot hear" (vv. 5-6). Our God can speak. Let us bow before him, give thanks, and worship the God who speaks.

We Worship Only God (8:14)

In the final verse of chapter 8, Amos refers to people who were worshiping at the shrines in Samaria, Dan, and Beer-sheba. The Old Testament affirms that idolatry was pervasive in Israel at virtually every stage in the nation's history. The people worshiped false gods at the locations Amos mentioned, and if they worshiped the one true God, they did so in addition to other gods. Amos refers to one of the gods sarcastically as "the guilt of Samaria." As they worshiped false gods, they may have thought they were being good, religious people. Amos said they were only increasing their guilt.

Regarding the worshipers of false gods, Amos proclaimed, "They will fall, never to rise again." Some have claimed that the Assyrian conquest of Israel and the exile cured Israel of idolatry. It is true that physical worship sites like those in Samaria, Dan, and Beer-sheba no longer existed for the Jews, but humans don't need a physical shrine to create an object of worship. People, including followers of Jesus, place their affections on a higher income, a loved one, or the opinions of others, and those things become idols for us. Only the one true God is worthy of our worship. That fact ought to change everything.

Reflect and Discuss

1. How does knowing the end is near change our lives?
2. How can God use a sinful nation like Assyria to accomplish his will?
3. Why should people believe the Bible's promise of future judgment will be fulfilled?
4. How does God's perfect justice relate to his final judgment of sin?
5. Describe the ways Israelites were oppressing the poor financially. What are some contemporary business practices that are unethical?
6. What are some ways God's law calls for compassion to the poor?
7. List some ways contemporary believers and churches are helping the poor. What are you doing to help the poor?
8. How does the object of our worship reveal the condition of our heart?
9. How does God's holiness relate to his judgment of sin? Why is his holiness an incentive for us to worship only him?
10. Why is the existence of the Bible a motivation to worship God?
11. What are some false gods people worship today? Why do people worship them?

Unavoidable

AMOS 9:1-6

Main Idea: The judgment of God is unavoidable; it is wise to be ready.

I. Will We Accept the Truth of God's Wrath against Sin (9:1)?
II. Will We Run to God or Away from Him (9:2-4)?
III. Are We Giving Praise to God for His Greatness (9:5-6)?

It's hard to like the word *unavoidable*. We would like to think that outcomes are not inevitable. The other team has a better record, and their players are bigger and faster than ours, so our defeat is unavoidable. No! We'll practice harder, find their weakness, and win. The cancer is in stage four and progressing. The end is unavoidable. We will *not* accept it; surely something more can be done. Even when we must accept an unhappy outcome as unavoidable, internally we rebel against it. We want nothing to be unavoidable. We want to be masters of our own fate.

The judgment of God is unavoidable—not for most people but for all people. Second Corinthians 5:10 says, "For we must all appear before the judgment seat of Christ, so that each may be repaid for what he has done in the body, whether good or evil." The verse says "all" and "each" of us. Standing before God in judgment is not optional; it's going to happen. Hebrews 9:27 says, "It is appointed for people to die once—and after this, judgment." After death comes judgment.

Will We Accept the Truth of God's Wrath against Sin?
AMOS 9:1

The greatest crisis facing humanity is not lack of education, the spread of disease, hunger and malnutrition, global warming, financial shortages, or even war. The greatest crisis facing humanity is the wrath of God against sin. God's wrath is universal; everyone has sinned, and no one can escape the penalty for sin. God's wrath is final and eternal; once it is applied, we don't have the opportunity to go back in time and live our lives over again.

The first verses of Amos 9 indicate that this passage records another vision Amos saw, the fifth vision of the book. It's a vision about God's wrath against sin. This vision includes no statement that "God showed me," and God does not address Amos directly as he does in the other visions. Also, this final vision has no wordplay based on an object in the vision, as in chapter 8. Still, the chapter opens with "I saw," and some of the sights Amos saw are not visible to the human eye without divine revelation. Just as the other vision reports, this is an announcement of God's coming judgment.

Amos saw God "standing beside the altar" (v. 1). This altar could have been at Bethel since Amos 7 records Amos's encounter with Amaziah there. But the final verse of Amos 8 mentions three additional worship sites. Therefore, any effort to identify the location of this altar would be speculative. Also, the other visions were symbolic in nature, so it's probably best to regard this altar and the actions in this vision as symbolic, representing "bringing down all of society" (Garrett, *Amos*, 257).

The action of this fifth vision happens at a place of worship, but no worship occurs. Instead, God describes a violent attack on this place of worship. He directed someone to knock down the support structures of the building—the pillars with their capitals and the thresholds—so that they fall "on the heads of all the people." Then God said, "I will kill the rest of them with the sword" (v. 1).

God is clearly demolishing this worship site and actively pursuing the death of the worshipers. What is not clear is whether people are willing to make such an image part of their conception of God. Many people like the idea of God as our Friend, and Jesus did say to his disciples, "You are my friends if you do what I command you" (John 15:14). People like the idea of God as a benevolent Father, Savior, and Provider, and all of those images of God are biblical images; they are true of God. But in the book of Amos, God appears as a Lion roaring from Mount Zion (1:2; 3:8) who says, "I will punish you for all your iniquities" (3:2). God tolerates sin for so long and then says, "That's enough; it's time for punishment." Amos makes clear that God's holy wrath against sin will not be erased by the changing standards of society, it will not be tamed by religious ritualism, and it will not be mollified by maudlin sentimentality about him.

Hosea's revelation of God as a spurned husband is likely more comforting to us than Amos's demolition God who smashes the sanctuary to pieces and comforts those who remain by thrusting a sword in their hearts. But this is the one true God of the universe, and our knowledge of God is incomplete, unbiblical, if it does not include this portrait. Some Christians limit their conception of God by only reading books about Jesus that describe him as strolling around Galilee delivering pithy maxims and showing compassion to the hurting. After reading such books, we should read Amos to see God swing a sword at the necks of unrepentant sinners. Then we may be ready to confess that there is more to this loving, holy God than we can get our arms around. Just when we think we have a definition of God pinned down in a tiny room of our own making, he shows up in unexpected places doing unexpected things, like using a street preacher we weren't impressed with to announce his judgment against sin we didn't think was all that bad.

We should not think depictions of God's judgment are limited to Amos or to the prophetic books. Descriptions of God's wrath against sin are from the beginning of the Bible to the end. At the beginning, God announced that Adam and Eve would die if they ate the fruit of the forbidden tree (Gen 2:17). They did eat of the forbidden fruit, God passed judgment against them, and then they died (Gen 3–5). At the end of the Bible, the apostle John wrote,

> *Then I saw a great white throne and one seated on it. Earth and heaven fled from his presence, and no place was found for them. I also saw the dead, the great and the small, standing before the throne, and books were opened. Another book was opened, which is the book of life, and the dead were judged according to their works by what was written in the books. Then the sea gave up the dead that were in it, and death and Hades gave up the dead that were in them; each one was judged according to their works. Death and Hades were thrown into the lake of fire. This is the second death, the lake of fire. And anyone whose name was not found written in the book of life was thrown into the lake of fire.* (Rev 20:11-15)

Those verses describe God's final wrath against sin, the eradication of sin, and the eternal punishment of unrepentant sinners. The names of all people who have been redeemed by Jesus are recorded in the Book of Life. Those whose names are not in the Book of Life are the unredeemed, and they are tormented forever. We should not have the impression that the reality of God's holy wrath against sin is limited to a few passages in the Bible; it is not. The question is, Will we accept this truth about God?

Every person should contemplate that God's wrath against sin is universal and unavoidable. Romans 6:23 says, "The wages of sin is death." Someone is going to die for our sin. If we have no one to take God's wrath against sin away from us, we will die for our own sin. But God has provided a way for us to avoid his righteous wrath. Jesus took our sin and its penalty on himself when he died on the cross as our sin substitute. First Peter 2:24 says of Jesus, "He himself bore our sins in his body on the tree," and 1 Peter 3:18 says, "Christ also suffered for sins once for all, the righteous for the unrighteous, that he might bring you to God." Jesus bore our sins; he suffered for our sins. People do not have to suffer for their sins if they put their faith in Jesus as Savior! However, if they do not put their faith in Jesus so that he bears their sins, they will bear their own sins and face God's eternal punishment for sin. God's wrath against sin is humanity's greatest crisis. Jesus is God's greatest gift to humanity. He's a really important gift because God's wrath against sin is unavoidable.

Will We Run to God or Away from Him?
AMOS 9:2-4

Psalm 139:1-18 says it's impossible. Jonah tried it and it didn't work. Nobody can hide from God. How can we hide from someone who's everywhere? Facing God is unavoidable. The book of Revelation says a day will come when people will try to hide from God's judgment. John saw that when the Lamb on the throne opened the seventh scroll, people

> hid in the caves and among the rocks of the mountains. And they said to the mountains and to the rocks, "Fall on us and hide us from the face of the one seated on the throne and from the wrath of the Lamb, because the great day of their wrath has come! And who is able to stand?" (Rev 6:15-17)

It's understandable that people will try to hide from God's judgment. The apostle John wrote that it's going to happen at the end, and the prophet Amos wrote that it's going to happen at the end of Israel. In verse 1 a temple building is crumbling on top of people's heads and God is pursuing the survivors with a sword. Of course people are running from that, but God says, "None of those who flee will get away; /

none of the fugitives will escape" (v. 1). Then, for the next three verses God offers a poetic expression of that reality.

First, God says, "If they dig down to Sheol, / from there my hand will take them." Where is Sheol? *What* is Sheol? A lot of speculative, unbiblical, inaccurate statements have been made about Sheol, even by serious students of the Old Testament.[15] The term occurs sixty-five times, and sixty of those occurrences are in poetic passages. *Sheol* is used as a reference to death forty-five times. The words *Sheol* and *death* are synonymously parallel seventeen times. *Sheol* is used to refer to hell twenty times (for example, Ps 9:18; Isa 14:4-21; Ezek 31; 32). So *Sheol* either refers to the eternal destination of the wicked or appears as a general, poetic reference to death (Moseley, "Sheol"). In Amos 9:2, it is surely the latter, meaning, "Even if they go all the way to the place of the dead, they cannot escape God."

Next, God says, "If they climb up to heaven, / from there I will bring them down." No matter how low they go and no matter how high they go, they cannot hide from God. It's ironic that Psalm 139 uses the same word pair (Sheol and heaven) as an encouragement, but in Amos they are a threat. The presence of God is a great comfort to his people; the presence of God is frightening to the wicked. So the first pair is Sheol and heaven—from low to high. The next pair is Carmel and the floor of the sea—from high to low (v. 3).

Of the four locations, Mount Carmel is the only one Israelites could travel to in real life. The other three locations are either metaphysical or inaccessible. A reader may ask why one accessible location was chosen and why *this* location, especially since Mount Hermon and Mount Tabor were higher. First, Mount Carmel is high, even though it's not the highest mountain in Israel. Second, it meets the Mediterranean, preparing for the next clause that refers to the depths of the sea. Third, it had spiritual significance as a sacred place of worship (see ch. 1).

Finally, God states, "If they are driven / by their enemies into captivity, / from there I will command / the sword to kill them." "Captivity" is a different kind of destination from the others. First, the other locations

---

[15] See, for example, Davidson, *The Theology of the OT*, 428–29; Baab, *Theology of the OT*, 212–18.

seem symbolic, but captivity was the future reality of Israel. Second, elsewhere in the Old Testament and throughout the history of Israel, captivity is something to be avoided. But here captivity seems like a desired place since it might offer shelter from God and his judgment. Even though it was in the presence of "enemies," it was still preferable to facing God.

The combination of all the possibilities in verses 2 through 4 provides a strong rhetorical emphasis on the impossibility of fleeing from God. First, a building was going to cave in on "all the people." Then, if any survive, God would slay them. If by some strange happenstance somebody escapes the collapse and the sword, God would find them and kill them, no matter where they went in all the earth, even if they attempted to blend into the crowd among their enemies in a foreign land.

Also, Amos wrote verses 2 through 4 in a structure that is obvious and dramatic. Verses 2 and 3 have two conditional sentences each, and verse 4 has one conditional statement. The structure is as follows:

> v. 2 – if they hide low . . . then. . . . if they hide high . . .
> then. . . .
> v. 3 – if they hide high . . . then. . . . if they hide low . . .
> then. . . .
> v. 4 – if captivity . . . then. . . . "I will keep my eye on them /
> for harm and not for good."

The imbalance of the structure at the end highlights the final statement, and the final statement supplies the reason for the entire chain of events: God intends to bring harm to these unrepentant sinners. Thus, readers are left with a bracing picture of God. He has determined for Israel a future of calamity, not goodness, and they cannot escape that future.

People still run from God. They fill their lives and their minds with multitudes of distractions so they can avoid facing God. They run from God by involvement in hobbies, by working, by staring at a screen, and they even do good things but run from God by pushing him out of those things. However, thank God that while we were running from God, he ran to us. He came to us as Jesus, God the Son, and Jesus said he came "to seek and to save the lost" (Luke 19:10). And we need Jesus's salvation because we cannot hide from God's righteous wrath against sin. It's unavoidable.

Are We Giving Praise to God for His Greatness?
AMOS 9:5-6

Amos 9:5-6 is the third hymn, or poem of praise, recorded in the book of Amos. The other two are Amos 4:13 and 5:8-9. In this hymn, Amos extols the greatness of God using the language of accommodation; he speaks of God's touching the earth (v. 5), building heavenly structures (v. 6), and pouring water (v. 6). The verbs create a mental image of God; he touches, builds, and pours. Those are things humans do, but God does them in ways that are beyond what humans can do. "He touches the earth; / it melts," and "it rises . . . / and subsides like the Nile" (v. 5). No human has power like that. God's building activity is "in the heavens" (v. 6), where no human can reach. And God pours like humans, but he calls to "the water of the sea" and pours it "over the surface of the earth"—probably a reference to rain. So God superintends the natural processes by his knowledge and power. The laws that regulate the created order are not laws of nature; they are laws of God. Humans can observe and even predict the weather; God controls the weather.

Why do we express worship to God? He has supernatural power to control the planet, and his jurisdiction ranges beyond the planet. The entire universe submits to his sovereignty. In the context of Amos 9, that's an important truth. What gives God the right to execute judgment on Israel? Only God has unlimited power, universal authority, and perfect holiness. We have none of that, so we do not have the prerogative to question God's judgment, even when it seems severe to us. We should remember our smallness in comparison to God. He is the God of the universe, and it's not spiritually healthy for us to limit our thoughts of him to what he does for us or to make him merely "our" God. He is Lord of all.

Jesus told a parable about God's ownership of the universe and therefore his right to judge (Matt 20:1-16). At the end of a workday, a landowner paid the workers in his vineyard. Some of the workers complained about how much he paid workers who were hired late in the day. The landowner replied, "Don't I have the right to do what I want with what is mine?" (v. 15). Why did the landowner pay his workers in that way? It was his vineyard, and that's what he chose to do. When we own something, we get to do what we want with it. Control is the prerogative of ownership. In the context of Matthew 20, the prerogative of ownership has to do with God's giving his salvation to undeserving people by his grace through faith in Jesus. That's his way of salvation, and he gets to choose the way of salvation because it's God's universe, his heaven. That's what Amos 9 also affirms. Why did God have the prerogative to decide when and how Israel would be punished for their sin? He's allowed to do what he chooses with what belongs to him. God says in his Word that we don't deserve a relationship with him because of his perfect holiness and our sin. But because of his great love for us and his great grace, he offers us salvation in Jesus. When we put our faith in Jesus, he takes away our sin, reconciles us to himself, and gives us the gift of eternal life. Praise his name!

God's judgment is coming. So we fall to our faces in worship and gratitude for the mercy of God that stirs him to give this broken world salvation in Jesus; we repent of the sins that continue to cling to us, and we turn to him in full faith and obedience. We train our minds to think biblically about the awfulness of sin and God's wrath against it, we speak that truth to the world, and we call the world to repent of sin and turn to Jesus now, before the time of God's mercy has passed. The word *unavoidable* may be hard to like, but facing God and his judgment really is unavoidable. It's wise to be ready.

Reflect and Discuss

1. Why is the wrath of God the greatest crisis facing humanity?
2. What Amos saw in this fifth vision, plus the verses that follow, can be seen as a narrative. Tell the story of what happens.
3. Why is it difficult to include passages of Scripture like this in forming our conception of God?
4. How can people avoid experiencing God's wrath against sin?
5. Do you know people you would describe as running from God? Why are they running?
6. Describe how this section summarizes Sheol.
7. In what ways do people hide from God? How can people hide from God even at church?
8. How does the hymn in Amos 9 portray the greatness of God?
9. Explain the relationship between the prerogatives of ownership and God's judgment of sin.
10. How does the message of this passage of Scripture motivate Christians to share the gospel?

A Promise of Hope in Dark Times

AMOS 9:7-15

Main Idea: Amos told the unfaithful they would soon suffer under the judgment of God if they did not repent, but he also prophesied the hopeful future that would be realized in Jesus.

I. **God Is at Work in Every Nation (9:7).**
II. **God's Judgment of Sin Will Not Be Thwarted (9:8-10).**
III. **Sin Breaks Our World (9:11).**
IV. **God's Plan Is to Restore This Broken World in Christ (9:11-15).**
    A. God will restore Jews and Gentiles (9:11-12,14-15).
    B. God will restore people and nature (9:13).

Amos lived in difficult times. On the surface some things seemed to be going well. Jeroboam II was on the throne of the northern kingdom of Israel, Uzziah was reigning over the southern kingdom of Judah, and both of those kings reigned for about forty years. In Judah, Uzziah completed multiple building projects and consolidated the strength of his kingdom. In Israel, Jeroboam enjoyed military successes that expanded the borders of Israel, and the economy seemed to be booming. But the people of Israel were supposed to be God's people who put their faith in him, and during the time when Amos preached, Israel was morally degenerate and spiritually apostate. Amos testified to sexual immorality, economic injustice, mistreatment of the poor, drunken revelry, and corrupt religion.

God allowed Amos to see that moral compromise and spiritual unfaithfulness would eventually be the undoing of Israel. So again and again Amos prophesied that God's judgment against sin was going to visit Israel. When God first gave his law to his people, he had promised that if they were unfaithful to him they would suffer. Amos saw all their unfaithfulness, and he told them they would soon suffer under the judgment of God if they did not repent.

Occasionally in the book of Amos, we see glimpses of hope for the future, but in chapter 9 it's as if the storm clouds part and we're allowed to see a future that's as bright as day—the future that began to be realized when Jesus was born, the future that will continue to unfold all the way into the age of a new heaven and a new earth. Consider a few truths God showed Amos.

God Is at Work in Every Nation
AMOS 9:7

In verse 7 God, through his prophet, asked Israel a question: "Israelites, are you not like the Cushites to me?" The Cushites were Ethiopians, and the answer the Israelites of Amos's day would have given to that question is, "No! No nation in the world is like us to you, God. We're your chosen people." The Jews *were* God's chosen people, but the problem was they had been perverting their election in two ways. First, they were twisting their election to mean they could behave any way they wanted and God was still obligated to bless them because they were his chosen ones. Second, they thought that because of their election they mattered to God more than other people groups mattered to God. In that situation, God let them know they *were* special to him, but that did not excuse sin, and it did not cancel his love for other peoples.

God then asked them, "Didn't I bring Israel from the land of Egypt?" (v. 7). Of course, the answer to that question is yes. And after God mentioned the exodus from Egypt, the Israelites probably expected God to say something about how unique they were: of all the nations in the world, God chose only them, delivered only them, and had a covenant with only them. But God did not say that next. He said, "Didn't I bring Israel from the land of Egypt, / the Philistines from Caphtor, / and the Arameans from Kir?" God was making his gracious activity in the history of Israel equivalent to his gracious activity in the histories of other nations. This is a powerful affirmation of the sovereign providence of God working in the histories of all nations. Yes, God worked miraculously in the history of Israel, delivering the Israelites from Egyptian bondage. But how did the Philistines arrive in Canaan? God brought them there from Caphtor. How did the Arameans arrive in Syria? God brought them there from Kir. God was telling the Israelites through Amos that he is actively involved in the history of every nation, bringing about his sovereign will. God cares about every person in every nation. Given all we know about the Israelites of Amos's day, it's likely they were astonished when Amos preached that God equated his work in Israel with his work in other nations and that he affirmed his care for those others.

Here's a question for us: **Do we care about every nation?** The gospel message is for all nations. On the night that Jesus was born, the angel said to the shepherds, "Don't be afraid, for look, I proclaim to you good news of great joy that will be for all the people. Today in the city of David a Savior was born for you, who is the Messiah, the Lord" (Luke 2:10-11). A Savior has been born, and that's good news of great joy "for all the people." God's salvation agenda is international. It always has been international, and it still is today. Jesus's commission to his church is, "Go . . . and make disciples of all nations" (Matt 28:19). "All nations," because, as 2 Peter 3:9 says, he is "not wanting any to perish but all to come to repentance." God's redemption program is for all people in all nations. "For God loved *the world* in this way: He gave his one and only Son, so that everyone who believes in him will not perish but have eternal life" (John 3:16; emphasis added). First John 4:14 says, "The Father has sent his Son as *the world's* Savior" (emphasis added).

The New Testament teaches that followers of Jesus are the elect. God chose us to be his children (Eph 1:4; 1 Pet 1:1). The New Testament also teaches that the gospel of Jesus is for all people. Theologians wrangle over how to reconcile those two truths, but the Bible never hints that they are incompatible with each other. May we never pervert the doctrine of election to justify disobedience to God's command to make disciples of all nations. Instead, let's follow Jesus and open our eyes to see the fields that are ready for harvest and pray that the Lord of the harvest would send workers into the harvest (John 4:35; Luke 10:2). What's your part in God's worldwide program of taking the gospel of Jesus to all nations so all can be saved through him?

God's Judgment of Sin Will Not Be Thwarted
AMOS 9:8-10

Verse 8 begins by stating that God's eyes are on us. We typically think that's good. We welcome God's watchful care over us. But if we're in sin, it's a different matter for God's eyes to be on us. In the case of sinful Israel, God said through Amos,

> *"Look, the eyes of the Lord GOD*
> *are on the sinful kingdom,*
> *and I will obliterate it*
> *from the face of the earth. However, I will not totally destroy*
> *the house of Jacob."*

God will act according to his perfect justice toward sin and toward righteousness. God will destroy wickedness, but the righteous will not be destroyed with the wicked. In verse 9 God said that he's going to shake the people of Israel like shaking them in a basket, and they're not going to fall out of the basket. They're not going to escape his judgment. In verse 10 God said that a violent death awaits the wicked. God quotes some of them as saying, "Disaster will never overtake / or confront us." They were denying God's judgment. But their denial was not going to stop it.

This is a word for our times. When confronted with the reality of God's judgment of sin, Israelites said, "Disaster will never overtake or confront us." Has there ever been a culture that has so widely denied the judgment of God as Western culture at this moment? The Bible teaches that hell is real, it is a place of torment, and it is eternal. Our culture mocks the idea of hell. "Disaster will never overtake or confront us." Please don't mock hell; it's real, and you don't want to go there. If people have not put their faith in Jesus to forgive their sin and reconcile them to God, and they're not scared of hell, they're missing something. Romans 2 says,

> *Do you think . . . that you will escape God's judgment? Or do*
> *you despise the riches of his kindness, restraint, and patience, not*
> *recognizing that God's kindness is intended to lead you to repentance?*
> *Because of your hardened and unrepentant heart you are storing up*
> *wrath for yourself in the day of wrath, when God's righteous judgment*
> *is revealed.* (vv. 3-5)

One day God will express his wrath against wickedness and the wicked, and on that day we all want God's grace, not his wrath. How do we avoid God's wrath? What is the way? Jesus said, "I am the way, the truth, and the life. No one comes to the Father except through me" (John 14:6). We get to heaven by putting our faith in Jesus. And Jesus wants us in heaven with him. In the same chapter, Jesus said,

Believe in God; believe also in me. In my Father's house are many
rooms. . . . If I go away and prepare a place for you, I will come
again and take you to myself, so that where I am you may be also.
(John 14:1-3)

Jesus told us to believe in him so we can be with him in heaven forever, in the place he has prepared for us. God's judgment against sin will not be thwarted, but praise his name, he has come to us in Jesus to save us from sin. God's wrath against our sin was placed on Jesus on the cross, so when we put our faith in him as our sin sacrifice, he saves us from sin, reconciles us to God, and gives us new and eternal life.

Consider two questions. First, **Are you trusting in Jesus for salvation?** If you have never put your faith in Jesus as your Savior and Lord, do that today. That's the best decision you will ever make. It is the only way to enjoy God's forgiveness for sin and to possess eternal life. Second, **Are we warning our neighbors about sin and judgment?** If heaven and hell are real, if everybody is going to spend eternity in one place or the other, and if faith in Jesus is the only way to avoid hell and go to heaven, what could be more important than getting that message to everybody we know and to the world? God's judgment of sin will not be thwarted.

Sin Breaks Our World
AMOS 9:11

Verse 11 refers to the "shelter of David" that was "fallen." That refers to Israel, and it was not the typical way to refer to Israel. Sometimes Israel was referred to as the "house of David," but this is the "shelter" of David. There was a significant difference between a house and this word translated "shelter," and everybody in Israel knew this. A shelter was just a hut made with tree limbs and branches, sort of a lean-to that was put together in the wilderness to provide temporary shelter. So God was referring to Israel as weak, but also this shelter was "fallen." Sin had broken Israel.

When Amos prophesied, Israel did not look broken—they had military and economic successes, a stable monarchy. But God, and Amos, knew Israel had a rotten spiritual core. The people and their leaders were unfaithful to God and morally corrupt. They were inviting the punishment of God, which God had promised if his people became unfaithful to him and disobedient to his law. When Amos prophesied destruction, Israel did not look broken, but it was, and in less than fifty years the Assyrians would conquer Israel and destroy the capital city Samaria.

The fall of Israel in the eighth century BC is just one example of the countless ways sin has broken our world and continues to break it. As sin continues to escalate, its devastating effects also escalate. The world in which we live is burning with disease and death, hatred and war, abuse and injustice; our world is fallen and broken. Here's a question: **Will people see the real problem?** People are constantly thinking that if they smooth over some surface problem, if they repair the consequences of the problem, then all will be well. But the root of every problem is sin and separation from God. We think that if we provide enough education, resources, or the proper environment, then people will improve and the world will improve. But that's only treating the symptoms, not the spiritual disease.

Picture a man who's down-and-out, homeless, and living around the railroad tracks. He steals food to eat and sleeps in boxcars at night. But if we could give him some financial help and an opportunity, then he wouldn't steal anymore, would he? So we clean him up and give him a job; we pay for a college education, and then he goes to law school. He runs for public office and is elected, and then he goes to Washington and steals a whole railroad company. (I am indebted to a famous saying by D. L. Moody for the idea of this illustration.) Why? Nothing has changed in the man's heart. He looks more respectable in every way, but his heart is still ruled by sin and rebellion against God. And our heart condition is the reason Jesus came. The night he was born, an angel said, "Today in the city of David a Savior was born for you" (Luke 2:11). "A Savior"—all of humanity needs a Savior because we're lost in sin and alienated from God. God gave us a Savior in Jesus.

God's Plan Is to Restore This Broken World in Christ
AMOS 9:11-15

Verse 11 refers to the shelter of David that had fallen, but God says he's going to rebuild the fallen shelter. "I will repair its gaps, / restore its ruins, / and rebuild it as in the days of old." And when is God promising to do all of that? The verse begins with "In that day." In what day? In the day of the coming of Christ and the establishment of his church.

That's what Acts 15 says. When the disciples of Jesus began to preach the gospel beyond Jerusalem, Gentiles as well as Jews were coming to faith in Jesus. That caused a controversy for the Jews. Shouldn't Gentiles be required to become Jews to be right with God? Church leaders gathered in Jerusalem to discuss that question and make a decision. The crucial moment came when the apostle James stood and quoted from Amos 9 as proof that the salvation of the Gentiles, the extension of the covenant blessings to all people, was God's plan all along.

So, when is the "in that day" to which Amos referred? It's the day of the spread of the gospel to all the nations; it's the day of the church, the day in which we are living. This is the time when **God will restore Jews and Gentiles.** Verse 12 refers to the Gentiles being brought into the blessings of the covenant. It mentions, "the remnant of Edom / and all the nations / that bear my name— / this is the declaration of the LORD." For the Jews of Amos's day, and the Jews in the early church, that was an astounding statement: "that bear my name." God used that phrase only two other places in the Old Testament with reference to people, and both of those refer to Israel (2 Chron 7:14; Isa 63:7). But God said through Amos, "In that day"—the day of the coming of the Messiah and the establishment of the new covenant in him—"all the nations" will be brought in. And now we can see more clearly what it meant for the angel outside Bethlehem that night to say the birth of Jesus is "good news of great joy that will be for all the people" (Luke 2:10). This was the inauguration of the new covenant in Jesus that would bring in all the nations.

Amos 9 also affirms that **God will restore people and nature.** Verse 13 is introduced with a new temporal marker: "The days are coming." That statement signals a shift to another time; Amos shifts here from the age of the church living in the new covenant to an age that is still future for us, the age in which God restores all things to their rightful place, when he creates what the New Testament refers to as a new heaven and a new earth. In those days, the harvest will be so abundant that we'll still be harvesting into the next year when it's time to start plowing and planting again. There will be so many grapes that we'll still be treading grapes into the next agricultural season. And the Lord said through Amos, "The mountains will drip with sweet wine, / and all the hills will flow with it."

God will restore the created order. Romans 8 says the whole creation is groaning in the present age, "subjected to futility" by the sins of humanity, and the creation longs for the day of redemption (Rom 8:19-22). God promises through Amos and through others that that day is coming. It was a promise of hope in dark times.

Do you live in dark times? Are you struggling with living in a broken world? Are you surrounded by wickedness? So was Amos. Hear his message. God will heal this broken world. Jews and Gentiles, people and nature, praise his name!

Reflect and Discuss

1. Amos lived in times that were spiritually and morally dark but bright in other ways. Would you describe the times in which you live as dark? Why or why not?

2. How do you think Israelites responded to Amos's equating God's activity in the history of Israel with his activity in the histories of other nations?

3. How were Israelites perverting God's choice of them as his people? How do Christians pervert God's election of believers?

4. God placed the Philistines and the Arameans in their locations. When we realize that God is somehow guiding every nation, how does that affect the way we think about the world and about history?

5. What should the church of Jesus be doing among the nations today?

6. How should individual Christians relate to the nations?

7. Have you personally encountered individuals who deny or question God's future judgment of sin? Why did they do so?

8. Why are some people unwilling to embrace Jesus as "the way, the truth, and the life"?

9. What evidence do you see today that sin is breaking our world?

10. How does it affect the way Christians live and think to realize that God will restore good and right in the end?

Obadiah

Introduction to the Book of Obadiah

Theme

The opening verse of the book of Obadiah states the theme of the book: "The vision of Obadiah. This is what the Lord GOD has said about Edom." It is also possible to translate the last two words of that verse as "to Edom" or "against Edom." Given the contents of the book, perhaps the last is best. The book of Obadiah is about Edom, and what it says about Edom is negative. Obadiah announced God's judgment of Edom, his punishment for their behavior toward the people of Judah and Jerusalem. As verses 10 and 11 express it, "Because of violence done to your brother Jacob. / On the day you stood aloof, / on the day strangers captured his wealth, / while foreigners entered his city gate." For crimes against their neighboring nation, through Obadiah God said to Edom, "I will bring you down" (v. 4).

Author

No justifiable reason exists for doubting that the book was written by the prophet whose name has been given to the book. As for Obadiah's identity, he has often been associated with the Obadiah who served as an administrator, or prophet, during the reign of King Ahab of Israel (1 Kgs 17–18). Such an identification seems to go beyond the evidence (Patterson, "Obadiah," 215). First, "Obadiah" was a common name in the history of Israel, demonstrated by its appearance several times in genealogies and lists in 1 and 2 Chronicles, Ezra, and Nehemiah. Second, nothing explicit in the Bible connects these two men named Obadiah. Third, the reign of King Ahab may be the wrong historical period in which to date the prophet Obadiah. Therefore, it is likely best to conclude that nothing is known about this prophet other than that he wrote this prophecy against Edom.

Historical Background

The history behind the book of Obadiah begins during the pregnancy of Rebekah, the wife of Isaac, the son of Abraham. That story is told in the first section of the exposition to follow: the descendants of Jacob were the Israelites, and the descendants of Esau were the Edomites. Jacob's name was changed as a result of his encounter with an assailant at the ford of the Jabbok River (Gen 32). After the two wrestled, Jacob's name was changed to Israel, which means something like "striving with God" or "God prevails." The assailant is not identified specifically (though see Hos 12:4), but Jacob knew he had encountered God. Esau's name was changed to Edom after Esau sold his birthright to Jacob for some stew. The stew is called "red stuff" (Gen 25:30), and the Hebrew word for red became Esau's name, "Edom." That sensual story stands in contrast with the divine story about Jacob's name change. Esau was named after a bowl of soup, not unlike being named "Brunswick." Esau was hungry after an unsuccessful hunt and said, "Give me some of that red stuff." So his name became Big Red.

The Date of the Book

The book of Obadiah refers to "violence done to your brother Jacob" (v. 10), and the sin of the Edomites was that they "stood aloof / on the day strangers captured his wealth, / while foreigners entered his city gate / and cast lots for Jerusalem" (v. 11). The question is, To which "violence" does Obadiah refer? Identifying the invasion of Jerusalem to which Obadiah refers is the key challenge in dating the book of Obadiah, since Jerusalem was invaded more than once.

First, in the late tenth century BC, Pharoah Shishak invaded Judah and Jerusalem during the reign of Rehoboam, and he looted the temple (1 Kgs 11:14-22; 14:25-27). Second, Philistines and Arabs invaded Jerusalem in the ninth century BC during the reign of Jehoram. Second Chronicles mentions that they ransacked the royal palace (2 Kgs 8:20-22; 2 Chron 21:8-10,16-19; cf. Amos 1:6). Third, Syrians attacked Jerusalem during the reign of Joash in the late ninth century BC. They killed leaders in the city and sent spoils to the Syrian king in Damascus (2 Kgs 14:8; 2 Chron 24:23-24). Fourth, in the early eighth century BC, Judah's king Amaziah attacked Edom and killed twenty thousand Edomites. After that battle, Amaziah attacked Israel. Israel not only defeated Judah, but King Jehoash of Israel marched to Jerusalem, damaged the city, and looted the temple and palace (2 Kgs 14:7-14). This invasion may not match the one mentioned in the book of Obadiah because Obadiah 11 mentions that "foreigners" invaded Jerusalem, and Israelites may not have qualified as foreigners to Judah. Fifth, During the reign of Ahaz in the late eighth century BC, Edom, the Philistines, Syria, and Israel attacked Judah (2 Kgs 16:5-6; 2 Chron 28:16-22). This invasion would partially fit the book of Obadiah since Edom participated, but no mention is made of the attack reaching Jerusalem. Sixth, during the early sixth century BC, in the reign of Jehoiakim, the Babylonians invaded Judah and Jerusalem when Jehoiakim rebelled against Babylonian rule. Syrians, Moabites, and Ammonites participated in the attack. Jehoiakim died during the siege, his son Jehoiachin took the throne, and the Babylonians conquered Jerusalem and carried Jehoiachin into exile along with the treasures of the temple and palace (2 Kgs 24:1-16). The Babylonians installed Zedekiah as a puppet governor.

Finally, ten years later, they returned when King Zedekiah rebelled against Babylon. During this invasion, the Babylonians burned the city and destroyed all the monumental buildings, including the temple. The extent of this destruction seems to fit most closely the kind of devastation Obadiah describes. Also, Ezekiel 25 refers to the Babylonian destruction of Jerusalem and states that Edom incurred guilt in that event (vv. 12-14). Ezekiel 35 refers to Edom's arrogance and the fact that Edom rejoiced over Judah's demise (vv. 13-15). That description, too, matches Obadiah's words about Edom. Lamentations 4:21-22 and Psalms 137:7 also refer to Edom in relation to Jerusalem's destruction. This commentary reflects the position that this final destruction of Jerusalem by the Babylonians in 586 BC is the destruction about which Obadiah wrote, the destruction over which the Edomites rejoiced. Dogmatism over the date of the book of Obadiah seems unwarranted since some of the other invasions of Jerusalem could possibly serve as the background of the book.

An Outline of the Book

God Wins

OBADIAH 1-21

Main Idea: God was about to bring the nation of Edom to an end because of its sin against its brother Judah.

I. Don't Make Sinful Substitutions.
   A. Don't substitute worldly wisdom for God's wisdom (8).
   B. Don't substitute human plans for God's plan (10-14).
   C. Don't substitute pride for humility (3,11-12).
   D. Don't substitute false gods for the true God.
II. Believe God's Future Reversals.
   A. Sin will receive God's punishment (15).
   B. Pride will lead to humiliation (3-4).
   C. God will be glorified over all (18,21).
III. Apply the Practical Implications.
   A. God avenges, so we can rest.
   B. God rules, so we can be patient.
   C. God's judgment is coming, so we must warn.

All adults over twenty-five or so remember what happened on September 11, 2001. It's such a common topic of conversation that we don't even refer to it as the terrorist attack on the World Trade Center; we just say, "9/11." Almost three thousand people died that morning. We saw the buildings burning and falling and people running and screaming. Those images are indelibly etched in our memories. That evening or the next evening I saw something else I'll never forget. On the news I saw video footage from Palestinian cities in the West Bank area of Israel, specifically the cities of Ramallah and Nablus. The year before 9/11 I had driven through Ramallah every day for about three weeks when I was in the area participating in an archaeological excavation. But on September 11, the people of Ramallah, Nablus, and other Palestinian cities were literally dancing in the streets, waving flags, giving out sweets, firing guns into the air, and shouting for joy. Three thousand innocent people died, and they were celebrating (Lerner, "PA Threatens").

During the lifetime of Obadiah, Israel had their own 9/11. Not to diminish the pain of ours, but theirs was worse. In 586 BC, the Babylonians besieged and destroyed Jerusalem. They burned the whole city to the ground. We could not overstate the significance of the city of Jerusalem to the Jews. Solomon's magnificent temple that had stood for 350 years was in Jerusalem. It was the most sacred space in the world to the Jews, but it was burned to the ground with the entire city. Still today, twenty-six hundred years later, Jews observe a day of fasting, mourning, and prayer on the ninth day of the Jewish month of Ab, the day when Jerusalem and the temple were destroyed.

When Jerusalem fell, the Jews mourned, but the Edomites did *not*. Like the people in Ramallah and Nablus, they *rejoiced* over the destruction of Jerusalem and the temple. Thousands of people in Jerusalem died, and thousands more were carried into exile, but the Edomites rejoiced. So God sent Obadiah to announce his judgment on the nation of Edom.

In verse 10 the prophet referred to Judah as "your brother Jacob." Again in verse 12, he called Judah "your brother." To understand why Edom and Israel were brother nations, we have to go back in time all the way to Abraham's son Isaac. Isaac's wife Rebekah conceived twins. The two babies struggled with each other in the womb. Rebekah asked the Lord about it, and he told her, "Two nations are in your womb; . . . / and the older will serve the younger" (Gen 25:21-23).

What God said came to pass. The older child was named Esau, and the younger was Jacob. Just as they had struggled in the womb, they continued to struggle throughout their lives. After they died, their descendants also struggled with each other. The descendants of Jacob were the Israelites, and the descendants of Esau were the Edomites. The Israelites, sons of Jacob, and the Edomites, sons of Esau, often clashed with one another. When Moses was leading the Israelites to the promised land, he asked permission to pass through Edom. Edom, the nation that was brother to Israel, said no and threatened to attack the Israelites if they entered Edomite territory (Num 20:14-21). After Israel was established as a nation in the promised land, the first two kings of Israel, Saul and David, had to fight against Edom (1 Sam 14:47; 2 Sam 8:14). Israel and Edom also fought in the days of King Jehoram (2 Kgs 8:20-24) and King Amaziah (2 Kgs 14:7). Israel prevailed in every battle. Just as the Lord had said, the Israelites, descendants of the younger Jacob, were dominant over the Edomites, descendants of the older Esau.

After all those years and all that bad blood between Israel and Edom, the Edomites still were unwilling to bury the hatchet. They didn't mourn when Jerusalem and the temple were destroyed. Both Obadiah (vv. 11-12) and the book of Lamentations (4:21-22) tell us that Edom *rejoiced* over the ruin of God's people. Psalm 137:7 says that when the Babylonians invaded Jerusalem, the Edomites said, "Destroy it! Destroy it / down to its foundations!" Obadiah also tells us that the people of Edom looted Jerusalem (vv. 11,13) and sold Israelites as slaves (v. 14). Obadiah wrote that God was going to bring the nation of Edom to an end because of their sin. God's words to Edom carry a powerful message for us because the sins of the Edomites are still with us.

Don't Make Sinful Substitutions

In place of what God wanted for the Edomites, they substituted what they wanted. We can identify four such substitutions. Edom made them, and so do people today.

Don't Substitute Worldly Wisdom for God's Wisdom (8)

God mentioned the wise men of Edom in verse 8. "Will I not eliminate the wise ones of Edom / and those who understand / from the hill country of Esau?" We think of wisdom as a good thing. But the Bible distinguishes between God's wisdom and the world's wisdom. The book of James contrasts wisdom that's "from above" with wisdom that is "earthly, unspiritual, demonic" (3:15-17). First Corinthians 1 asks, "Hasn't God made the world's wisdom foolish?" And it says that when we know Jesus as Savior he becomes "wisdom from God for us" (1 Cor 1:20,30).

Most ancient Near Eastern cultures included a scribal class that excelled in the wisdom arts. They debated by telling parables and taught their children by using proverbs. The Edomites practiced the same wisdom skills. Contemporary Western culture also has become known for its high degree of education. But when education is divorced from the wisdom that comes down from above, the wisdom that is in Christ, the result is a man-made wisdom that incurs the judgment of God. Don't substitute worldly wisdom for God's wisdom.

Don't Substitute Human Plans for God's Plan (10-14)

After the Hebrew slaves left Egypt and were in the wilderness, God's plan was for his people to enter the promised land. The Edomites opposed God's plan and told the Israelites they could not go through Edomite territory. Instead of helping God's plan, they hindered it. They considered Israel their enemy, and that took precedence over God's plan. The Edomites substituted human plans for God's plan, and God was going to pass judgment against them for it. People still oppose God's plan—his plan of salvation and his plan for the sanctification of his people.

Don't Substitute Pride for Humility (3,11-12)

God was condemning Edom to death because of what verse 3 calls "your arrogant heart." Verses 11 and 12 also state they "stood aloof" and gloated and boasted. Pride continues to be a problem today. At least pride is a problem for you. Not for *me* because I've grown beyond that, and I'm trying to help you with *your* problem with pride. No, if I believed that, I would truly be arrogant. Pride is a universal problem. We want to be our own gods, masters of our own lives. Jesus left the glories of heaven to live as a servant who died for sinful people, and he calls us to that life of humble service. But service is hard; we prefer leadership and ownership. We want to be the hero, in the limelight. When boys watch a Batman movie, they fantasize about being Bruce Wayne, not Alfred the butler. Girls want to be the leading lady, not the housekeeper. That proclivity for pride often controls not only persons but also nations. It controlled Edom.

Are nations proud today? It's possible for citizens in every country to cross the line between patriotism and nationalism. David Allan Hubbard wrote about how nations sometimes commit atrocities, but they remain proud and don't apologize:

> What would probably shock the United Nations most would be for a nation to stand before the solemn assembly and make a public apology. You can hear the speech now: "Mr. Secretary, ladies and gentlemen. I have been instructed by my government to tell you that we have made a serious mistake. We had no right to move our troops across the borders of our neighbors to invade their land. . . . We did it purely from greed and selfishness. . . . And to this august gathering, which has been justly angry at our action, my government wants to tender a sincere apology." (*Will We Ever Catch Up*, 51)

That's clearly an imaginary scenario. Edom, as far as we know, never confessed their wrongs against the people of God. Edom had substituted national pride for humility.

Don't Substitute False Gods for the True God

The Old Testament refers to the religion of Edom. Those references are in 2 Chronicles 25, and both of them refer to Edomite gods in the plural. The Edomites were polytheists; they worshiped multiple gods, and they were false gods. Second Chronicles 25 also says that the real God was going to send his judgment for worshiping them.

Edom came from Esau, and Esau was the grandson of Abraham. How had the sons of Esau, the Edomites, strayed so far that they worshiped pagan gods? All nations in the ancient Near East had their own gods. Evidently, the descendants of Esau wanted to be independent from the descendants of Jacob, a separate nation with their own gods, like the other nations. Submitting to the God of Israel seemed equivalent to submitting to Israel, and the Edomites were not going to do that. The independence of their nation had become more important to them than right worship. Their freedom to believe what they wanted trumped the truth about God.

Eclipsing the truth about God by exalting one's nation remains common today. Many people in the world put their hope in their sovereign state instead of the sovereign God, or they put their faith in both equally, resulting in a civil religion that exalts the nation and debases God. It's another form of idolatry. What are the gods of Western culture? In Western culture, the dominant explanation of the origin of the universe is that it began by the chance interaction of naturalistic causes; the god is chance. Western culture is worshiping the wrong god. The Bible claims to be the perfect revelation of the one true God that is absolutely true. But the cardinal sin in Western culture is to claim the existence of absolute truth. Western culture worships the god of relativism, the wrong god. Western culture also worships individual freedom to the point of *moral* relativism, so every person does whatever he or she pleases without the restraint of moral absolutes. The Bible, however, is full of moral absolutes that come from the one true God. Our culture is worshiping the wrong god. Let us pray that God will protect us from making that sinful substitution.

Believe God's Future Reversals

God was not ignorant of Edom's sin, nor was he passive. God knew Edom had celebrated the calamity of God's people. He was about to intervene and introduce some divine reversals.

Sin Will Receive God's Punishment (15)

In verse 15 God says to Edom, "As you have done, it will be done to you; / what you deserve will return on your own head." Sin will receive God's punishment, and the punishment will be suited perfectly to the sin. What the Edomites had done was going to return on their heads. We refer to that kind of punishment as *lex talionis*, a principle according to which punishment is appropriate to the sin. The severity of the punishment fits the severity of the crime. The Edomites had participated in the destruction and exile of another nation; they had treated the Israelites with violence. Therefore, Edom would be defeated, and they would cease to exist as a people. "No survivor will remain / of the house of Esau" (v. 18). God said what they had done was going to come back on them. Sin will receive God's punishment. That will always be true.

Pride Will Lead to Humiliation (3-4)

Proverbs 16:18 says, "Pride comes before destruction." The Edomites were saying, "Look at how great we are! We live up here in the mountains. Who could ever bring us down?" God said, "I'm going to bring you down" (vv. 3-4).

God Will Be Glorified over All (18,21)

Edom gloated over the defeat of Judah and the destruction of Jerusalem. They celebrated the suffering of God's chosen people, and that was just one of their many sins. What happened to Edom? Verse 18 says, "No survivor will remain / of the house of Esau, / for the LORD has spoken." That prophecy about Edom came to pass. The nation of Edom is no more, and the territory of Edom is now occupied by the country of Jordan.

Verse 21 states, "The kingdom will be the LORD's." When the book of Obadiah was written, many of the Jews were in exile in Babylon after the fall of Jerusalem. In Babylon, the Jews would have heard the gods

of Babylon extolled. Obadiah reminds them that the one true God of
Israel, and no other god, will reign over all. That one true God has now
come to us in Jesus, who is King of kings and Lord of lords (Rev 17:14;
19:16). "The dominion belongs to YHWH incarnate in Jesus Christ!"
(Block, *Obadiah*, 116).

When Jesus was born, wise men from the east informed King
Herod that a king had been born in that area. King Herod ordered
the deaths of all male babies so he would be sure to kill that one
baby, the baby Jesus. King Herod was an Idumean. "Idumean" was
a Hellenized version of "Edomite." Herod was an Edomite. Jesus,
God's Messiah, escaped Herod's plan to murder him. Herod died.
Jesus manifested himself as the Messiah, died on the cross for the
sins of humanity, rose from the dead, and today his gospel is spread
worldwide by his church. One day he will return and reign over all,
and when he returns, he will come to Mount Zion. So, when verse 21
says, "Saviors will ascend Mount Zion / to rule over the hill country
of Esau, / and the kingdom will be the Lord's," that's referring to
something more than the Jews returning from exile and occupying
their ancestral land. Obadiah was writing about a coming kingdom
that would be universal, beginning with the coming of Jesus and ending with the return of Jesus to reign over all. When all the kingdoms
that were going to last forever have passed off the scene, when every
nation that thought it would rule the world has been destroyed, Jesus
will be on the throne. God will be glorified.

Apply the Practical Implications

What difference do the truths of the book of Obadiah make? How
should we be different because of this part of God's Word? Consider
three practical implications.

God Avenges, so We Can Rest

When we see something that's wrong, we don't have to get vengeance.
God took care of passing judgment against the Edomites for their
sin. God will take care of all judgment of sin, so we need not worry
about seeking vengeance. Romans 12:19 says, "Friends, do not avenge
yourselves; instead, leave room for God's wrath, because it is written,
Vengeance belongs to me; I will repay, says the Lord." In every situation

of wrong, God will bring his judgment. That's his job; ours is to trust his sovereign rule and rest. In the end God wins.

God Rules, so We Can Be Patient

God's judgment moves slowly, but he is in charge. So, when we read all the horrible news, we don't ricochet emotionally from one crisis to another, wring our hands, and wonder what is going to become of this world. We *know* what this world is coming to, and we know God is on his throne as the sovereign Lord of the universe. We can have patience instead of panic.

God's Judgment Is Coming, so We Must Warn

God announced his judgment against the nation of Edom, and that judgment came. God has also announced his judgment against those who reject his Son Jesus. That judgment also will come. If we love people like God loves them, we'll warn them of the coming judgment. Our prayer should be, "Lord, use me to call people to you." We know God wins, so in the end all that matters is whether people are right with God through his Son and our Savior Jesus.

Reflect and Discuss

1. Consider the condition of the relationship between Judah and Edom that resulted in the conflicts reviewed in this section. Does such enmity exist today between nations or persons?
2. The Edomites were descendants of Abraham but evidently did not worship the one true God. What can we do to preserve faith in the truth in coming generations?
3. In what ways do people substitute worldly wisdom for God's wisdom?
4. How can legitimate and godly acquisition of knowledge become worldly wisdom?
5. In what ways do Christians hinder the fulfillment of God's plan for his church today?
6. How do Christians elevate love for country so high that it competes with allegiance to God? Where do we draw the line between patriotism and nationalism, between love for country and worship of country?

7. What is an idol? What are some false gods in your heart?

8. When you think about the fact that God wins in the end and sinners are punished, what actions do you feel are urgent for you to take before this age passes?

9. How have you been doing at resting in faith in the knowledge that God is in control of the destiny of the world?

10. What contributions are you currently making to warn your generation of coming judgment and to tell people the way to be saved?

The Pride Pandemic

OBADIAH 1-9

Main Idea: The book of Obadiah serves as a warning from God to avoid the disease of pride.

I. **Do I Have It? Take God's Test.**
   A. Test for self-deception (3).
   B. Test for a sense of invincibility (3-4).
   C. Test for blindness to the truth.
II. **What Can I Do about It? Apply God's Remedy.**
   A. Remember God's opposition to pride (1,3).
   B. Submit to God's people.
   C. Consider the outcome of pride (3-4).

The Corona virus was labeled COVID-19, short for Coronavirus disease of 2019. Its effects began to spread in 2020. All over the world, hospitals filled to overflowing. Millions of people died. People also typically referred to it as "the pandemic" because it spread virtually everywhere. The human toll of the disease was incalculable—sickness, death, grief, and financial hardship all over the world.

Pride is also a sickness. And it's a pandemic: people everywhere are sick with it. It sounds like hyperbole, but throughout history pride has led to more human suffering than COVID-19. First, it has been around since the garden of Eden. Second, its consequences are not only universal but also potentially eternal.

Edom had a problem with pride. When God spoke to Edom, he referred to "your arrogant heart" (v. 3). The Edomites lived among the mountains, and God made their lofty location a metaphor for their lofty thinking about themselves. He quoted them as saying, "Who can bring me down to the ground?" (v. 3). The word translated "arrogant" in verse 3 occurs only eleven times in the Old Testament. The Bible makes clear that it's a sin with grave consequences. For example, Deuteronomy 17:12-13 says,

> *The person who acts arrogantly, refusing to listen either to the priest who stands there serving the LORD your God or to the judge, must*

die. You must purge the evil from Israel. Then all the people will hear about it, be afraid, and no longer behave arrogantly.

Sin is a serious matter, but to sin arrogantly results in more severe judgment by God. If we are proud when we commit sin, we won't even see ourselves as sinners in need of God's forgiveness. "Me? A sinner? I'm just fine; I'm a good person!" We'll remain unrepentant.

Proverbs 11:2 says, "When arrogance comes, disgrace follows, / but with humility comes wisdom." The book of Obadiah announces that disgrace was about to come on Edom because of their pride. Obadiah serves as a warning from God to avoid the disease of pride.

Do I Have It?
Take God's Test

Throughout the COVID-19 pandemic, people were being tested for the virus. A major challenge of the pandemic was securing an adequate number of tests so people could determine whether they had the virus. How can we determine whether we are infected with the virus of pride?

Test for Self-Deception (3)

God said to the Edomites, "Your arrogant heart has deceived you" (v. 3). Pride deceives us into thinking we're better than we are. When people are proud, they can have obvious character problems, but they don't see the problems because of pride. Proverbs 30:12 refers to "a generation that is pure in its own eyes, / yet is not washed from its filth." That verse describes people who are dirty but think they're clean. Such delusion is the essence of pride.

A lot of people who reject the gospel of Christ think this way: "Repent of sin? Need the new birth? That's for the bad guys. I take care of my family, I'm a respectable neighbor, and I even give to charities." People who think that way are proud—pure in their own eyes yet not washed of filth. But when we look at the cross and see that a sacrifice for sin was necessary to atone for our sin and reconcile us to the holy God, pride should melt away. The truth is that no one is so good that he doesn't need to be saved, and no one is so bad that Jesus cannot save him (Moseley, *Living Well*, 117–19).

Edom was a small, desert kingdom. Its only real significance in the region was related to the fact that it was located on a major trade route.

But somehow Edom had developed an inflated sense of self-worth. Pride had deceived them. It happens so easily. A health-and-wealth preacher tells us we should practice positive confession—saying out loud that we're saints not sinners, winners not losers. Pride makes us forget that the only reason we're saints is because of Jesus's saving work, not our worth, and all we contributed to our salvation was our sin. We should regularly test ourselves for self-deception.

Test for a Sense of Invincibility (3-4)

"Who can bring me down to the ground?" Edom asked (v. 3). They were deceived, and more specifically, they were deceived that they were invincible. They were saying, "We live up here in the mountains, unreachable, unassailable, invincible." Yet God said they were vulnerable to his judgment. He said, "I will bring you down" (v. 4).

Pride prevents us from thinking about our own demise in time or in eternity. It's difficult or impossible to feel proud when we contemplate the fact that one day disease will weaken us and death will overtake us. Proud people don't think about that; they're thinking about this moment in which they feel strong, invincible.

The movie *Black Hawk Down* is about a real battle that was fought in Mogadishu, Somalia, in 1993. Jeff Struecker was in that battle. I heard Jeff tell the story of what happened. Jeff was a Christian, but most if not all of his fellow soldiers were not believers. They were tough guys, and Jeff said they were not inclined to admit they needed anything or anybody. When he spoke with them about Christ, they didn't seem to think they needed him either. Then during the "Black Hawk Down" incident, some soldiers in their unit were killed, and the rest were under such heavy fire that it's virtually a miracle they survived. Jeff Struecker distinguished himself and fought bravely during that battle. His fellow soldiers saw the way he behaved under fire, and after the battle they began to come to him to ask about his faith in Christ and his assurance of eternal life. Jeff said their brush with death impressed on them the reality of their own mortality and their need to prepare for death.

When I heard about Jeff's opportunity to share Christ with his fellow soldiers, I was delighted at their interest in the gospel. I was also astonished that for those men to think seriously about the reality of their deaths it took being in a situation in which dying was an imminent possibility. We don't have to almost die to know we're going to die. Everybody dies. Since the beginning of time, every single person has died. The mortality rate is 100 percent. The only way we can feel a sense of invincibility is if we're blinded by pride so that we don't think about our own approaching death. Edom, perched in the mountains, thought they were invincible and did not consider the judgment of almighty God. They were proud.

Test for Blindness to the Truth

The people of Israel and Judah—the descendants of Jacob—were God's covenant people. That was the truth. The Edomites—the descendants of Esau—should have known that since Abraham and Isaac were their ancestors too. Jerusalem was where God had chosen his name to dwell (Deut 12:10-14). Therefore, the destruction of Jerusalem was a tragedy. That was another truth the Edomites should have known. Babylon, the nation that conquered Judah and destroyed Jerusalem, was wicked. Edom should have known that too. Instead of seeing and accepting all that truth, the Edomites rejoiced over the demise of Judah, God's people, and the destruction of Jerusalem and God's temple. The Edomites were proud, and pride was blinding them to the truth.

Pride blinds a lot of people to the truth. They don't seek God's way of salvation because they think they have a better way. They think, *I'll get into heaven on the merit basis; I lived better than that murderer, so I should get into heaven.* Or, *I'll get into heaven because I was religious, regardless of which religion.* Or, *I'll probably get a second and third chance to get into heaven.* A lot of people think they can come up with a better way to get to heaven their way. Don't we get to choose? No, we don't. But ungodly pride will blind us to that truth.

What Can I Do about It?
Apply God's Remedy

Pride is not like polio; there is no vaccine against pride that our parents can give us at birth so we'll never contract it. Even when we're born again, pride continues to be part of the old self that we must put to death continually (Rom 6:11-13; Col 3:1-5). But the revelation God gives us in his Word provides a daily dose of help in our struggle against pride. The prophet Obadiah motivates us to take at least three steps to eliminate pride.

Remember God's Opposition to Pride (1,3)

James 4:6 says, "God resists the proud but gives grace to the humble." We don't want God to resist us. Proverbs 6:16-19 lists seven things the Lord hates, and the first is "arrogant eyes." Edom had an "arrogant heart" (v. 3), and in the book of Obadiah, God announced his opposition to Edom. God was sending an envoy to say, "Let's go to war against her" (v. 1). God goes to war against pride.

God also gives us a direct command against pride; James 4:10 says, "Humble yourselves before the Lord, and he will exalt you." Is that something we do daily—humble ourselves before the Lord? The act of obedience to God's commands, including this one, helps cure pride; obedience is an act of submission to God, and submission is the opposite of pride. Either we'll oppose pride and submit to God, or God will oppose us. Remembering God's opposition to pride should motivate us to humble ourselves.

Submit to God's People

In his prophecy, Obadiah included statements made by other prophets. For example, Jeremiah 49:14-16 is virtually identical to Obadiah 1b-4. Jeremiah prophesied before the fall of Jerusalem. If the book of Obadiah is dated to a time after the fall of Jerusalem, then it appears that Obadiah read the words of the prophet Jeremiah, learned from him, and included some of Jeremiah's words in his prophecy.

Obadiah 17 states, "There will be a deliverance on Mount Zion." Joel 2:32 says, "There will be an escape / for those on Mount Zion and in Jerusalem." In the original Hebrew, the statement in Obadiah is identical to the statement in Joel, except that Joel adds, "and in Jerusalem." Again, if the book of Obadiah is dated after the prophecy of Joel, then Obadiah used language that originated with another prophet. It seems that Obadiah was a student of other prophets, and he integrated some of their words into his message.

Obadiah's inclusion of phrases used by other prophets was not plagiarism since every true prophet preached and wrote words the Lord gave to him (2 Pet 1:20-21). Instead, it's an illustration of learning from other faithful followers of the one true God. Contemporary followers of Jesus are also not independent from other Christians. We are part of the body of Christ, the church, in which all members are dependent on one another. The Bible says that in the church we're to love one another

(Rom 12:10; 1 Pet 4:8), serve one another (Gal 5:13), encourage one another (1 Thess 5:11), pray for one another (Jas 5:16), confess our sins to one another (Jas 5:16), bear one another's burdens (Gal 6:2), forgive one another (Eph 4:32), and instruct one another (Rom 15:14). Of course we'll learn from other believers. Maintaining the desire to learn from other believers will help guard against pride.

Consider the Outcome of Pride (3-4)

Edom was asking, "Who can bring me down to the ground?" (v. 3). But God said to the Edomites, "Though you seem to soar like an eagle / and make your nest among the stars, / even from there I will bring you down" (v. 4). God was going to bring down those proud people. That's the outcome of pride. "Pride comes before destruction, / and an arrogant spirit before a fall" (Prov 16:18). God has brought down every proud kingdom. When we're proud, we should get ready for God to bring us down.

The supreme example of rejecting pride and humbling ourselves is the Lord Jesus. He took a towel and washed the feet of sinful disciples, the work of a servant (John 13:4-5):

> *He emptied himself*
> *by assuming the form of a servant,*
> *taking on the likeness of humanity.*
> *And when he had come as a man,*
> *he humbled himself by becoming obedient*
> *to the point of death—*
> *even to death on a cross.* (Phil 2:7-8)

That's a total rejection of pride: abandoning the worship of angels in heaven, taking the form of a servant, and humbling himself all the way down to a criminal's death on a cross. And he didn't die there because of his own sin; he died for our sin. Therefore, Jesus's death is so much more than an example of humility; his death is the atoning sacrifice for our sins that reconciles us to God when we put our faith in him. We won't be able to overcome the pandemic of pride without his salvation and his daily help.

Reflect and Discuss

1. What manifestations of pride can you see among nations today?
2. Tell your "pride testimony." When you were saved, what happened to your pride?
3. Why is pride such a dangerous sin?
4. How is Edom an example of misplaced pride—pride with no justification for pride?
5. Can you think of examples in the Bible or in history of pride leading to humiliation?
6. How does thinking about our death help eliminate pride? Why do so many people neglect to think about their death and what comes after death?
7. Why do you think God opposes pride?
8. How can involvement in the church help eliminate pride?
9. What does the life of Jesus teach us about humility?
10. Make a list of ways you struggle with pride, a list of manifestations of pride. Confess them to God. Renounce them and ask fellow believers to pray that you will practice service and humility.

WORKS CITED

Allen, Ronald B. *Joel.* Bible Study Commentary. Grand Rapids: Zondervan, 1988.

Andersen, Francis I., and David Noel Freedman. *Amos: A New Translation with Introduction and Commentary.* The Anchor Bible. New York: Doubleday, 1989.

———. *Hosea: A New Translation with Introduction and Commentary.* The Anchor Bible. New York: Doubleday, 1980.

Baab, Otto Justice. *Theology of the Old Testament: The Faith behind the Facts of Hebrew Life and Writings.* Nashville: Abingdon, 1949.

Barna Group. "Meet Those Who 'Love Jesus but Not the Church.'" March 30, 2017. Accessed December 28, 2020. https://www.barna.com/research/meet-love-jesus-not-church.

Barney, Morgan, McCall Barney, Brianna Copeland, Elise Griffin, Kristie Watkins, and Maleah Weir. *Save Our Sisters: How God's Heart for Justice Transforms High School Girls and Human Trafficking Survivors.* CreateSpace Independent Publishing Platform (August 9, 2017).

Barstad, Hans M. *The Religious Polemics of Amos.* Leiden: E. J. Brill, 1984.

Barton, John. *The Theology of the Book of Amos.* Cambridge: Cambridge University Press, 2012.

Bayly, Lewis. "I Am the One to Blame." Pages 202–3 in *Piercing Heaven: Prayers of the Puritans.* Edited by Robert Elmer. Bellingham, WA: Lexham, 2019.

Block, Daniel I. *Obadiah.* Exegetical Commentary on the Old Testament. Grand Rapids: Zondervan, 2013.

Bright, John. *A History of Israel.* 4th ed. Louisville: Westminster John Knox, 2000.

Bronner, Leah. *The Stories of Elijah and Elisha as Polemics against Baal Worship.* Leiden: E. J. Brill, 1968.

Brown, Francis, S. R. Driver, and Charles A. Briggs. *The Brown-Driver-Briggs Hebrew and English Lexicon (BDB)*. Peabody, MA: Hendrickson, 2006 (orig. 1906).

Chrysostom, John. *Homilies on Genesis 46–67*. The Fathers of the Church, vol. 87. Translated by Robert C. Hill. Washington, DC: Catholic University of America, 2010.

Cohen, Gary G. *"sha'nan." Theological Workbook of the Old Testament*. Chicago: Moody, 1980, 2:893–94.

Conway, Joseph P. *Broken but Beautiful: Why Church Is Still Worth It*. Eugene, OR: Wipf & Stock, 2020.

Coppes, Leonard. *"qînâ." Theological Workbook of the Old Testament*. Chicago: Moody, 1980, 2:798.

Cunningham, John M. "Did Marie-Antoinette Really Say 'Let Them Eat Cake'?" Accessed January 12, 2021. https://www.britannica.com/story/did-marie-antoinette-really-say-let-them-eat-cake.

Davidson, A. B. *The Theology of the Old Testament*. Edinburgh: T&T Clark, 1904.

Dearman, J. Andrew. *The Book of Hosea*. The New International Commentary on the Old Testament. Grand Rapids: Eerdmans, 2010.

Dickens, Charles. *Great Expectations*. In *Charles Dickens, Four Novels*. New York: Barnes & Noble Books, 1992.

Eidevall, Göran. *Amos: A New Translation with Introduction and Commentary*. The Anchor Yale Bible. New Haven: Yale, 2017.

Ferguson, Sinclair. "The Day of the Locusts." *The Gospel Coalition*. Accessed February 15, 2024. https://www.thegospelcoalition.org/sermon/the-day-of-the-locusts.

Firmage, Edwin. "Zoology." *The Anchor Bible Dictionary*. New York: Doubleday, 1992, 6:1150.

Fletcher, Louisa. *The Land of Beginning Again*. Boston: Small, Maynard and Company, 1921.

Galli, Mark, and Ted Olsen. *131 Christians Everyone Should Know*. Nashville: Broadman & Holman, 2000.

Garrett, Duane A. *Amos: A Handbook on the Hebrew Text*. Waco: Baylor, 2008.

———. *Hosea, Joel*. New American Commentary. Nashville: Broadman & Holman, 1997.

Harper, William Rainey. *A Critical and Exegetical Commentary on Amos and Hosea*. The International Critical Commentary. New York: Scribner's, 1905.

Hoerth, Alfred J. *Archaeology and the Old Testament.* Grand Rapids: Baker, 1998.

Hubbard, David Allan. *Will We Ever Catch Up with the Bible? The Minor Prophets Speak to Us Today.* Glendale, CA: Regal, 1977.

Hurowitz, Victor Avigdor. "Joel's Locust Plague in Light of Sargon II's Hymn to Nanaya." *Journal of Biblical Literature* 112, no. 4 (Winter 1993): 597–603.

Kaiser, Walter C., Jr. *A History of Israel: From the Bronze Age through the Jewish Wars.* Nashville: Broadman & Holman, 1998.

Keller, Tim. *Counterfeit Gods: The Empty Promises of Money, Sex, and Power, and the Only Hope that Matters.* New York: Penguin, 2016.

———, and Ed Clowney. "Preaching Christ in a Postmodern World." *The Gospel Coalition.* Accessed February 21, 2024. https://www.thegospel coalition.org/course/preaching-christ-postmodern-world.

Kidner, Derek. *Love to the Loveless: The Message of Hosea.* Downers Grove, IL: InterVarsity, 1981.

King, Philip J. *Amos, Hosea, Micah—an Archaeological Commentary.* Philadelphia: Westminster, 1988.

Koehler, Ludwig, and Walter Baumgartner. *The Hebrew and Aramaic Lexicon of the Old Testament (HALOT).* M. E. J. Richardson, trans. Leiden: E. J. Brill, 2001.

Lerner, Aaron. "PA Threatens to Kill News Workers of Broadcast Photos of Celebrating Palestinians." *Independent Media Review Analysis.* September 12, 2001. Accessed April 13, 2022. http://www.imra.org .il/story.php3?id=8147.

Lewis, C. S. *The Lion, the Witch and the Wardrobe.* New York: HarperCollins, 1950.

———. *The Problem of Pain.* New York: HarperCollins, 2001.

———. *The Voyage of The Dawn Treader.* The Chronicles of Narnia. New York: HarperCollins, 2004, orig. 1952.

Leithart, Peter J. *The Kingdom and the Power: Rediscovering the Centrality of the Church.* Phillipsburg, NJ: P&R, 1993.

Liederbach, Mark. *Chasing Infinity: Discipleship as the Pursuit of Infinite Treasure.* Orlando: Cru Press, 2017.

Maclaren, Alexander. "Ezekiel, Daniel, and the Minor Prophets; St. Matthew 1–8." *Expositions of Holy Scripture.* Nashville: Sunday School Board, n.d.

Matthews, Victor H. *Social World of the Hebrew Prophets.* Peabody, MA: Hendrickson, 2001.

———, and Don C. Benjamin. *Old Testament Parallels: Laws and Stories from the Ancient Near East.* 3rd ed. New York: Paulist Press, 2006.

Merrill, Eugene. *A Kingdom of Priests: A History of Old Testament Israel.* 2nd ed. Grand Rapids: Baker, 2008.

Mirsky, Steve, "A Staggering Discovery." *Scientific American* 318, no. 3 (March 2018), 74.

"Mom Rescues Son from Jaws of Alligator." *Gainesville Sun.* September 27, 1986, 10A. Accessed June 24, 2023. https://news.google.com/newspapers?nid=1320&dat=19860927&id=Xj1WAAAAIBAJ&sjid=7OkDAAAAIBAJ&pg=6965,3272158.

Morgan, G. Campbell. *Hosea: The Heart and Holiness of God.* Grand Rapids: Baker, 1974.

Moseley, Allan. "Baalism and Hebrew Worship." *Biblical Illustrator* 46, no. 1 (Fall 2019), 22–25.

———. *A Critical Evaluation of the Methods and Motifs in the Polemic against Baalism in Hosea.* Unpublished dissertation, New Orleans Baptist Theological Seminary, 1987.

———. *Living Well: God's Wisdom from the Book of Proverbs.* Bellingham, WA: Lexham, 2017.

———. "Sheol and Differentiated Destinies in the Old Testament." Unpublished essay.

———. "When God Repents." *Biblical Illustrator* 18, no. 3 (Spring 1992), 65–67.

Nadeau, Sophie. "The Real Story behind Marie Antoinette's 'Let Them Eat Cake.'" December 7, 2016. Accessed January 12, 2021. https://www.solosophie.com/real-story-behind-let-them-eat-cake-marie-antoinette.

National Weather Service. "Hurricane Camille 1969." Accessed December 11, 2023. https://www.weather.gov/jan/1969_08_17_hurricane_camille.

Niehaus, Jeffrey. "Amos." *The Minor Prophets: An Exegetical and Expositional Commentary.* Edited by Thomas McComiskey. vol. 1. Grand Rapids: Baker, 1992.

Nissinen, Martti. *Prophets and Prophecy in the Ancient Near East.* Writings from the Ancient World. Atlanta: Society of Biblical Literature, 2003.

Oswalt, John. *The Bible among the Myths.* Grand Rapids: Zondervan, 2009.

Owens, Ron. *Return to Worship: A God-Centered Approach.* Nashville: Broadman & Holman, 1999.

Packer, J. I. *Knowing God*. Downers Grove, IL: InterVarsity, 1973.

Patterson, Richard D. "Joel." Pages 229–66 in The Expositor's Bible Commentary, vol. 7. Frank E. Gaebelein, general editor. Grand Rapids: Zondervan, 1985.

———. "Obadiah." *Minor Prophets: Hosea-Malachi*. Cornerstone Biblical Commentary. Carol Stream, IL: Tyndale, 2008.

Piper, John. *Brothers, We Are Not Professionals: A Plea to Pastors for Radical Ministry*. Nashville: Broadman & Holman, 2013.

———. "Future Grace for Finishing the Task," part 4. *Desiring God*. Accessed February 21, 2024. https://www.desiringgod.org /messages/future-grace-for-finishing-the-task-part-4.

Raines, Robert Arnold. *Lord, Could You Make It a Little Better?* Waco: Word, 1972.

Riggs, Jack R. *Hosea's Heartbreak*. Neptune, NJ: Loizeaux Brothers, 1983.

Roberts, Alexander, and James Donaldson. *Ante-Nicene Fathers*. vol. 7. Peabody, MA: Hendrickson, 2004 (orig. 1886).

Robertson, O. Palmer. *Joel: Prophet of the Coming Day of the Lord*. Leyland: EP Books, 1995.

Schaeffer, Francis. *He Is There and He Is Not Silent*. Downers Grove, IL: InterVarsity, 1972.

Shakespeare, William. *The Complete Works of William Shakespeare*. Boston: Ginn, Heath, & Company, 1881.

———. *The Tragedy of Hamlet, Prince of Denmark*. New York: Simon & Schuster, 2012.

Skaist, Aaron. "Ancient Near Eastern Law Collections and Legal Forms and Institutions." Pages 305–18 in *The Oxford Handbook of Biblical Law*. Edited by Pamela Barmash. New York: Oxford, 2019.

Smith, Billy K. *Amos, Obadiah, Jonah*. The New American Commentary. Nashville: Broadman & Holman, 1995.

Smith, Gary V. *Hosea, Amos, Micah*. The NIV Application Commentary. Grand Rapids: Zondervan, 2001.

Smith, George Adam. *The Book of the Twelve Prophets*, rev. ed. New York: Harper & Brothers, 1928.

———. *The Historical Geography of the Holy Land*. New York: Harper & Row, 1966 (orig. 1894).

Spurgeon, Charles H. "Hitherto hath the Lord helped us. 1 Samuel 7:12." *Morning and Evening*. Accessed February 19, 2024. https://www.blue letterbible.org/devotionals/me/view.cfm?Date=1229&Time=am.

Steinbeck, John. *East of Eden*. New York: Penguin, 2002.

Strange, Philip. "Goat Island and the Great Chasm—the Day the Earth Moved." *Philip Strange Science and Nature Writing*. August 29, 2019. Accessed July 1, 2023. https://philipstrange.wordpress.com/2019/08/29/goat-island-and-the-great-chasm-the-day-the-earth-moved.

Stuart, Douglas. *Hosea–Jonah*. Word Biblical Commentary 31. Waco: Word, 1987.

———. *Hosea–Jonah*. Word Biblical Commentary. Grand Rapids: Zondervan Academic, 2014.

"3 Circles." NAMB (North American Mission Board). Accessed February 22, 2024. https://www.namb.net/evangelism/3circles.

United Nations Office on Drugs and Crime. "Human Trafficking." Accessed August 12, 2020. https://www.unodc.org/unodc/en/human-trafficking/what-is-human-trafficking.html.

Wall, Joseph Frazier. *Andrew Carnegie*. Pittsburgh: University of Pittsburgh Press, 1989. Quoted in Timothy Keller. *Counterfeit Gods*. New York: Penguin Books, 2009.

Wilhite, Jud. *Pursued: God's Divine Obsession with You*. New York: Faith Words, 2013.

Winslow, Octavius. *Christ's Sympathy to Weary Pilgrims*. Pensacola: Chapel Library, 2008.

Wolff, Hans Walter. *A Commentary on the Book of the Prophet Hosea*. Hermeneia: A Critical and Historical Commentary on the Bible. Translated by Gary Stansell. Philadelphia: Fortress, 1974.

Yadin, Yigael. *Hazor: The Rediscovery of a Great Citadel of the Bible*. New York: Random House, 1975.

Young, Gordon D., ed. *Ugarit in Retrospect: Fifty Years of Ugarit and Ugaritic*. Winona Lake, IN: Eisenbrauns, 1981.

SCRIPTURE INDEX